GOD'S YES WAS LOUDER THAN MY NO

God's Yes Was Louder than My No

Rethinking the African-American Call to Ministry

William H. Myers

WILLIAM B. EERDMANS PUBLISHING COMPANY
GRAND RAPIDS, MICHIGAN

AFRICA WORLD PRESS, INC.
TRENTON, NEW JERSEY

Copyright © 1994 by Wm. B. Eerdmans Publishing Co.

Published jointly 1994 by Wm. B. Eerdmans Publishing Co.
255 Jefferson Ave. S.E., Grand Rapids, Michigan 49503
and by Africa World Press, Inc.
15 Industry Court, Trenton, N.J. 08638

Printed in the United States of America

Library of Congress Cataloging-in-Publication Data

Myers, William H., 1947-
God's yes was louder than my no: rethinking the African American
call to ministry / William H. Myers.
p.   cm.
Includes bibliographical references and indexes.
ISBN 0-8028-0109-9 (pbk.)
1. Clergy — Appointment, call, and election. 2. Afro-American clergy.
3. Afro-American women clergy. I. Title.
BR563.N4M945 1994
253'.2 — dc20   93-46991
CIP

Africa World Press ISBN 0-86543-427-1 (pbk.)

For all those
who, in spite of the liminality,
have struggled, are struggling, and will
struggle with self, others, and God
to hear and answer the call of God

Contents

Acknowledgments   xi

Introduction   1

I. THE CALL AS STORY   15

1. Early Religious Exposure   17
2. The Call Experience   24
3. The Struggle   37
4. The Search   47
5. The Sanction   54
6. The Surrender   61

II. THE CALL AS NARRATIVE   67

7. The Narratology of Story   69
   Types of Call   71
   Point of View   74
   Narrative Time   81
8. The Narratology of Story: Plot   93

III. THE CALL AS RITES OF PASSAGE   117

9. The Liminality of the Call to Ministry   119
   The Preliminal, Liminal, and Postliminal Phases of Call   123
   The Liminality of the Call as Story   126
   The Pastor as the Primary Portal   129

IV. **THE CALL AS HERMENEUTICAL RETROSPECTION**   133

10. The Call as Hermeneutical Retrospection   135

  Carey McCreary   135

  Joseph L. Roberts   147

  Ernest W. Newman   155

  Lucille Abernathy   158

  Vashti M. McKenzie   178

  Manuel Scott, Sr.   185

  Some Observations and Hermeneutical Implications   187

V. **THE CALL AS THEOLOGICAL AND CULTURAL PERSPECTIVES**   193

11. The Call as Theological and Cultural Perspectives   195

  Biblical Perspectives   195

  Theological Perspectives   202

  Black Religious Experience Perspectives   206

VI. **THE CALL AS HERMENEUTICS AND MINISTRY**   215

12. Betwixt and Between: Rethinking Call to Ministry —
    Call, Called, and Calling   217

13. Betwixt and Between: Women,
    the Black Church, and the Call to Ministry   227

14. Betwixt and Between: Where Have We
    Come From and Where Do We Go?   233

Appendixes

  A. Demographics   240

  B. Call Stages   243

  C. Narrative Sequences   246

Indexes

  Names   260

  Subjects   263

Acknowledgments

I am grateful to a host of people for their participation in the life of this work. First and foremost is African-American churches where I came to appreciate the significance of the call to ministry. The AME church in Meridian, Mississippi, and the Baptist church in Cleveland, Ohio, nurtured my desire to understand more about the ministerial call in the black church. To this list I add all of those who gave their story in the first book that made this work possible.

Matriculation at three schools prepared me for this work. For their constant encouragement I am grateful to my colleagues, a few of whom were my teachers, at Ashland Theological Seminary (Ohio) where my studies began. My studies ended when I received my Ph.D. from the University of Pittsburgh in the joint program with Pittsburgh Theological Seminary. I am especially grateful to Doug Hare (PTS) who helped me polish my New Testament focus, John Wilson (PTS) and Larry Glasco (Pitt) who shaped my historical perspectives, and Tony Edwards (Pitt) who gave me a new appreciation for narrative theory.

I cannot overlook my teacher, friend, and constant supporter, Ronald Grimes of Wilfrid Laurier University (Canada), who introduced me to the importance of ethnography and ethnobiography for this work. I cannot thank him enough for his suggestions, encouragement, and critique through all the years that this work was unfolding.

Special thanks goes to my extended family who endured this "possessed" man as he worked on "the book."

And then God came through a person who helped to put it together for me and helped me to claim that call, because I kept saying, "No, God, not me. One, I've got another door that's open. How will I do it? I'm female. How am I going to respond in the midst of a male-dominated world and all of the other pieces of it?" I mean, all of those things were in my head. No, no, no, no. I found all the reasons for no, but **God's "yes" was louder than my "No."**

REVEREND YVONNE V. DELK
Executive Director
Community Renewal Society
Chicago, Illinois

I got on my knees that night, and I asked the Lord if he had called me to the ministry. I wanted to know. And, Doc, I woke up; I think it was about the crack of day and I felt pretty nice about it because I hadn't felt anything and I didn't see anything in a dream. I don't know whether I went half way back to sleep or what. But the Holy Spirit jumped on me and it felt like to me it was going to choke me to death. . . . I had woke up and the Lord hadn't called me. I was a little disappointed, but I was partly glad too, because I felt I wasn't gonna do it. So I was **betwixt and between.** I was kind of worried that I misled myself.

REVEREND CAREY McCREARY, Pastor
New Mount Zion Baptist Church
Cleveland, Ohio

I think that [women's] presence in the ministry forces the church, forces us, forces our colleagues to have to **rethink ministry**, rethink gifts, rethink the notion that in the Black church only the preaching ministry is the ordained ministry in our churches.

DR. RENITA WEEMS
Professor of Old Testament
Vanderbilt University Divinity School
Nashville, Tennessee

Introduction

Gerald Davis's book *I Got the Word in Me and I Can Sing It, You Know*, is his attempt to argue that the African-American sermon is a genre, a unique phenomenon in the black community worthy of serious analysis. His penetrating analysis of the sermon, which utilizes nontraditional methodologies such as ethnography and narrative theory, offers insights into the African-American sermon that make his work the best on the subject to date. It is noteworthy, then, that he opens the book with a narrative from Bishop Cleveland about his "call to preach." Bishop Cleveland believes preachers are born.

> When you're born, preaching is in you. And when the time comes it stirs, God stirs it up. . . . And I went for a couple of years maybe without acknowledging it. I had to get up to testify and speak and I'd go ahead. I could preach. They said, "Preach!" Oh when they said that, I'd say, "Oh, oh, that isn't the way I want it" and I'd stop. And it just went so bad so long 'til I had to do it, you know. . . . And at night, at night I'd go home to bed, I'd go to sleep, I'd go to preaching. I'd wake up in the morning, I'd be tired. Preaching all night. . . . So that's the way it is, and I've been knowing it from a boy. And I used to play, me and my sister and other kids would play church, and I'd always be the preacher. And I'd get in the wagon, they'd have boxes and things all around on the ground, and I'd get in the wagon and preach.[1]

1. Gerald L. Davis, *I Got the Word in Me and I Can Sing It, You Know: A Study of the Performed African-American Sermon* (Philadelphia: Univ. of Pennsylvania Press, 1985), ix.

1

Many things are significant about this narrative. It is a retrospective oral accounting of the Bishop's self-understanding of his call to ministry that both the investigator and the narrator interpret as a "call to preach." Its brevity, omissions, and structure make it clear that the narrative is only part of the story. Hence, what we have is a tape-recorded call story that is more than story. It is story, narrative, and hermeneutics; about this we shall say more later. In addition, although it reads like many of the narratives on which this study depends, Bishop Cleveland belongs to an African-American church not represented in this study — the Church of God in Christ. Hence, it is evidence that the oral transmission of call stories is known in African-American communities of faith other than those represented in this study.

Oral transmission of tradition has a long history in African-American churches, as is evidenced by slave narratives, conversion narratives, Negro spirituals, black preaching, and the antiphonal call and response dynamic in African-American worship. Call narratives are a significant aspect of this oral tradition. Legitimation, acceptance, authority, and ordination are all dependent, though in different degrees, upon an oral articulation of a divine call. Irrespective of the changes observed in African-American religion from that of a preliterate to a literate community, the oral articulation of a call still has a place in that community.

In view of the longevity[2] of this phenomenon in the African-American church, the goals of this study were two. First it sought to collect and transcribe a variety of these oral narratives in one place for present and future study; and second, to describe and analyze the content and structure of the narratives. The first objective was accomplished in the companion publication, *The Irresistible Urge to Preach: A Collection of African American "Call" Stories;*[3] the second goal is accomplished in this work. The books are not only companions in their dependence upon each other, but together they highlight the need for us to rethink this entire subject. The titles of both are significant. The first tries to be true to the majority view (i.e., call to ministry is interpreted as "call to preach") that emerges out of the stories, while the

---

2. For documentation of call narratives more than a century old see Charles S. Johnson, ed., *God Struck Me Dead* (Philadelphia: Pilgrim Press, 1969). See also Roland Steiner, "Sol Lockheart's Call," *Journal of American Folk-Lore* 13 (Mar. 1900): 67-70. Though obviously meant as a pejorative parody, Booker T. Washington, *Up from Slavery* (Boston: Houghton Mifflin, 1928), 82, gives evidence of oral call stories among African Americans prior to and after the Civil War.

3. William H. Myers (Atlanta: Aaron Press, 1992).

second takes seriously the challenge of the minority view (i.e., call to ministry is interpreted as something significantly more than a "call to preach"). Moreover, the companion works are singularly dedicated to offering an African-American perspective on this matter. In this regard, the dialogue has been restricted as much as possible to those sources.

The significance of this study manifests itself when placed in the context of similar studies. A few scholars have collected and described similar African-American oral phenomena, and a number of classic works are dependent upon these collections. Slave narratives, conversion narratives, Negro spirituals, and sermons are but a few oral phenomena collected, transcribed, and described by one group of scholars, yet subjected to further analysis and interpretation by a later group of scholars.[4]

A complete call narrative published as such is rare.[5] Usually it is part of a different work such as a biography or an autobiography.[6] Thus, if the call narrative is to be recognized as such, it must be lifted from these sources and reconstructed. There is no published work that col-

4. On works that collect and/or analyze and interpret slave narratives, see George P. Rawick, *The American Slave: A Composite Autobiography*, vols. 2-17 (Westport, Conn.: Greenwood Press, 1973); Mechal Sobel, *Trabelin' On: The Slave Journey to an Afro-Baptist Faith* (Westport, Conn.: Greenwood Press, 1979); and Robert B. Stepto, *From Behind the Veil: A Study of Afro-American Narrative* (Chicago: Univ. of Illinois Press, 1979). For conversion narratives, see Charles S. Johnson, ed., *God Struck Me Dead*. For spirituals, see Alan Lomax, *The Folk Songs of North America* (Garden City, N.Y.: Doubleday & Co., 1960); and James H. Cone, *Spirituals & Blues* (New York: Seabury Press, 1972). The most penetrating study of the sermon as genre is Gerald L. Davis's, *I Got the Word in Me and I Can Sing It, You Know: A Study of the Performed African-American Sermon*.

5. See, however, Roland Steiner, "Sol Lockheart's Call."

6. Some interesting call stories can be reconstructed from the following works: Lerone Bennett, Jr., *What Manner of Man: A Biography of Martin Luther King, Jr.* (Chicago: Johnson Publishing Co., 1976); Martin Luther King, Sr., *Daddy King: An Autobiography* (New York: William Morrow & Co., 1980); Howard Thurman, *With Head and Heart: The Autobiography of Howard Thurman* (New York: Harcourt Brace Jovanovich, 1979); Benjamin E. Mays, *Born to Rebel: An Autobiography* (Athens: The Univ. of Georgia Press, 1987); *Adam by Adam: The Autobiography of Adam Clayton Powell, Jr.* (New York: The Dial Press, 1971); Granville W. Reed, *Known and Yet Unknown* (Los Angeles: Reed College of Religion, 1963); Reverdy C. Ransom, *The Pilgrimage of Harriet Ransom's Son* (Nashville: Sunday School Union, n.d.); W. H. R. Powell, *Illustrations from a Supervised Life* (Philadelphia: The Continental Press, 1968); Otha M. Kelly, *Profile of a Churchman: The Life of Otha M. Kelly* (Jamaica, N.Y.: K & C Publishers, 1976). King, Sr., King, Jr., Thurman, Mays, Powell, Jr., Reed, and Powell were Baptists. Ransom was AME, and Kelly was Church of God in Christ. Although Thurman was later recognized for the nontraditional, nondenominational structure of his church, he was called, licensed, and ordained Baptist.

lects, describes, analyzes, or interprets a corpus of African-American "call" narratives *qua* narratives.[7]

The importance of this study stems also from the fact that, although collections of African-American slave narratives, conversion narratives, Negro spirituals, and sermons are available, collections of call narratives are not. The companion volume makes a collection of call narratives available in one place that was heretofore unavailable. This book relies mainly on that collection of eighty-six stories recorded by the author.

The collection consists of tape-recorded interviews with a diverse group of African-American preachers across the United States. The corpus was randomly selected, and it has the following components: (1) The corpus is 25 percent female. (2) It contains a cross section of ministerial contexts in the United States which represents seven of the eight geographical regions. (3) It includes a significant number of well-known informants (i.e., nationally), as well as some not so well known

---

7. A few doctoral dissertations have looked at call narratives from a variety of perspectives. William Loyd Allen, "Spirituality among Southern Baptist Clergy as Reflected in Selected Autobiographies" (Ph.D. diss., Southern Baptist Seminary, 1984), examines call stories in an attempt to understand spirituality among called clergy of the Southern Baptist church. Samuel Southard, Jr., "The Counseling of Candidates for Church Vocations" (Th.D. diss., Southern Baptist Seminary, 1953) utilizes some call narratives in his effort to better understand how candidates for the ministry should be counseled. Thomas B. Milligan, "A Psychological Study of the Call to Christian Service" (Th.D. diss., Southern Baptist Seminary, 1947) utilizes some call narratives in his effort to understand the psychological aspect of a call. None of these study African-American calls, nor do they make the narratives on which the study is based available.

Only Victor T. Glass, "An Analysis of the Sociological and Psychological Factors Related to the Call to Christian Service of the Negro Baptist Minister" (Ph.D. diss., Southern Baptist Seminary, 1952), has examined African-American call narratives and this from a sociological and psychological perspective. Glass, p. 14, says about his study: "As far as I know, this is the first attempt to explore the call of Negro Baptist ministers." None of the actual narratives are made available in the study. And the mixture of methodologies used to obtain the data (e.g., questionnaires) makes narrative analysis virtually impossible.

What is even more intriguing about Glass's study is that the title of the dissertation belies the actual goal of the study. A close reading of the study makes it self-evident that Glass is interested in the lack of education of Baptist ministers who are called. Of the 41 tables that Glass includes in his appendix, 37 relate to the education of the ministers studied. Moreover, his study was part of a larger national study about the lack of education among ministers in the black church. Glass attempts to argue that it is sociological and psychological factors that allow the Negro to claim a call even though he does not have the education that Glass feels he should have in order to fulfill that role.

(i.e., locally). (4) The corpus contains callees from three different generations. (5) It contains callees from ten different denominations. Names were obtained as a result of the author's prior contact as well as recommendations made by interviewees and colleagues across the country.

The interviews were done between winter 1985 and spring 1990. The largest portion was recorded during summer 1989. All interviews were recorded in person, except seven. These seven were interviews tape-recorded over a speakerphone because of scheduling difficulties with people deemed significant for the study. Interviews took place either in the informants' city, or in cities that they were visiting for other reasons (e.g., conventions, revivals).

The methodologies utilized in this study are drawn from several disciplines: hermeneutics, narrative theory, ethnography, biblical criticism, and theology. It is of particular importance that the study describes this phenomenon from the "native's point of view." Significant for the hermeneutical task[8] is an honest effort to capture the subjectivity and individuality of the callee's self-understanding of his or her call, while juxtaposing it to the community's traditional understanding of call. Significant for the narrative-theory task is to discover something about the content and structure of these narratives, especially whether there are content and structural similarities or differences due to gender, generation, geography, or religious tradition (i.e., denomination). Significant for the theological task is to discover how this discussion fits into the historical dialogue about call in the larger religious community, mainly American Protestantism.

I am persuaded by ethnographers like James Spradley, Alan Dundes, Kenneth Pike, and others that an emic approach[9] is best suited

8. Ong says, "To interpret . . . is to bring out what is concealed in a given manifestation, to make evident what in the manifestation is not evident to the milieu in which the interpreter's audience lives. Interpretation can be applied to anything that bears information. . . . To interpret verbal utterance is to bring out what the utterance does not of itself reveal to a given audience. . . . Verbal discourse regularly calls for interpretation." Walter J. Ong, "Text as Interpretation: Mark and After," in *Oral Tradition in Literature: Interpretation in Context,* ed. John Miles Foley (Columbia: Univ. of Missouri Press, 1986), 147.

9. An etic-nomothetic approach reports the view of the outsider, often imposing the outside frame of reference on the informant. In contrast, an emic-idiographic approach reports the informant's ("native") subjective view.

Maria Barbara Watson-Franke and Lawrence Watson, *Interpreting Life Histories: An Anthropological Inquiry* (New Brunswick, N.J.: Rutgers Univ. Press, 1985), 26, in their discussion of the phenomenology of subjective experience say, "The etic-nomothetic orientation described by Allport emphasizes generalizing and model building in an for this type of analysis. In addition, I am greatly influenced by Watson and Watson-Franke's merging of ethnographic techniques with phenomenological hermeneutics as a method of unveiling an informant's own subjective truth.[10] Furthermore, I have been informed by a variety of narrative theorists such as Gerard Genette, Seymour Chatman, and Roland Barthes.

Spradley informed my approach to interviewing.[11] The procedure followed this sequence: (1) All informants were asked the same initial question, "Would you tell me about your call?" (2) The informants were allowed to tell their story without interruption. (3) Questions of clarification were asked at the completion of the story. (4) Some selected informants were asked questions about the call process as independent support of documented procedures. Some informants' (e.g., Baptists') testimony served as primary data because no written procedures existed.

One of the most divisive matters facing black churches in our time focuses on the hermeneutical issue of the call to ministry, especially the role and function of women in leadership positions in the church. The Bible is the chief battleground where this war is waged. Opponents come fully armed to their favorite prooftexts, sometimes the very same text, to do battle over who has the right to speak for God. In rare instances the discussion takes as its point of departure something other than Scripture, but for the most part that is where the axe gets ground. In other words, the past intersects with the present at the nexus of an ancient text. Hence, hermeneutics is paramount in this debate.

---

abstract frame of reference that is externally imposed on phenomena. On the other hand, the *emic-idiographic* approach, which he contrasts to the etic-nomothetic, concerns itself with the specific and unique richness of a phenomenon, so that we understand the particular (the individual, the subjective) rather than the general."

Moreover, Marvin Harris, ch. 20, "Emics, Etics, and the New Ethnography," in *The Rise of Anthropological Theory* (New York: Crowell, 1968), gives us background information on the terms when he asserts, "The terms themselves were coined by the missionary linguist Kenneth Pike . . . on analogy with the 'emic' in phon*emic* and the 'etic' in phon*etic*. In conformity with this analogy, Pike stressed 'the structural results' obtained by phonemic analysis as opposed to the 'nonstructural' results characteristic of phonetics." Cf. Clifford Geertz, " 'From the Native's Point of View': On the Nature of Anthropological Understanding." *Bulletin of the American Academy of Arts and Sciences* 28/1 (1974): 221-37.

10. See particularly Maria Barbara Watson-Franke and Lawrence Watson, *Interpreting Life Histories: An Anthropological Inquiry.*

11. James P. Spradley, *The Ethnographic Interview* (New York: Holt, Rinehart & Winston, 1979).

Since call stories are individuals' claims to be commissioned as spokespersons for God, and since these stories have held a place of prominence, power, and authority for legitimation in the ritual of ordination in the black church, it is striking that no one has asked what place they have in this hermeneutical debate. This study is an attempt to help the academy and the church rethink this issue; it hopes to serve as the launching pad for discussion of some key hermeneutical issues that affect black churches today.

It is noteworthy that while the hermeneutical point of departure in this debate tends more often than not to be Scripture, such is not the case in these stories. In fact, neither in the life of the religious community nor in these stories does the call to ministry begin by debating Scripture. The call to ministry begins as a story; a story of an encounter between an individual and God. Irrespective of the potential for abuse in such claims or suspicion about human-divine encounters, it would be difficult indeed to argue that calls to ministry do not begin in this manner.

Scholars as diverse as literary critics, narrative theorists, folklorists, anthropologists, and biblical critics — to name a few — have highlighted the importance of stories while bringing together a story, a storyteller, and a hearer. Recently, scholars in biblical and theological disciplines in particular have accentuated the significance of story. They have taken seriously the equal importance of how stories are told with what is told. Especially among narrative theorists, "story" refers to the content — what is told — while narrative refers to the discourse — how it is told. Story is the storyteller's attempt to reconstruct the chronological account of what happened. Narrative is the oral or written words that the hearer experiences as articulated by the storyteller.

The first indication of hermeneutics in the call to ministry is when the claimant comes to the community of faith for confirmation. At this point the story is transformed into a narrative in order to persuade the community of the authenticity of the call. The difference between story and narrative is not necessarily to be seen as error or deception; rather, story is an individual's attempt to wrestle, as did Jacob and Paul, with God and self, and later narrative is the attempt to explain the transformative encounter in a way that makes sense to others; it is retrospective interpretation.

The transformed claimant presents the transformed story, now narrative, to the religious community in order to pass through that community's rites of passage, usually culminating in the ritual of ordination. However, the call to ministry and especially the rites of passage do not end there, because the call is a process that may change in its scope and mission throughout the life of the individual who is called.

It is at this point that theological reflection, the traditions of the community, the debates over "call-to-ministry" understandings in the larger community, interpretation of Scripture, and the community's knowledge of the claimant are brought to bear on the specific claim. Someone who may have been completely embraced within the community may encounter hostile rejection for making such a claim.

Therefore, it should be evident that a discussion of call to ministry does not begin with a debate or discussion about relevant or irrelevant passages of Scripture. It begins with call as story. This study is structured to take this notion seriously. Many people in this study go searching for answers as they struggle with the call, not only in terms of accepting it, but in an effort to better understand it.

This study joins the struggle and search for a more inclusive understanding of call to ministry by utilizing these subjective retrospective interpretations of call as the point of departure for a discussion of call to ministry.

In part one the analysis of call to ministry begins with call as story. The content of the stories is examined and six major stages are uncovered: early religious exposure, call experience, struggle, search, sanction, and surrender.

Chapter one argues that early religious exposure greatly influenced the vocational choice of individuals in this collection. The home and church were the key places where this exposure took place. Further, the mother or some other female family member (e.g., grandmother) tended to be the primary source of this exposure.

Chapter two describes the call experience stage. An irresistible urge toward ministry is a key aspect of this stage. Validation comes in a variety of aural, ocular, and other sensory signs such as visions, voices, accidents, and being awakened at unusual times. In addition to a variety of unusual phenomena, a number of callees emphasize that being groomed in a Christian home was a key element in their vocational choice.

Chapter three describes the struggle stage. The majority of callees encounter some conflict engendered by their inclination toward ministry. Some of the conflict is internal, while other aspects of it are external. Some callees struggle with self as well as others over whether God will call them. Ambiguity permeates this stage. Even supernatural phenomena are not always sufficient for removal of the ambiguity. Resistance is a prominent response to the call during this stage.

Chapter four examines the search stage. The call experience and struggle to understand the call send the callee on a search for answers. What this stage demonstrates more than any other is how important human validation is in the call process, and how important the pastor's role is in validating a callee. No matter how much divine validation a callee receives, human validation is still desired and sought.

Chapter five describes the sanction stage. Through the process of struggling and searching for understanding the callee receives both divine and human confirmation. Family members, the community of faith, others who have been called, and especially the pastor are key persons in helping to sanction the call. In addition, a variety of extraordinary events such as visions, voices, and providential occurrences also help to sanction the call.

Chapter six describes the surrender stage. Finally, the callee decides to accept the call. Acceptance comes in the form of a private and public acknowledgment, to self and the community of faith. Quite often, the pastor is the first one in the community of faith to be told. Some callees express great relief, as if a burden has been lifted from their shoulders and peace, joy, and fulfillment now reign.

In part two the analysis focuses on call as narrative. Unlike call as story where content takes center stage, in narrative it is the structure that is examined in order to categorize call types. Three types are discovered: type A — cataclysmic/reluctant; type B — noncataclysmic/reluctant; type C — noncataclysmic/nonreluctant. Each of these types has its own plot.

Chapter seven describes the types and their narrative perspectives. The types are described at both the story and narrative levels. Type A (cataclysmic/reluctant) rarely omits any of the six story stages, but has its primary locus in stage two (call experience), with stages three (struggle) and six (surrender) holding secondary importance. Extraordinary events in the form of ocular, aural, and sensory phenomena are important in this type. These phenomena are very important for sanctioning the callee. At the story level it may be one event or a series of events; however, at the narrative level it tends to be one event. Further, resistance and relief are key aspects of this type. These callees did not seek the call; it was thrust upon them. They were reluctant callees who resisted the call and felt great relief, peace, joy, and fulfillment when they finally surrendered to it.

Type B (noncataclysmic/reluctant) rarely omits any of the six story stages, but has its primary locus in stage two (call experience) with secondary importance in stages three (struggle) and five (sanction). It is like type A in that the callee resists the call, but unlike type A in that the callee has no cataclysmic moments at the story level and rejects the interpretation of the call at the narrative level as due to a single event. This call unfolds gradually and its sanctioning is seen as a series of events occurring within the community of faith.

Type C (noncataclysmic/nonreluctant) has the least number of story stages. Its primary locus is in stage one (early religious exposure). Unlike type A, it has no cataclysmic moment; unlike those of type A and B, the callees of type C are not reluctant. They did not resist the call because, at the narrative level, they never wanted to be anything else; they always saw the call as their destiny, something they were born and nurtured to do. Hence, their narrative awareness of being called is unlike that of type A, which is more sudden, and, though gradual, different from that of type B, which is more gradual.

Three stories, one of each type, are examined more closely in order to compare and contrast narrative points of view and narrative times. These stories present similar points of view. Each perspective is primarily that of the main character (the callee) telling his or her own story in the first person singular. Narrative time, however, does offer some significant differences. Narrative time is different from story time in that the narrator has altered the story to accomplish his or her purpose, and the narrative allows the narrator the opportunity to do things that cannot be done in story time. For example, one can begin *in medias res* and flashback. Chronology can be modified and some events given more attention in terms of time and space than others. Whereas many of the narrators attempt to set their call in a larger life-history, the attempts differ in terms of order and duration, two primary components of narrative time. The reason they differ emerges in the next chapter.

Chapter eight continues analysis of the three types by looking at the plots of their corresponding narratives. Plot, though not an easy term to define, is the narrative theorists' way of describing what happens in a story. It is the theme that holds the entire narrative together. These narrators more than anything else want the community of believers to believe their story, and narrative is structured to do just that. Plot is primary in that regard. Parts of the story are left out, while other parts are greatly emphasized, all in an effort to make the theme as clear as possible. Hence, though there might be broad similarities, each narrator's theme is uniquely his or her own.

Part three addresses call as rites of passage. Arnold Van Gennep argues in his classic work, *The Rites of Passage*, that there are three phases (separation, margin or limen, and aggregation) of rites of passage. Throughout life people go through these phases in a variety of instances (girl to woman, boy to man). The call is an example of rites of passage as individuals move from layperson to clergy.

Chapter nine demonstrates how call to ministry can be viewed as a rite of passage by focusing on the liminality of the call. The key phase in Van Gennep's theory is the middle passage or threshold (limen) through which one must pass. In order to move from a preliminal phase to a postliminal phase, both of which are stages of stability, one must go through the instability and ambiguity of the liminal stage.

The six stages of call as story are classified as preliminal (stage one — early religious exposure), liminal (stage two — call experience, stage three — struggle, and stage four — search) and postliminal (stage five—sanction, stage six — surrender). It is argued, however, that since these stages do overlap and a degree of circularity is evident in the call process, the call as a rite of passage represents a challenge to the linear assumption of Van Gennep's theory.

An analysis of the liminality of the call helps us to appreciate again the important distinction between call as story and call as narrative. At the narrative level, hermeneutical retrospection allows the narrator to claim far greater knowledge, understanding, certainty, clarity, and stability than is evident at the story level. Juxtaposing the story to the narrative uncovers more instability, ambiguity, confusion, and limited knowledge than the narrative suggests.

Further analysis of the liminality of the call to ministry makes it clear that an individual cannot past through this phase alone. Divine confirmation and intervention are not enough; human validation and support are necessary. In this regard the pastor tends to be the primary portal between the preliminal and postliminal stages. This awesome power to give or withhold support and confirmation needs to be used wisely and with great sensitivity.

Part four examines call as hermeneutical retrospection. Call is not only story and narrative, it is an illustration of callees' retrospective interpretation of a series of events in their life in an effort to explain to themselves and others how they understand their call to ministry.

Chapter ten examines six stories, two from each type, in a more detailed manner in order to further highlight what has been learned in earlier parts of the analysis. Having focused on the larger corpus in earlier parts of the analysis, this section allows us to look at the flow of selected individual stories from each type. It is evident that theme development at the narrative level has dictated how the story needed to be told and how liminality is different when story is juxtaposed to narrative. These narratives are replete with hermeneutical insights that can be valuable to our further appreciation and understanding of call to ministry.

Part five addresses the theological and cultural perspectives of call to ministry. The objective is to examine the concept of call in the larger historical context. A call does not come in a vacuum. Additionally, no Christian call in American Protestantism emerges without reference to, dependence upon, or relation to a biblical basis for call.

Chapter eleven helps us to understand the historical trajectory — both theologically and culturally — for this tradition of the black call to ministry, as well as the unity within the tradition on the one hand, and its diversity on the other hand. Our goal is to determine if there are any theological and cultural traditions to which it can be linked. Old Testament prophetic calls as well as the New Testament call of Paul are examined for similarities to the black call in structure and content.

The theological perspectives of the church from the first century to the present among a variety of Christian traditions are looked at briefly for a broader perspective of call. The triple interest in the call to ministry as a personal call (inner call), a congregational call (outer call), and the education necessary to fulfill the call sets the stage for different perspectives of call throughout the church's history. In this regard a black perspective of call to ministry has its own unique contributions to this discussion that may have some trajectories leading us back to Africa.

Part six ends the discussion where it should end, on the hermeneutical implications, conclusions, and directions of further dialogue about call to ministry. Call narratives are interpreted stories about a call to ministry. In that respect they are communication about hermeneutics and ministry. The argument in this section is that black churches are in a liminal state — betwixt and between — on a host of issues related to this call. Three issues overlap the discussion in this section: testing the call to ministry, the issue of women's ministerial role in black churches, and rethinking our understanding of what is meant by call to ministry.

Chapter twelve addresses the difficult but much needed discussion engendered by three questions: Who does the calling? How is the call to be certified? What is one called to do? The call is both an inner and outer call that necessitates vastly different kinds of training depending upon the ministry one is called to do. Black churches have joined other Protestant denominations throughout their history in the debate over what is the proper balance between the inner and outer call. In addition, various denominations have taken a variety of positions on educational requirements for the ministry. In view of the plight of the masses of black people in the country, however, these questions, especially the last question, need further attention.

Chapter thirteen addresses what may be the most important question of our time facing black churches: What should the position of black churches be regarding women's call to ministry and the leadership roles they can hold in the church? Hermeneutically the usual point of departure for this debate is Scripture. However, this study begins the debate at a different point by juxtaposing women's stories to those of men, as story, narrative, and hermeneutical retrospection. In the life of the community as well as the rhetoric of the Bible, that is the usual process, not the former. Since these stories are similar, irrespective of gender, what happens to the value of this call phenomenon in the community when it is rejected or accepted on the basis of gender? The needs of the church and the community as well as the gifts that women bring to ministry require us to rethink the issue of women's role in ministry.

Chapter fourteen closes the book with a broad summary of where we have come from in the discussion and where we should be headed. The call is not as clear when it first comes as it is later in life looking back. There are aspects of the call that are culturally defined, but there are also aspects that transcend cultural restrictions. We must rethink any understanding of call to ministry that would reduce it to merely the preaching task, something usually restricted to the male gender. We need to recognize call in a much broader way if we are to address the many ills that are afflicting our people. One way to begin that recognition process (something this study has helped us to achieve) is to understand call as story, narrative, and hermeneutical retrospection and benefit from the differences that each perspective offers.

PART I

THE CALL AS STORY

CHAPTER 1

Early Religious Exposure

The call is first and foremost a story — an oral accounting — about a human-divine encounter. It is the narrator's retrospective attempt to articulate a divine mission — a call to ministry. In addition, the "call as story" is the interpreter's attempt to reconstruct the chronological account of what happened. It is a preverbal view of events in temporal and causal order. This chapter will examine the content of the stories as a corpus.

Narrative theorists make distinctions between "story" and "narrative" for analytical purposes.[1] This study will follow that analytical approach. Narrative, for this study, refers to the oral tape-recorded account articulated by each interviewee. Story refers to my attempt to reconstruct the preverbal account of what happened. Hence, reconstruction of story is not limited to the narrative. The reconstruction will depend primarily on internal clues (e.g., the narrative); however, when appropriate I will draw upon external data (biographical information and recorded follow-up questions) as well.

This section will analyze six recurrent stages that are dominant in this collection of call stories. This focus is not meant to suggest that all of the stages appear in all of the narratives, or that they have equal quantitative or qualitative weight, or that the stages are completely linear in their occurrence. Indeed, there are significant differences between the types and on occasion slight differences within types. Furthermore, these stages are not meant to be taken as exhaustive. Rather, this focus is meant to call attention to those stages contained in

---

1. See more on this distinction in part II.

the story material that occur often enough to be crucial for understanding the content of call narratives.[2]

The six stages are: early religious exposure, call experience, struggle, search, support, and surrender. All of these stages contain other components that the study will highlight.

Early religious exposure is the most common stage in the story. Explicit reference to this element does not appear in every narration of the call. However, when the biographical data — a crucial part of the story — are included in the analytical material, it is clear that every person in the corpus was exposed to an early religious environment.[3] This background provided callees with images, models, symbols and relationships that helped to shape their vocational choice.

The home is the key. In the home, the most important influence is a particular person, usually the mother or father.[4] The importance of this environment is captured by Bishop John Hurst Adams's (AME) narrative:

> I guess the best way to start this story is to tell you that I grew up in a very religious home. My father was an AME minister before me. My mother was a very, very avid and devout Christian woman. The combination of those two parental influences was always there. This was always very, very important; and I assume in many respects that the nurturing which they gave me as a child groomed me to be called to preach.[5]

2. Glass, 117. In his dissertation on the psychological and sociological factors related to the call of Negro Baptists, Glass draws the following conclusions about the crisis of the call. "One or more of the following factors should accompany a valid call. It should be cataclysmic, supernatural, emotional, different from secular vocations, and it should be resisted. These phenomena usually follow a definite pattern of 'visions and dreams, seasons of unrest, and giving up to God.'" This is true, however, only for certain types of calls, as we shall discover later.

3. Glass, 170, says, "There were two important discoveries concerning the home, in the thesis. One was the fact that the home was the most important agency in the recruitment of ministers. The second fact was that the Negro home is not as adequate as the white home in influencing the call of its youth to Christian service." While I would agree with the former conclusion, my study would raise serious questions about the latter conclusion.

4. Glass, 61, says, "Another work in this field, with regard to white Baptists, points out the fact that, in the homes where the parents are Christian, attend church regularly, and have family prayer, the call to Christian service is ten times as high as over against these homes which do not have these Christian activities." My study adds data that probably helps to substantiate this claim.

5. Myers, 16.

The importance of the home transcends geographical location, gender, and denominational affiliation, as demonstrated by Yvonne Delk's (UCC) story:

> First, I was nurtured in a family whose stories about how I came into this world and whose connection to powerful women, namely, my grandmother and also my mother, made me feel that there was something special about my life. It was a plain family and it was a church-going family. The whole symbolism of the community of faith surrounding us was just so powerful. The spirit of being a part of the faithful community was sewn [sic] really strong in my family. That was the first beginning of my wrestling with call.[6]

It should be noted, however, that this influence does not require that both parents be religious. In many cases the father was only nominally religious or even nonreligious, but the mother was quite religious and influenced the child by exposing him or her to the community of believers. In some cases it was neither mother nor father, but another family member. Delores Carpenter (Disciples), though she had a religious mother, describes her grandmother's influence on her early religious development:

> When I was born we went back to Towson, and I spent a lot of time with my grandmother. She was a woman who prayed a lot. . . . I saw my grandmother writing religious tracts, and I helped her look up the correct spelling. . . .[7]

The importance of a religious influence in the home cannot be underestimated. It can transcend race and the absence of blood relatives. Earl Cotton (Baptist) says:

> I grew up as an orphan. My father passed away when I was four years old; my mother, when I was eleven. Therefore, I had no particular person to guide and direct me. I lived with some Southern white people. They were Christians, and being in this Christian atmosphere, it kind of kept a sparkle of the Christian life moving in my direction.[8]

6. Ibid., 89.
7. Ibid., 65. Cf. Arlene Churn (Baptist), pp. 78-80, who had neither a religious mother nor a religious father, but whose religious grandmother influenced her.
8. Ibid., 84. Observe certain similarities in the story of a white extended family influencing the religious development of Cain Felder, pp. 104-10.

The church is equally influential. In the five cases where neither parent was religious, the church held the primary role in shaping four of the callees' religious identities.[9] After describing the family as the primary source that influenced her religious development and direction, Yvonne Delk describes the role of the church in that process:

> The second [influence] was really planted in that church that I grew up in. It was my church — Macedonia Congregational Christian Church. It was as much a part of my life as going to school, as living in the community that I lived in. It was the nurturing, supportive community that surrounded us.[10]

The dynamics — models, images, symbols, and relationships — at work within this broader community of faith are powerful indeed. Its most explicit manifestation is imitation — by some callees — at early ages. Male callees are especially explicit about how they "mimicked," "mocked," or "marked" the male preacher.[11] Joseph Blake (Baptist) describes this phenomenon well: "My father was a Baptist minister, and every Sunday when we come from church, I would get in the wagon and have the other children to sit down. I would verbally do my father's whole sermon."[12]

9. Myers: The four callees are Jim Holly (169ff.), Ann Lightner (220ff.), Renita Weems (338ff.), and Alfreda Wiggins (350ff.). Wiggins (UM), 350, relates how her inactive parents contributed to her church involvement. "So I guess it was divine providence, or whatever, that I joined the Disciples of Christ church where I grew up. [My parents] didn't feel like going to church, so they sent me there. Of course, I became very active in their Sunday school. . . ."

Arlene Churn, the fifth person, received her primary religious exposure from her grandmother.

10. Myers, 89. The significance of the church is captured throughout the corpus in different ways. For example, Jim Holly (Baptist), 169, states: "When I was growing up as a kid, I always worked in the church." Vashti McKenzie (AME), 226, makes a similar assertion: "I can tell you now that the call to the ministry began as a girl growing up in church. I can't remember a time when I was not in church."

11. The context in every instance makes it clear that these terms are being used as synonyms of *imitate*, and thus should not be viewed pejoratively.

12. Myers, 38. See also Earl Cotton (Baptist), 84, who says: "I developed a great love for preachers and preaching. From a child on, preachers were my idols, and everything that I did in life was directed towards preaching the gospel. I found myself, as a young child, imitating preachers, preaching to myself going through the woods. . . ." Roderick Pounds (Baptist) had a similar experience: "Even as much [sic] as grade school, people were calling me a little preacher. And I remember mocking the preacher a lot. My friends wanted to play church. They could play church with me." See also E. K. Bailey, who talks about "marking" and "mimicking" the preacher (34ff.), Henry Mitchell (264ff.), among others.

I shall say more later about the consequences of adequate or inadequate role models for female callees. However, it should be noted at this point that imitation of adults in the community of faith is not the exclusive domain of males. Carpenter connects this activity to her call:

> My grandmother said I preached my first sermon when I was five years old. . . . I would have all the children sit down, and I would tell them these stories. Well, this would turn out to be very important to my call — playing church. . . . We imitated people in church and we took different roles, my cousins and I.[13]

The influence of early religious exposure in the extended community of faith (home, church, larger religious community) is graphically depicted in the life of callees who were PK's, or preacher's kids. Though clearly this early exposure has its negative side, in most instances this atmosphere engendered positive influences immediately.[14]

Bishop John Bryant (AME) is very direct about the positive influence this atmosphere had on him. "I've wanted to be a preacher all my life. My father's a preacher and that had a lot to do with it."[15]

This same environment engendered early childhood predictions. They may have been associated with the fact that you were a PK who imitated his or her father and everywhere you would go the people would say, "You gonna be a preacher,"[16] or perhaps you weren't a PK, but just had the "marks in your forehead."[17] Maybe you had been dedicated back to God by your mother.[18] Nonetheless, all of these are manifestations of a powerfully influential environment.

As Cornelius Henderson's (UM) story makes clear, the import of this type of influence encompasses an even larger religious community than one's local church or denomination:

13. Ibid., 65-66.

14. Ibid., 307ff. Joe Roberts is an example of the negative side: He was bothered by the "poverty of ministry" he observed in their home, the "demeaning" position his family was placed in by church trustees and the "demeaning nature" of the bishopric system.

15. Ibid., 58. Similarly Andrew Newberry (AME), 277: "I was reared in an AME parsonage, my father being a minister, and knowing nothing but the ministry all my life, there was a considerable amount of influence that being a PK [preacher's kid] had on my desire to become a minister."

16. Ibid., 38.

17. Ibid., 211. See Myers, 204, where Kemp says: ". . . persons in my family had predicted that I was going to be a preacher. I had a head like a preacher, I looked like a preacher, I acted like a preacher."

18. Ibid., 89.

If I think about it, seeds were planted back almost to my early child-hood development. . . . Charlayne Hunter, the first black female graduate of the University of Georgia, who is now a TV reporter — Charlayne's daddy was an AME chaplain, a minister of an AME church, and I lived next door to his parsonage. When I was two and one-half, three years old, he started planting seeds in my mind about ministry, as I think about it. In high school, ministers would often make similar kinds of comments, Sunday school superintendents, school teachers, etcetera.[19]

The combination of the early influences in the home, church, and larger religious community sometimes led to very unusual circum-stances: Julia Brogdon (Disciples) was made assistant teacher to the deacon board chairman when she was nine years old, and began teach-ing Sunday school every other Sunday;[20] Mack King Carter (Baptist) was placed on the deacon board in his church at age ten;[21] Cheryl Gilkes (Baptist) was given a key to the church at age twelve,[22] and Delores Carpenter (Disciples),[23] Carey McCreary (Baptist),[24] and Arlene Churn (Baptist)[25] preached their first sermons at five years of age.

It should be evident from this testimony that early religious ex-posure influenced greatly the vocational choice of individuals in this collection.[26] Furthermore, the primary place where such exposure oc-curred was the home and church, and in some instances the larger community. PK's are striking examples of the kind of influence — posi-tive or negative — a religious environment can have on children. Whereas some fathers played a role in influencing the child, the mother (or in her absence an extended-family female figure like a grandmoti.er) was the key source of this exposure. Preachers were key persons that were imitated, though other religious people in the church were in-

19. Ibid., 150.
20. Ibid., 49ff.
21. Ibid., 22ff. Glass, 88, records a similar incident: "One church ordained a nine-year-old boy with no religious experience who had been in the church only a few months."
22. Ibid., 124.
23. Ibid., 64ff.
24. Ibid., 233ff.
25. Ibid., 78ff.
26. This is contrary to Glass's conclusions about Negro Baptists. "The home, mother, and father together were given by only fourteen [out of 128] as the factors most helpful in interpreting the call." By *interpreting* Glass also means *influencing*. He asserts that such is not the case with white families.

fluential also. Early childhood predictions about a future life in ministry were dynamics that could occur in the home, church or larger community. These influences on occasion led to unusual responsibilities for some callees at very early ages.

CHAPTER 2

The Call Experience

The second stage is the stage that describes the actual call experience. The stories contain fragments of data that shed light on what actually happened that influenced vocational choice. The three most recurring elements are: an internal urge, signs, and being groomed or nurtured for this vocation. The internal urge and signs often appear in various combinations, thus serving as strong forms of validation for the callee. The signs include a variety of aural, ocular, and other sensory phenomena such as voices and visions.[1] Those who felt that they were nurtured or groomed for this vocation usually did not associate a sign with their call experience. On the contrary, some of them made it explicitly clear that their experience did not include such phenomena. However, just as internal urge and signs appear in combination, so too do internal urge and nurture, though not nearly as frequently.

Urge

There are forty-four narratives that specifically include the "urge" as an important component of the call experience.[2] Urge is often used to describe the call experience, without further explanation of its meaning.[3]

1. Glass, 121, drew this conclusion about visions in his study. "Out of 516 active pastors, a total of sixty-eight had either a dream or a vision. There were fifty-five others who had a revelation which is closely associated with a dream-vision."
2. See the following stories in Myers: 3, 5, 6, 7, 8, 9, 12, 16, 17, 19, 20, 24, 25, 26, 29, 30, 31, 32, 33, 35, 36, 37, 41, 42, 45, 46, 48, 51, 52, 55, 57, 58, 61, 62, 63, 65, 67, 68, 71, 72, 74, 77, 78, 79, 81.
3. Glass, 121, also addresses urge in his study. He says, "One hundred and

Thus, Sharon Austin (Baptist) equates it with "urgings and tugging" at her "heart strings, mind and soul."[4]

Similarly, Alfreda Wiggins (UM) refers to the urge as "nudgings." "But there was still that gentle little nudging going on, and it's something that makes you know that indeed this is a call on your life."[5]

Other terms are often substituted for urge as the callee attempts to explain the experience. However, as with Austin and Wiggins, these terms do not necessarily shed more light on the meaning of "urge." For instance, the call experience is sometimes described in terms of a feeling.

E. K. Bailey (Baptist) describes urge as "feelings that were churning underneath my skin";[6] Renita Weems (AME) maintains that, "There has never been a time in my life when I have not known that God's hand was on me,"[7] and as Alvin Jackson (Disciples of Christ) explains, "I just felt God leading me in the direction of ministry."[8]

Moreover, some people make it clear that, at least at the time of the experience, there was just as much ambiguity for the callee. For example, L. Venchael Booth (Baptist) asserts, "There was an inner urge to proclaim the truth even before I knew much of what the truth was,"[9] and Cynthia Hale (Disciples) says, "I sensed God's call upon my life and not knowing what to do with that. . . ."[10]

Other ambiguous terms used to describe urge are: "inclination,"

---

nine [out of 516] were called by the Holy Spirit and 161 had an inner urge, which can almost be equated with a vision, because a vision is so subjective it can be anything." This conclusion by Glass is most unfortunate, especially since he made no attempt to understand the relationship between the two.

4. Myers, 26.

5. Ibid., 353.

6. Ibid., 35.

7. Ibid., 338. See also ibid., 275, where Otis Moss, Jr. (Baptist), says, "I cannot remember when I did not carry in the inner core of my being the urge to preach"; ibid., 114, where Johnny Ford (Baptist) says, "But down through the years I've always had this deep yearning to be a spokesman for God"; and ibid., 320, where Manuel Scott, Sr. (Baptist), recalls, "My call to the ministry was a consciousness that I felt at the earliest stages of my life."

Contrary to these and others who suggest that their "urge" was something gradual, always there, William A. Jones (Baptist) emphasizes the suddenness of his urge. "I was never aware of any gradual urge to [preach]. It was an overwhelming thing." Ibid., 202.

8. Ibid., 184.

9. Ibid., 44-48. This statement was made during follow-up questions not recorded in the book.

10. Ibid., 144.

"divine seizure or intuition," and "awareness" or "inner, compelling daily thought," among others.

Some terms, though not totally clear, broaden our understanding of the term "urge." Among these are "desire," a sense of "restlessness" and "emptiness," "uneasiness," and "lack of fulfillment" with any other vocational choice.

Sometimes the urge affects the entire life of the person. Bishop Herman Anderson (AME Zion) says, "During those days [i.e. moving from one career to another], I felt a restlessness that would not go away, along with an emptiness or lack of purpose. There was an absence of purpose to my life."[11] On other occasions it influences career decisions in school. Cornelius Henderson (UM) says, "In 1952, when I arrived on the campus . . . there was not a major in physical education. . . . My second choice was that of music. . . . At the end of my first year in music, I still felt a tremendous sense of restlessness and started chatting with some of the student and faculty leaders, some of whom felt that I might have had some of the gifts and graces that a minister possessed."[12]

The use of the term "desire" helps in our attempts to further flesh out the meaning of "urge." E. Theophilus Caviness (Baptist) speaks for many in this collection when he says, "It has never been my desire to do anything else but preach. I mostly articulate it with words of a divine call motivated by an inward urge to preach the gospel. And I could say a ton more of words, but I don't think it will come any more crystal clear than a divine urge to preach the gospel, a divine call. . . ."[13] We are moving ever closer to clarity on this "urge."

11. Ibid., 19.
12. Ibid., 147-48.
13. Ibid., 74-75. As with the term "urge," "desire" is spoken of as something gradual by some and instant by others.

See, e.g., Manuel Scott (Baptist), who recalls, "I never dreamed or proceeded to desire any other type of life pursuit other than preaching. . . . The call didn't come at any ecstatic moment. It came with growing and gradual awareness. . . ." Ibid., 320; T. Oscar Chappelle (Baptist), who says, "I didn't have no cataclysmic call, just always wanted to be a preacher. Never wanted to be anything but a minister." Ibid., 76-77. This quote comes from follow-up questions not recorded in the book. Andrew Newberry (AME) adds, "There was a considerable amount of influence that being a PK had on my desire to become a minister. My calling would not be, per se, the dramatic, one-night event. I would say it was more or less a series of experiential things that took place over the years that led me into that desire to be a preacher." Ibid., 277.

Compare, however, among others, stories like that of Roderick Pounds (Baptist), who says, "Later, as I think about the call and as I have been relating it to other people, I associate it with an overwhelming desire, an overwhelming burden sort of desire. And I had that desire. And that basically depicts what happened that night." Ibid., 288.

James Young (Baptist) sets "desire" in apposition to "urge" as he attempts to shed further light on his experience. "One of the assured ways of one knowing that he has been called is that he wants to preach. It's that longing desire. It's an urge. It is something that you can't ignore."[14]

Odell Jones's (Baptist) juxtaposition of three key phrases in his story sheds additional light. "My calling was that there was an inner voice or inner urge or inner dissatisfaction with doing anything else except the ministry."[15] The context of this statement as well as the follow-up questions make it clear that Jones is using the terms "inner voice," "inner urge," and "inner dissatisfaction" as synonyms.

Perhaps the best description of the concept of "urge," however, comes from Caesar Clark, one of the older (born 1914) and more renowned callees of the corpus. Clark (Baptist) uses biblical call stories and words of his former professor to clarify his urge.

> When Paul was called, you know what crisis he went through. Dr. E. L. Harris used to tell us that if a man can keep from preaching he ought not to preach, because if he can keep from preaching, that is a sign that he hadn't been called to preach. You don't preach because you want to; you preach because you can't help yourself. . . . So you have that inner urge, it haunts you, and you only have a sense — a feeling — of satisfaction when you yield to it.[16]

A number of conclusions may be drawn about the term "urge" found in these narratives. The term encompasses a "consciousness," "inclination," "awareness," and "desire" that ministry is to be one's vocational choice. It may manifest itself as feelings of "restlessness," "dissatisfaction," "uneasiness," and "lack of fulfillment" with any other pursuit in life. It may be variously interpreted by the callee as his or her divine destiny, influenced partially or wholly through human channels. The human channels include a variety of possibilities, such as being a PK,[17] having contact with other preachers,[18] even having an

14. Ibid., 378.

15. Ibid., 200.

16. Ibid., 82.

17. Ibid., 58; Newberry, n. 13. John Bryant (AME) offers, "I could say that my first recollection is made up of my desire to be a preacher. I've wanted to be a preacher all my life. My father's a preacher and that had a lot to do with it."

18. Ibid., 377. Alfred Waller (Baptist) says, "My call to the ministry I would classify as an indwelling desire to promote the cause of Christianity as I had observed it. . . . As a very small lad, I took an interest in the preacher of the church. It seemed as though after he paid my family a visit, that everything around the home seemed to be more happy and more pleasant."

encounter with a prostitute.[19] This urge is described by some as emerging suddenly, but by others as emerging gradually.

Signs

Another important component of the call experience is signs. The attempt by the callees to describe and explain the call experience as an "urge" to preach is the single largest component of the call experience. However, when all sign phenomena are lumped together, signs have an equal place in the narratives. Indeed, this phenomenon is larger (forty-nine cases). Signs include voices, visions, and other concomitant events.[20] As the following discussion will reveal, "voices" refers to the perception of divine communication, and "vision" is used as a synonym for dream or trance. Other concomitant events are varied in nature, including such phenomena as car accidents, bright lights from the sky, and hospital operations.

Voices

Voices heard by the callees are the sign that appears most frequently in the parts of the story that discuss the call experience itself. They occur in a variety of forms. In some instances the callee could not be clear in retrospect about the nature and character of the voices, the meaning of the message conveyed, and how he or she felt obliged to respond. However, the callees speak with absolute certainty and consistency about some aspects of the voices — that they heard a voice, what it said, and when they heard it.

There is a group of callees who assert that the voice was internal, and they suggest that the voice had no gender. Lucille Abernathy (UCC) maintains, "The voice said, 'You can't do what I want you to do and keep teaching school.' I didn't understand it. But it came back again."[21] When

19. Ibid., 157-68. See the story of Samuel Hines (Church of God).
20. Glass, 127, discovered the following: "In a group of 516 ministers, 433 had experiences related to dreams, voices, or visions. . . . Out of 128 students, ninety-five of them had visions or dreams in connection with their call. In these phenomena, Negroes reveal a major difference with white ministers." This conclusion is supported by the work of Mechal Sobel, *"Trabelin' On": The Slave Journey to an Afro-Baptist Faith* (Westport, Conn.: Greenwood Press, 1979), 98-122.
21. Myers, 3.

probed further about the character of the voice, Abernathy says that the voice didn't have a gender and that it was internal and inaudible. "The inner voice is more like a mental voice, if you could put it that way. It's a thought that comes to your mind, not a voice like we are talking now. . . . It's like carrying on a mental conversation with God. . . . It's a thought more than an actual voice."[22] However, on yet another occasion she claims to have heard the voice sounding as if it were external and audible. "I was sitting there and I heard my name. I just heard my name real loud. And I looked around to see if anybody was calling me. It was just the first name.[23] And that was the only time I could actually say that it was audible."[24]

Agnes Alston (Community Church) says, "Just as clear as we're sitting here now, I heard 'Use what you have,' because I had been very apprehensive about [the preaching ministry]. It was as though he was really speaking to my mind telling me to 'use what you have.'" After further probing Alston says the voice had no gender but that its uniqueness would allow her to recognize it from any other voice. She further asserts that it spoke to her "consciousness." "I keep saying 'voice' because it comes to my mind in the form of communication, so we're talking to each other." When asked whether the voice was audible, Alston says, "No, not like your voice coming over to me right now. Into my mind."[25]

22. At this point during the interview Abernathy told me that God was, at that moment, invading her thought to tell her that I had been called to preach, but had not yet acknowledged it. She said that she decided to tell me because the thought kept invading her mind as we talked, so much so that she had no choice but to tell me. She contended that I would acknowledge it after I finished the book on the call. Abernathy was so insistent about hearing this message that was meant for me that after the interview was complete, she asked me if I would do her a favor, which was as follows: (1) Go into the sanctuary and pray to God to reveal to me that I had been called to the ordained ministry. (2) When I finally accept notify her wherever she is because she wants to be at my ordination ceremony.

There is another interesting phenomenon that I have observed about many of those who have been called. They recognize it in others, often before the person does — or at least before the person has verbalized it — and they are very rarely wrong.

23. Martin J. Buss, "An Anthropological Perspective Upon Prophetic Call Narratives," *Semeia* 21 (1981), n. 33 says, "the voicing of a name as the substance of an Eskimo call, and the triple calling of a name in Nepal are similar to biblical call." This biblical pattern would be readily recognized and nonthreatening to someone in the black church.

24. Myers: See the stories of Gilkes (124-35), Williams (360-61), and Churn (78-80) for other instances when their names were called.

25. Ibid., 20-24. Quotes are from follow-up questions during Alston's inter-

Another group of callees asserts that although the voice was internal and meant only for them to hear, it sounded as if it was audible. However, they knew this was not the case. In most instances, this group also claims that it was a masculine voice. Julia Brogdon (Disciples of Christ) heard the voice say, "You know that you have work to do for me." In addition, she asserts that the voice sounded audible to her. "It sounded so loud to me, as though it had consumed the entire room, yet I knew that it was only for me and that no one else had heard it but me. . . . I was totally consumed by that voice. . . . As I laid there, the voice was adamant, and I guess out of my own tradition I would say the voice was masculine."[26]

Mack King Carter (Baptist) helps us in clarifying the internal and external connection of the voice raised by Brogdon's assertions. He maintains, "A voice spoke within me and said, 'Now that your grandmother is gone, you must move up now. You must get eager in your commitment, you must get eager in the faith.'"[27] "It was not an audible voice, but it was so overwhelming until it was almost audible."[28]

James Earl Massey (Church of God) corroborates the internal aspect of the voice but not the gender. He heard the voice while sitting in a worship service one Sunday morning. He says, "In an almost transfixed state, I heard a voice insinuating itself in my consciousness, saying, 'I want you to preach.'"[29] Upon being questioned further about the voice, he says, "It was an internal voice but with the decibel level that would make me sense it from outside. There was no gender. It was just a level of awareness. And the sense of claim was so strong that I

---

view. See the story of Sterling Glover (Baptist), 139, who also claims that the voice spoke to his conscience. "'. . . while I was embalming, something spoke to my mind.' It said, 'You no longer are to work with the dead, but with the living dead.' That was the exact quotation to my mind." Joseph Blake (Baptist), 38-41, adds in follow-up questions that, "It was one of the softest, yet most clearly understood voices I have ever heard." Cf. Churn (Baptist), 78-80, who says the voice was "firm though gentle."

26. Ibid., 49-53. Quotes come from follow-up questions. Arlene Churn (Baptist) also heard the voice as male and external. The voice called her name three times. However, she was also aware that she was the only one that could hear it. McCreary (Baptist; story 52), Vivian Bryant (AME, story 14), William Johnson (Baptist, story 41), and Ron Williams (Brethren, story 80) make similar claims. Williams, Churn, Abernathy, and Gilkes all assert that the voice called their names, in most instances multiple times.

27. Ibid., 72.

28. This quote is from follow-up questions.

29. Ibid., 230-31.

knew I was being spoken to. It was not in the voice of anyone that I had ever heard before, and yet it was not so strange that it startled me. . . . But I've never forgotten the voice. I talk about it now, and it is very clear and is as fresh in my memory as if it happened this morning."[30]

One of the more intriguing accounts is told by Carey McCreary (Baptist), who heard voices through a variety of objects.

> I heard a voice saying, "I want you to leave here and go tell your pastor that you have been called to preach. . . ." I went on down to the church and knocked on the back door. Rev. Fuller opened that door and a voice said to me, "Look at the clock." And it got so tight, my plate would talk to me, my pillow would talk to me. . . . I'd have my plate, sitting there looking at it, and I was about to put my food on it and it would tell me, "You got to preach, you got to preach. . . ." And when I'd lay down at night, my pillow would tell me, "You got to preach." Sometimes it would say, "You must preach." Boy, you talking about being sick.[31]

The concomitant crisis and ambiguity that such a phenomenon engenders are captured well by Cheryl Gilkes's (Baptist) experience. ". . . I was sitting in the house; I heard someone call my name. I looked around and I said, 'Oh boy, I've been working too hard. I'm having an auditory hallucination.' So I signed up to go see a psychologist. I went to therapy."[32] Gilkes was unable to say whether the voice sounded internal or external or whether it had a gender. Yet it was sufficiently unique that she could recognize it if she heard it again.

It is now possible to draw some conclusions about the "voice" that the callees in this corpus discuss. It is not possible to speak with absolute clarity about the nature and character of the voice heard by these callees. There appears to be as much ambiguity for the callees as for the interpreter of these stories. However, this does not mean that nothing can be said. For example, the voice communicates to the mental consciousness in language that is absolutely understandable. Although

---

30. Quotes are from follow-up questions during interview.
31. Ibid., 235.
32. Ibid., 127. James Young (Baptist) says, "something just as plain as I'm speaking now. 'I have a mission for you to do, and that is to proclaim the word of God to a dying world.'" He said the voice sounded like it was external and it was "a calm, mild voice, just a small voice," but he was not able to tell whether it was male or female. Ibid., 378-82, follow-up questions. See also Johnny Youngblood (Baptist). Ibid., 388-91, and follow-up questions.

there may be difficulty in comprehending the full import of the message, not one of the interviewees implies that the communication could not be understood. On the contrary, it is the absolute clarity of the message that caused consternation in most instances.

In a number of cases, the voice so overwhelmed the callee's consciousness that it sounded as if it was external rather than internal. It is this aspect of the communication that causes confusion in some callees' attempts to articulate whether the voice was internal or external. Moreover, some callees know that the voice is meant only for them, even when it sounds external. This suggests that they are probably accurate in their assessment that the voice is actually internal, even when it sounds as if it is external.

There is great consistency among the callees' experiences; in each case, the voice is unique enough that the callee would recognize it among all other voices. The voice is most often described as gentle, smooth, and calm, yet at the same time strong and firm. The fact that it is on some occasions described in decibels as deep or light does not contradict the former characterizations. The voice is not easily ignored. On the contrary, it is very assertive in its purpose.

The messages do not seem to be foreign to the callees. They often come framed in biblical rhetoric or theological overtones. The message may be disturbing because of other factors (e.g., the callee is not ready to accept it for a variety of reasons), but not because the message or mission is unrecognizable. Sometimes the message is no more than calling the person's name, whereas in other instances more elaborate messages are conveyed.

The matter with the greatest ambiguity is the gender of the voice. The majority claim that it is a male's voice. Women make this claim as well as men. However, a number of callees assert that the voice has no gender, and still others say that it is not discernible. This appears to have no resolution, nor does it necessarily require one. The fact that the voice is perceived by people in different ways as regards gender can be explained by cultural predispositions or other factors.[33] The plain fact of the matter is that some say, retrospectively, that they heard the communication in the masculine gender, some in a gender-free form, still others are unable to say. No one, male or female, asserts that the voice communicated in the female gender. To say more would be mere conjecture.

---

33. Buss, 16, claims, "The specific form of a call report is clearly shaped by cultural patterns."

Visions

A second category of signs is visions. There are six narratives in which visions, dreams, or trances are mentioned as a significant part of the call experience.[34]

John Bryant (AME) saw Jesus, who spoke to him in a dream,[35] and Leroy McCreary (Baptist), while in a trance, saw the person that spoke to him. Although he describes the person, he does not call him Jesus as Bryant does.[36] Delores Carpenter (Disciples of Christ) entered a trance in which she was led on a journey.[37] Ann Lightner (AME) had visions in which she saw herself transformed into the person she saw or heard preaching.[38] Ed Wheeler (Baptist) had a dream of his childhood pastor reaching for him with one hand and holding the Bible in the other. Wheeler says, "I knew that was confirmation that I had been called."[39] One of the more incredible cases is that of Carey McCreary (Baptist), whose narrative includes all four extraordinary events — visions, voices, signs, and concomitant crises. Like Wheeler, McCreary had someone handing him a Bible, and like Carpenter, he was led on a long journey. In the journey of his vision he was the one elected to save people who were trapped in a river.[40] It appears as if the callees are using the terms "vision," "dream," and "trance" synonymously.[41]

Concomitant Signs

There are twenty cases in this group. Sixteen of these cases are concomitantly linked to a significant event in the callee's life that influenced his or her response to the call.

Six signs were ocular observations. Three people saw what they perceived to be an unusual light. Jeremiah Wright's (UCC) call received

---

34. This phenomenon played a much larger role in the study done by Glass, 122, who concludes, "Dream-vision was the main event that brought the call to the minds of 128 theological students, with the Bible ranking third and a talk with the minister far down the list. Of these 128 men, ninety-five of them either had a dream or a vision of their call."

35. Myers, 58.

36. Ibid., 242-44 and follow-up questions.

37. Ibid., 64-70. See Sobel for support of journeys in visions.

38. Ibid., 220-25.

39. Ibid., 347.

40. Ibid., 233-41.

41. Ibid. See especially the stories of Carey McCreary (233-41) and Lightner (220-25).

its initial impetus from an unnatural light shining in his college dorm.[42] As a child Cecelia Bryant (AME) experienced a light in the sky shining down on her and her friend. She told her friend that it was God.[43] Barbara Essek (UCC) experienced the whole sanctuary brighten with a white light when she said to herself that she could preach the sermon just as well as the preacher that was preaching.[44] Lucille Abernathy (UCC) saw a cross in the sky.[45] Carey McCreary (Baptist) went blind temporarily and shortly thereafter had the Holy Spirit direct his attention to a clock that registered 12:00 noon.[46] Marvin McMickle's (Baptist) call emerged out of a situation in which a white candle that he had under his pillow turned red overnight.[47]

Six signs described the sensory perception of feeling. Two are related to a crisis moment in the hospital in which the individual's physical health was in doubt. W. Franklyn Richardson's (Baptist) entire nervous system was disrupted,[48] and Charles Tunstall summoned his cousin to his hospital bed to inform her that he was about to die because he had rejected his call.[49] Two others signs are related to sleep. Vivian Bryant (AME) was awakened every morning at 3:45 and had the call to preach impressed upon her mind.[50] Walter Kimbrough's (UM) call required that God wake him up between 3:00 and 4:00 in the morning as a sign that he had been called.[51] William Johnson (Baptist) felt as if his entire body was on fire, burning, but it was a pleasant, enjoyable type of heat.[52] While lying down, as a child, Henry Payden (Baptist) felt the hand of God on his shoulder.[53]

Five of the signs described are linked to unusual motor vehicle events. Julia Brogdon (Disciples of Christ) considers the car accident in which she was injured her "Damascus road experience." It was in an emergency room that she yielded to the voice that told her, "You know

42. Ibid., 363.
43. Ibid., 55.
44. Ibid., 100.
45. Follow-up questions.
46. Ibid., 235.
47. Ibid., 254-55.
48. Ibid., 305.
49. Ibid., 331-32.
50. Ibid., 61. See also ibid., 175: In the case of Susan Newman Hopkins (UCC), it was not her being awakened at an unusual hour, but her awaking her mother at an unusual hour.
51. Ibid., 212.
52. Ibid., 195.
53. Ibid., 283.

that you have work to do for me."[54] Two very similar accidents are those of Henry Jones (Baptist)[55] and Eugene Morgan (AME Zion).[56] Each man was involved in two accidents, the second accident being similar to the first and both escaped serious injury. Both decided that the connections between the two accidents were too strong to be mere coincidence. They interpreted these events as significant parts of their call experience. Gardner Taylor's (Baptist) story is similar in many respects, although there was only one accident.[57] Suzan Johnson (Baptist) was not involved in an accident. However, it was getting stuck in a traffic jam when she needed to be at two other places that forced her to make a vocational choice for ministry.[58]

Two signs described are connected to the callee's intervention on behalf of others. Ronald Fowler's (Church of God) call emerged out of his observation of a young child who had to come to school every other day without shoes.[59] Sam Proctor's (Baptist) call arose out of the brutality that he observed in black fraternity groups on the college campus.[60]

A final sign was Susan Hopkins's (UCC) mother giving her permission to preach at eighteen upon being awakened at the unusual time of 2:00 a.m.[61]

Nurture

The final component of the call experience is nurture. Six interviewees specifically characterize their call experience as "nurture," "tradition," or being "groomed" for it. They come from a variety of denominational groups: Bishop John H. Adams (AME), Yvonne Delk (UCC), Cain Felder (UM), Thomas Hoyt (CME), Ella Mitchell (Baptist), and Ernest Newman (UM). Important elements that distinguish this group are observed in the stories of Adams, Newman, and Hoyt. Bishop Adams says, "I wasn't struck by lightning, and didn't fall off no mountain top. I think I was groomed and nurtured, and I was converted."[62] Bishop

---

54. Ibid., 53.
55. Ibid., 197-98.
56. Ibid., 270-74.
57. Ibid., 328-30.
58. Ibid., 188-94.
59. Ibid., 116-23.
60. Ibid., 289-98.
61. Ibid., 172-78.
62. Ibid., 17.

Newman asserts, ". . . at the age of sixteen when I completed high school, I had a sense of call. Of course, it's been pretty much understood as far as my entire life up until that time, that I was going into the ministry. I did not see any other profession or calling as to what would be my life's commitment."[63] Hoyt adds an important emphasis as well when he contends, "When I was seventeen years old, I accepted the call to preach. And I felt that the call to preach, at that point, was something that I had been nurtured in. It was always an urge to deal with freedom and liberation for people. . . . That has always been a strong urge in me."[64]

Although there is an absence of any extraordinary event of concomitant crisis in this group of call experiences, there does appear to be a "sense of call," an "urge to preach." The difference between this group and the larger "urge group" is that this group seems to place the heavier emphasis on the nurturing process than on the phenomenological events. There appears to be an interdependent relationship between their nurturing and their urge — both of which influenced their vocational choice — that is difficult to disentangle in terms of cause and effect. However, they do seem to imply that, to some extent, their nurturing contributed to their urge.[65]

The call experience is a key part of these call stories. A key component is an irresistible urge to preach that does not abate until fulfilled. It is often validated by a variety of aural, ocular, and other sensory signs such as visions, voices, accidents, and awakenings at unusual times.[66] In addition, certain circumstances in life that cry out for intervention are signs for others to take up this vocation. A final group denies that they had any extraordinary sensory encounters, but says they were nurtured and groomed for ministry in a religious setting that pushed them toward that vocation.

63. Ibid., 280.

64. Ibid., 181.

65. I say this with much reservation, because Newman says some things that on the one hand appear to affirm this conclusion, yet on the other hand appear to deny it. See more on this later.

66. Glass, 125, concludes: "It is a favorite theme of Negro Baptist ministers to recite their conversion and call experience which, in many cases, are cataclysmic. Young men are advised by some pastors to wait until they see or hear something."

CHAPTER 3

The Struggle

The liminality[1] — i.e., ambiguity — of the call experience sets in motion an intense struggle within the callee that may be both internal and external. This is the third stage. The stories contain material that suggests callees struggled with accepting the call to ministry for a variety of reasons. The passages discussing struggle often focus on family conflict, church conflict, and personal conflict manifested as ambivalence, ambiguity, and loneliness. Resisting the call is one of the most prevalent aspects of the struggle. Conflict does not always engender resistance in the callee. However, there are instances when a specific aspect of conflict (e.g., gender for women, youth for some, and the expectations of one who is called for others) becomes the main reason for resistance. In other instances it is a combination of conflicts that causes the individual to resist the call. The discussion that follows will not only address what engendered the resistance, but also how the resistance was carried out. Suffice it to say that most of the narratives in this corpus include a discussion of conflict and resistance as part of the struggle.

Conflict and Crisis

Conflict due to the call into the ministry is a prevalent part of the story.[2] Only a few narratives can be objectively interpreted as having no con-

1. See part III for a full discussion of liminality in these call stories.
2. Glass, 117, says, "From a psychological standpoint, the call of many men is a crisis in their lives."

flict or crisis element in them at all. There are a number of different ways in which the interviewees describe their conflict or crisis.

One way of describing the conflict is much more internal in nature. Callees emphasize a sense of restlessness, emptiness, or unhappiness with any other pursuit or vocation in life.[3] Bishop John H. Adams (AME) is an example of a number of callees across denominational lines for whom the call created both an internal and an external conflict with other preferred vocational choices:

> The intense struggle in my life between the call to preach and my decision to go to law school became more than I could handle. . . . I tried to go other routes and the Lord interfered, circumstances interfered, my own happiness interfered.[4]

Women represent a different group that felt great internal conflict because of their gender.[5] The conflict that developed in some women was so intense it forced them to argue with God. Vivian Bryant (AME), who was Baptist at the time, says

> I would leave my bedroom and go into the family room and just sit there. I just couldn't believe it. I would talk to the Lord and tell him why he couldn't call me; . . . I would tell him I was a woman; I kept telling him that. That was the first thing I would say all the time, "Lord, don't you know I'm a woman?"[6]

Cynthia Hale's (Disciples) story illustrates the enormity of the internal conflict even when there is external support:

> I was during this time a biblical literalist, and I didn't believe that God called women to preach. . . . But others saw that in me. . . . Then my pastor, Alvin Jackson, [and] my local congregation confirmed [my calling into the ministry]. I told them they were crazy, because God didn't call women to preach.[7]

---

3. See, e.g., the following stories in Myers: 3, 4, 8, 21, 25, 27, 32, 33, 35, 38, 40, 41, 42, 50, 51, 55, 62, 82, 85, 86.

4. Ibid., 17 and follow-up questions during interview. Bishop Adams is among a number of people in this collection who intended to pursue vocations in law as opposed to ministry. Gardner Taylor (Baptist) says, "I had been admitted in my senior year of college to the University of Michigan Law School. . . . And I wanted to be a criminal lawyer." Ibid., 328.

5. See the following stories in ibid.: 1, 5, 6, 14, 15, 22, 24, 31, 36, 79.

6. Ibid., 61.

7. Ibid., 144. Of course, there are the obvious instances in which women are

This is particularly striking because most of the denominations cited in this study have a history of accepting women in the preaching ministry.[8]

A third group felt conflict as a result of being preacher's kids (PK's).[9] The fact that PK's who experience conflict as a result of the call are from different denominations illustrates why it is an important aspect of the struggle. It occurs in nonconnectional churches, as attested to by Sterling Glover (Baptist):

> So, early on, I began to talk about being a businessperson. I'd seen a lot of the difficulties that my father had with [the church] membership, because he used to take me around with him when I was very, very young. . . . That kind of orientation really had something to do with my desire not to be a preacher.[10]

Joe Roberts, though a Baptist now, describes what it was like being a PK in a connectional church (AME):

> I was bothered by the poverty of ministry, the lack of material acquisitions, as was evident in my father's life. I was bothered by the solicitous nature and stance (which I felt was demeaning) that was laid upon him not only as he had to deal with trustees who would determine what kind of furniture we had in "their house" — not our house but the house that was theirs — the parsonage. . . . The third thing that I found offensive was the demeaning nature of the black African Methodist Episcopal bishopric assistant, which was definitely a plantation sort of pecking order.[11]

---

aware of prevailing views of the time. Alfreda Wiggins (UM), who was Disciples at the time, says, "First of all, it was unheard of in 1959 that a woman would even think about preaching. . . ." Ibid., 350.

8. Perhaps the problem is not merely denying women ordination in certain denominations, but the level of placement and participation even when ordination is allowed. Essek (UCC) says, "I had an inkling that God was trying to tell me something, but I did not want to think that I was actually being called into the ministry. I didn't know any women in the ministry. I had no role models, no ministers in my family." Ibid., 100.

9. See the following stories in ibid.: 7, 13, 26, 30, 44, 54, 58, 65, 67, 80, 81, 84.

10. Ibid., 137.

11. Ibid., 307-8. E. V. Hill (Baptist), though not a PK, talks about the poverty of the vocation as a reason for conflict. "I not only told the Lord that I wasn't ready to preach, I told him that I hadn't ever planned to, and that I didn't want to be a preacher. All the preachers I knew were very poor, with the exception of a few. We paid them off (preachers) in our community with eggs and bacon and chickens and

A fourth group emphasizes their youth.[12] Restriction on their freedom due to early predictions about their vocations was a source of major conflict for them.[13] McKinley Young (AME) explains how early childhood predictions engender untold conflict in a young person.

> From early childhood — five, six, seven, perhaps even earlier — I would be tagged or labeled by peers or by neighbors or by parents, adults, and others who would see me and say, "He's going to be a preacher. He will be a preacher. He sounds like a preacher." I think there is nothing that created in me more of an anxiety than that, because I think that any young person who is pegged to be something . . . it is almost like you are "wanted to be" yet unable to be, to determine what you want yourself. Someone already knows what you are going to be. That naturally threatens you. It threatens your freedom, your own personal sense of autonomy.[14]

Ed Wheeler (Baptist) describes the social conflict that can emerge for the young preacher.

> It was a struggle at fifteen, because I wasn't sure what was expected of me. . . . I used to love to dance and, you know, all of a sudden, I was being told I couldn't do that anymore. . . . girls at fifteen, fourteen, fifteen-year-old girls, they don't understand going with a preacher. So at first I wouldn't even tell them. Eventually they would find out and the phone conversation usually went something like, "May I speak to Eddy?" And I would say, "This is Eddy." They'd say, "I just want to ask you just one question. Are you a preacher?"

---

peanuts." Ibid., 155. Cf. Glass's study, 48. "Negro Baptist theological students listed the economic reason as first in importance out of eight factors which hindered their call. However, Glass, 135, also concludes, "Economics may be a fundamental deterrent of prospective candidates, but, in many cases, to a person who can receive the call and get ordained, the way is open to economic power. The average Negro Baptist preacher, except the few who are highly trained, is better paid in the ministry for his training than he would be in other fields of work."

12. This is contrary to Glass's, 68, findings: "Negro Baptists are called relatively late in life. . . . Out of 516 men, forty per cent were not called until they were twenty-five and above. Only twelve per cent were called between the ages of 16-18."

In the present study nearly 60% of the callees were called before they reached the age of 20, and 20% of the total were called before the age of 10. The statistics are as follows: less than 10 years old = 15 callees; 10-19 = 32; 20-29 =23; 30-39 = 9; over 40 = 1 and one could not date it.

13. See the following stories in ibid.: 17, 19, 20, 43, 46, 52, 66, 78, 81, 84, 85.

14. Ibid., 384.

I'd say, 'Yeah." They'd say, "Why didn't you tell me? I ain't going with no preacher. We're through." After that [I'd say], "That's why I didn't tell you."[15]

A fifth group encountered conflict because of certain aspects of the actual call experience.[16] Cheryl Gilkes (Baptist) describes for us what perhaps many of the callees in this collection would like to have done, because of certain aspects of their experience, but didn't.

> After all this, I was sitting in the house; I heard someone call my name. I looked around and I said, "Oh boy, I've been working too hard. I'm having an auditory hallucination." So I signed up to go see a psychologist. I went to therapy. . . . Remember, I didn't know at this point that what I was dealing with was God. . . .[17]

Another way of viewing the struggle is from a more external perspective. In these instances, the callees experience conflict with a host of people who exacerbate the internal conflict that the callees are already experiencing. The people that callees had conflict with upon acknowledging a call are varied. They include parents, spouses, pastors, ministers, church members, potential dates, in-laws, friends, and strangers.[18] You would expect that parents, of all people, would be the last to participate in escalating this conflict. However, sometimes they are an indication of more conflicts to come. Sometimes it is well meaning; they want more for their children than they think a vocation in ministry will bring. Upon informing her father that she was going to seminary in order to be a preacher, Cynthia Hale's (Disciples) father responded: " 'You can't go to seminary. You need to go take this job in a bank and be prosperous,' that kind of thing. He said, 'I won't support you.' And I said, 'I'm going anyway, because God has called me.' "[19]

There are other occasions, however, as in the case of L. Venchael Booth (Baptist), when the parents just don't believe the callee:

15. Ibid., 348.

16. See the following stories in ibid.: 29, 45, 49, 68, 83.

17. Ibid., 127.

18. See the following stories in ibid.: 1, 4, 5, 6, 8, 10, 11, 14, 15, 19, 20, 22, 24, 29, 31, 36, 52, 56, 78, 79, 82, 85.

19. Ibid., 145. It should be observed that, as in the case of Cynthia Hale, those who don't support the callee initially often come around later and are quite supportive. Hale says, "I went to seminary out of sheer obedience to God. When I did that, my father came back and was tremendously supportive." 145.

So at seventeen I wrote a letter to my parents informing them of my call to the ministry and expressing the hope that they would permit me to go into the ministry. The letter was not answered, but I did hear them discussing it one night as I laid in bed. My father said, "Well if he's called to the ministry, Fido has been called." That was our little dog.[20]

As with internal conflict the variety of people that women encountered in external conflict due to their call was because of their gender. Lucille Abernathy (UCC) was Baptist at the time she acknowledged her call. Her story captures the full spectrum of people that create external conflict for women in accepting the call because of their gender.

I remember my pastor saying, "Well, you had better be quiet about this, because you don't know what you are talking about and you can't tell anybody. . . ." So every time I would go to prayer meeting I felt like I needed to tell people. . . . So finally I just told them. Everybody got real quiet, and nobody said anything. . . . When I announced my call to ministry it was a total turnoff. . . . Some of the ministers threatened to stop supporting the school because they allowed this woman [Abernathy] to be president of this group. . . . Even in my family, my in-laws more than my family, it was awful. Because they don't believe that God calls women. And my mother went through this thing that my husband was awful because he was going to let me go to school and do all this other stuff. It was terrible. . . . But in seminary people kept saying, "You're not going to be ordained. Who's going to ordain you?"[21]

Delores Carpenter (Disciples) was Free Will Baptist when she experienced similar treatment, and her case illustrates that women were also subjected to abuse by other women.

Now, the first person that I told this to was a woman in our church. And she told me that was the devil, because God did not call women to preach. I was fourteen then, and I cannot tell you the devastation I felt. I was plunged into a very, very deep depression.[22]

---

20. Ibid., 45. It is interesting to note that despite his father's initial assessment Booth went on to become the founder of the Progressive Baptist Convention, one of the largest and most prominent black Baptist conventions in existence today.

21. Ibid., 2-10, passim.

22. Ibid., 68.

Other kinds of external conflicts connected to the time of struggle include accidents,[23] encounters with injustices that require action,[24] and occasions of illness or death.[25]

Resistance

Resisting the call is another prominent aspect of the struggle over the call. The callees provide us with data that help us understand why they resisted the call. On occasion we get a glimpse of how they resisted as well.

Perhaps the largest single group of resisters is PK's. Their resistance is often engendered by the poverty, the lack of freedom, and the expectations that they had to live up to as children of preachers.[26]

A second group of resisters is women. Their resistance is most often connected to the lack of a woman as a model and the rejection of the idea of women preachers by family, parishioners, friends, and others. In some instances they held the belief themselves that a woman could not be called.[27]

A third group of resisters is those who felt that they were either too young or not ready to accept the restrictions that the perception of the call demanded. In some instances it was merely their age that was the source of the resistance. However, in other instances it was the freedom that they would have to give up at that age.[28]

Johnny Youngblood (Baptist) describes this form of resistance well. "I can remember, you can't dance — my mama got into 'You can't laugh too loud, you can't hang out with the girls, you can't play ball.' So, I mean, man, I am going into my teenage years. Who wants those kinds of restrictions? So I figured God and everybody else could wait until I was through that kind of stuff."[29]

A fourth group resisted because they were afraid of being inadequate for the task.[30] Walter Kimbrough (UM) captures this well when

23. Ibid., stories 12, 73.
24. Ibid., stories 28, 34, and 66.
25. Ibid., stories 47, 56, and 74. See also examples in Glass, 119.
26. See the following stories in ibid.: 4, 7, 26, 28, 30, 34, 44, 47, 54, 57, 58, 60, 62, 65, 67, 73, 80, 81, 84.
27. See the following stories in ibid.: 1, 6, 14, 15, 22, 24, 29, 31, 36, 79.
28. See following stories in ibid.: 5, 17, 19, 42, 43, 50, 52, 78, 85.
29. Ibid., 389.
30. See the following stories in ibid.: 46, 49, 82.

he says, "I did not want to preach. I suppose one of the reasons I did not want to preach was because I was scared. I thought it would be so tough to get up before the same people Sunday after Sunday after Sunday and to have something prophetically to say to the people. . . . I thought it was so tough, and I was, frankly, scared."[31]

Others resisted because they had other desires for their life,[32] or no model of ministry that they emulated.[33]

The most prominent way of resisting the call is the attempt to replace it with another vocation.[34] Often professional fields, such as medicine or law, were sought as a suitable substitute. Other ways of resisting it were simply to ignore it, deny it, delay it, or defy it.[35]

It may be that the callees who chose the medical or legal profession as a substitute thought that the prestige and service aspect of the profession would appease God and others. People who attempted to ignore the call were simply hoping that it would go away. People who denied it usually did so publicly when others suggested that they had been called. Additional support for the call was not something that they wanted to hear while they were struggling with it, especially when they wanted to resist it. Those who attempted to delay it usually did so because of the effect that accepting it would have on their freedom at an early age or before they were ready to make such a transition. Some callees' defiance took the form of attempting to make themselves unworthy. The callees did so by becoming gamblers, drunkards, pimps, or the like, in the hope that God would reject them and withdraw the call.

Arthur Kemp's (Baptist) story describes this kind of resistance in more graphic form than any other:

> When it sometime later dawned on me that that would have been a call for me to go into a preaching ministry, then I determined that I was not going to do that. Because preaching was the furthest thing from my mind. . . . I was going to make sure that I would not preach . . . , because I had been taught that if you are going to be a

---

31. Ibid., 212. Glass, 119, says, "Other studies have shown that fear is active in the call."

32. Ibid., stories 51 and 66.

33. See the following stories in ibid.: 22, 55.

34. See the following stories in ibid.: 3, 4, 22, 24, 25, 26, 27, 32, 36, 38, 40, 41, 42, 54, 66, 68, 78, 82, 84.

35. See the following examples in ibid.: ignore it (52); deny it (14, 29, 49, 79); delay it (5, 11, 17, 19, 20, 42, 43, 50, 52); defy it (7, 8, 13, 28, 33, 45).

vessel for God you've got to be a fit vessel and you got to have good behavior, good morals, and good ethics. So I determined that I was going to be the worst possible human being that you could be, to make myself unfit to be a minister of the gospel. . . . I wasn't drinking then, but I started drinking. I had been gambling occasionally, but I became an avid gambler. And subsequently drove getaway cars for thieves. While I did not ever use narcotics, I participated in those kinds of things — money raising ventures if you will, criminal money raising ventures that would get money for those persons. . . . Well, in short, I had prostitutes working for me. I had just become a dyed-in-the-wool rascal through and through, with the avowed intention and purpose that I was never ever going to respond to that call in that hospital room, "Go feed my sheep."[36]

Ambiguity, Loneliness, and Doubt

Ambiguity, loneliness, and doubt: There are occasions in which callees emphasize that the struggle was due to ambiguity or doubt. Had a call actually occurred? What did it mean?[37] They experienced feelings of loneliness as they struggled to understand the call.[38] Julia Brogdon (Disciples), who was Baptist at the time, describes this well: "She would ask me how I felt about being called by the Lord. That was something that at that time I really could not explain to her. I just knew down in my spirit that God wanted me to do something special. What that would be, I would have to wait and see."[39]

Abernathy (UCC), also Baptist at the time of the call, describes the loneliness that one feels as a woman struggling with the call. "Going back to deal with the call itself, I guess the hardest part is being alone in it. Being alone in it and not having anybody else around you to say, yeah, this is wonderful, celebrate it."[40] Yet Carey McCreary (Baptist), who is male, also describes a form of loneliness: "And with me, I was in a strange place and fooling with these old preachers up here. I didn't get any encouragement and it was a hard thing."[41]

There is one final observation that should be made about the

36. Ibid., 208.
37. See the following stories in ibid.: 6, 11, 25, 31, 41, 55, 56, 68, 74, 86.
38. See the following stories in ibid.: 1, 10.
39. Ibid., 53.
40. Follow-up questions during interview.
41. Ibid., 238.

stage of struggle. Some narratives do not contain a discussion of a struggle.[42] Other callees are very specific about not having a resistance to the call, even if they acknowledge having a conflict of some sort regarding the call.[43]

As with the call experience, the struggle is indeed a significant part of these narratives. Conflict and resistance are overwhelmingly consistent as the dominant component of the struggle with the call. Ambiguity, loneliness, and doubt are part of the struggle also, though not as common.

Conflict is frequently depicted internally as a sense of restlessness, unhappiness, and emptiness with the pursuit of any other vocation. Women experience internal conflict because of their gender. PK's experience conflict because of the way their fathers are treated economically, socially, and politically. Others experience conflict as they become aware of the lost freedom and restrictions that the vocation entails. This is especially the case if the callee is young. Each of these conflicts serves as the basis for the resistance of the call.

Some encounter conflict because of the nature of the call experience, especially those that have extraordinary phenomena as a part of the experience. Experiences similar to these are crisis moments due to accidents, illnesses, deaths, or injustices. It would be better in these instances to describe the response as ambiguous, lonely, and uncertain, rather than "resistant." Sometimes in situations like this, fear emerges as a form of resistance. The ambiguity creates doubt in the mind of the callee about his or her competence to fulfill the vocation.

In addition, conflict is depicted externally as encounters with parents, spouses, in-laws, pastors, friends, parishioners, and others who question the authenticity of the call. This challenge may be due to gender, age, prior behavior, or some other reason.

Finally, callees attempt to resist the call as follows: ignore it, deny it, delay it, defy it, or substitute another vocation for it.

42. See the following stories in ibid.: 12, 16, 37, 39, 48, 53, 59, 61, 63, 71, 76.
43. See the following stories in ibid.: 9, 18, 20, 21, 69, 77.

CHAPTER 4

The Search

The struggle puts the callee in a state of disarray. It propels him or her on a journey in search of understanding and a sympathetic ear. This is the fourth stage. In some instances the callee merely wants to share the call with someone, especially someone close. In other instances, however, he or she seeks greater clarity and understanding of the experience. What the callees desire most is help with interpreting the experience. Therefore, people who know something about this kind of experience are sought out, whether they are relatives or not. Sometimes the callee's reasons overlap and are not easy to disentangle. The most frequently sought out people on this occasion are pastors and parents. Although it is necessary to appeal to the biographical data and follow-up questions on some occasions, most callees have a search element in their call story.[1]

Instances in which the callees wanted to tell someone, not for the sake of clarity, but because they just couldn't hold it back any longer are frequent in the stories. The people they choose to tell vary. The person most frequently told is the pastor.[2] This is true whether he or she is the first person told or not. There are a number of reasons why pastors are told. First, since callees are aware of or assume that the pastor had a call also, the pastor is the most logical person from whom to seek help in any attempt to interpret the call experience. In addition, it might be assumed that he has the most theological knowledge about

1. See especially the following stories in Myers: 9, 10, 16, 17, 18, 20, 21, 26, 28, 33, 34, 37, 39, 42, 48, 61, 69, 76, 77, 83, 84.
2. See especially the following stories in ibid.: 5, 8, 15, 16, 17, 19, 21, 24, 33, 34, 35, 46, 48, 66, 69, 76, 77.

it. Another reason, however, is the "rites of passage."[3] More than anyone else, the pastor holds the key to passage in the community of the called. He can help or hinder the callee in receiving the validation needed from the community of believers. It is noteworthy, then, that on occasion there is great hesitancy on the part of the callee to go to the pastor.

Leroy McCreary (Baptist) went to at least three other people before going to his pastor, even though his pastor was also his cousin. He says, "I had anticipated some difficulty there. I did not think that [the pastor] would accept it as easily as he did. I had some reluctance in going to him initially."[4]

Fear of rejection by the pastor is perhaps part of the reason for the callee's hesitancy. Rejection by the pastor makes it most difficult for the callee to get sanctioned in the community. However, Cheryl Gilkes (Baptist) uncovers another reason. In response to the question, "Why weren't you ready to talk to your pastor?", she said, "Because talking to your pastor was like saying, I'm called to the ministry, let's get it on."[5]

Callees are aware of the fact that momentum takes over when you tell the pastor about your call, because he is in a position to do something about it, positively or negatively. If he believes the callee, this will usually start a move toward confirmation that is very difficult to stop. Therefore, if the callee is not sure of the call and wants to consider turning back, it had best be done before mentioning it to the pastor. After the pastor is told, it is a most difficult matter to reverse.

Ron Williams's (Brethren) experience is not unusual. He was AME Zion at the time. He contends: "I called my father [who was also his pastor] and I said, 'Dad, don't tell anybody, but I've decided to enter the ministry. I'm tired of fighting.' He did not honor my word. . . . He got up in front of eight hundred people the next Sunday and told all of them that I had entered the ministry. Then I was caught. I couldn't get out. Not only did he do that, but he set a date for me to accomplish my trial." [6]

3. See part III for a fuller discussion of the call as rites of passage.
4. Ibid., 244.
5. See Gilkes's story (29) in ibid. This quote comes from follow-up questions during the interview.
6. Ibid., 361. The "trial" sermon has reference in the black church to the initial sermon given by one acknowledging a call before any license is issued. In many communities a license is issued to preach upon the completion of that sermon. What this event may once have represented — a true trial — has long been lost, since no one having reached this point is now turned back.

The other large group that is told are parents. It should not be surprising that PK's often tell their fathers first; other "non-PK's" do this also.[7] However, all PK's do not tell their father first; a number of them tell their mothers; other non-PK's do this also.[8] This may be due to a variety of reasons. Particularly in the case of PK's the callees come from Christian homes; telling one parent about this great experience is like telling the other. In some cases, of course, the father is not alive, and some are closer to their mothers. Charles Booth (Baptist) describes why some callees tell parents first. "I had come at that point to a place of not being able to contain it. . . . It was just bubbling over. . . . I remember sitting at the kitchen table in my mother's home, saying, 'Mama, I have been called to preach and I've got to do it.' "[9]

Often another person, who just happens to be available when the callee needs to tell someone, is told before the pastor. Most callees seek out someone with a sympathetic ear who is safe; a person who will understand what they are talking about is a bonus, but first and foremost they merely want a nonjudgmental listener. Many callees assume that this is possible with parents, especially Christian parents. However, such a bonding may also exist with a best friend, a roommate, a spouse, or another relative or acquaintance.[10] Sometimes the experience is so overwhelming that the callee just has to tell someone even if no close bond exists — even if he or she does not get a sympathetic ear.[11]

Therefore, when the call experience happened to James Massey (Church of God) in church, he merely turned to the person sitting next to him and told her. Later he told his mother, father, and pastor, respectively.[12] After a car accident that compelled him to accept the call, Gardner Taylor (Baptist) told the college president whom he had been chauffeuring when the accident occurred that he "felt called to the ministry."[13]

7. See the following stories in ibid.: 27, 28, 30, 39, 42, 44, 54, 61, 65, 80.

8. See the following stories in ibid.: 9, 10, 12, 18, 20, 22, 63, 71, 78, 86.

9. Booth's is story 9 in ibid. This quote comes from follow-up questions during the interview.

10. See the following examples in ibid.: best friend (6); spouse (83), and a variety of other relatives and acquaintances — cousin (74); grandmother (84); bishop (26, 33).

11. Ibid., 260. Ella Mitchell (Baptist) says, "I felt very much the call to ministry. I grew up in it, and felt nurtured by my father and very much encouraged by him. All the while my mother was just dying inside, and when I went to seminary she just about flipped. . . . She wasn't happy that I would go to seminary. . . ."

12. Ibid., 230-32.

13. Ibid., 329.

Equally prominent in these stories are instances in which the callees went searching for help in understanding the call. The people they went to for clarity are also varied. Again, the most frequent person sought out is the pastor.[14] Carey McCreary's (Baptist) story captures a variety of reasons why callees go to a pastor seeking clarity in understanding their call experience:

> As I was telling Rev. Fuller what the Spirit told me — "I was downtown looking for a job and the Spirit told me to come and tell you I was called to preach." — he said, "Well, that's one thing you got to be sure of." Then I said, "Well, maybe I won't have to do it," because he didn't seem to believe me. . . . Now, that Sunday night after I went to Rev. Fuller and I asked him about what the Spirit told me when I was downtown . . . he asked me to come to his house. I went down to his house. He told me, "Now you got to be sure that the Lord called you to preach." In the way he talked to me and what the folks had told me about him, I felt like whatever he told me, that would be what God wanted. . . . So I said to myself, all right, maybe it's not so. Well, I felt kind of good because I thought I didn't have to preach.[15]

First, ambiguity exists about the experience as well as the interpretation of the experience. Callees go to the pastor because they perceive that he or she, above all others, can help interpret the struggle in which the callee is involved. Since the pastor had a call experience, and since he or she is the resident theologian for that local church as well as the key person in the rites of passage process, the callee expects that he or she can help experientially, theologically, and politically in dealing with the experience. Obviously, if the pastor validates the call, this aids the callee tremendously. Yet, at the same time, if the pastor questions the call, it provides a way out for callees who wish to rationalize their resistance.

The callees that have the greatest difficulty are those who go to their pastor hoping that he or she will say something that will validate their resistance. Ann Lightner's (AME) story exemplifies this well:

> So, after that, I called Reverend Bryant up and I told him, "I need to make an appointment to come talk with you." . . . I told him, "I think the Lord is calling me to preach." . . . So, he said, "Have you accepted

14. See the following stories in ibid.: 14, 15, 24, 32, 40, 41, 49, 50, 52, 55, 58, 86.

15. Ibid., 235, 237.

it?" And I said, "Well, at this point I realize that that's what's happening but I don't know what to do." "Well, you either say yes or no." "Well I can't say no. Because it is haunting me. But I don't know what to do." "You do what the Lord is calling you to do." "But I can't do it." . . . "Reverend Bryant, I never wanted to be a preacher." . . . "I'll give you a trial sermon date if you want it." "Right now?" "Yes." "But you make people wait." "Not when I already know." . . . Well, then I was floored. I said, "Well why didn't you tell me." He said, "It wasn't my place to tell you. The Lord had to show you." . . . He went to his book and he said, "I'll give you December fourth." That was my trial sermon date. . . . I said, "Reverend Bryant, I've got a son. I don't have any money to go to school. I've got to support my son. I need to go to seminary, and dah-dah-dah." He said, "Don't worry about all that."[16]

In addition to seeking the pastor, callees go to fathers, mothers, spouses, other relatives, and friends seeking help in understanding and interpreting the experience.[17] Again, although callees may start with these people, they do not end with them but proceed seeking greater clarification. Sometimes the callees are even sent to others by the one to whom they are talking. Perhaps the person doesn't feel that he or she can help the callee experientially, theologically, or politically with this experience. Leroy McCreary's (Baptist) pilgrimage is a good example. After first going to the public auditorium to talk with a visiting evangelist in town about his call, McCreary went to others as well.

And it was a short time after that I went to my aunt with whom I was living. And I said to her that God has called me to preach. She expressed some surprise and shock, and I told her he had and she said to me, "Well you better go and see Rev. Carey McCreary. . . ." However, I do need to backtrack for a minute. Just before going to her, my aunt, I believe I spoke to a minister, a minister who someone had told me was very good in helping young men get started in the ministry, whose church was on East 79th or 89th and Wade Park. It's a Methodist church. . . . And I went there and told him that I had been called to preach. And he told me the first step in getting started is to go see my pastor. . . . I went to Rev. McCreary and I told him.[18]

16. Ibid., 223.
17. See the following stories in ibid.: for fathers (3, 7, 13, 60, 67, 80, 81); mothers (11, 31, 47, 51, 57, 85); spouses (1, 62); other relatives (53); and friends (29, 36).
18. Ibid., 243-44.

What is even more intriguing about Leroy McCreary's story is that while we have been best friends who have shared almost everything with each other for more than a quarter century, I knew nothing about this sequence of events until sixteen years later when I recorded his experience. Callees who first share their call experience with someone who is safe, but perhaps unable to help them understand it, thereafter search for people whom they believe can help them interpret and understand their experience. Usually this is someone who has either firsthand theological knowledge about the matter (e.g., a seminary professor)[19] or firsthand experiential knowledge (e.g., a preacher).[20] Ultimately, the callee's pastor is the best person, because he or she has both theological and experiential knowledge to help the callee interpret the experience. Moreover, he or she has the political knowledge necessary to help move the callee to the next step, though this may not be part of the callee's motive for going to the pastor. His or her initial motive may be merely to get a better understanding of the call experience, not necessarily verification or validation of the call.

The struggle propels each callee into what is sometimes a tortuous search, looking for someone adequate with whom to share his or her experience, especially someone who can help him or her interpret and understand it better. Parents, relatives, friends, especially those who have not experienced a call themselves, are probably contacted because they are often close, safe, and sympathetic. Such people are always needed and sought out when struggles arise in a person's life. Seminary professors and preachers, whether relatives or not, are probably sought out more for theological interpretation and clarification than anything else. Yet, in the final analysis, the most important and dominant person in the search for understanding is the pastor.[21] The pastor combines the political, theological, and experiential knowledge necessary to move the callee through the rites of passage. It matters little whether the callee speaks to the pastor first; ultimately he or she must go to the pastor. And this may create an incredible amount of anxiety, some justifiable and some unjustifiable.

Perhaps the most revealing aspect of the search is what it says about the power and role of the pastor. We have observed some heavily

19. See the following stories in ibid.: 38, 43.
20. See the following stories in ibid.: 53, 54, 59, 79, 82.
21. This is contrary to Glass's study, 82-83. He claims that the pastor was not a factor among Negro men called to the ministry, but was the most important person among white Baptist students called to the ministry.

laden experiences in which callees believe that they have had an encounter with God. Yet the solitary experience with God is not enough to validate the call. Those called seem to need human validation. Even if they don't get it and instead receive validation from some event that clinches the call experience for them, they still seek human validation from people in the community of faith, especially those who have had this kind of experience and subsequently were validated themselves.[22]

Further, although callees may start with someone close, such as a family member, even if they get confirmation from that person it is not enough. They need or want additional validation. Vivian Bryant (AME) is an excellent example. She says, "But first I'm going to talk to my daughter and my husband, and see what they say about it. If they say no, then that's going to do it. Or if they say yes, then I'll speak to my pastor."[23]

Although Bryant starts with her family, she decides beforehand that even if they say yes she will go to her pastor. Perhaps this is evidence of the recognized role of the pastor as the political power broker in the rites of passage process. However, it may indicate more the need for confirmation from someone who has experienced the existential struggle that the call places upon a person.

22. Paul is the best biblical example of this dynamic. See Gal. 1:11 and 2:10.
23. Ibid., 62.

CHAPTER 5

The Sanction

Sanction in the sense of validation and confirmation of the call is the fifth stage. This element refers to those portions of the story that discuss the set of circumstances and people who helped to confirm the callee's call to ministry. We discovered in chapter four that the callee goes on a search for understanding. Usually that search brings him or her into contact with a variety of individuals as well as a variety of circumstances. It is out of those experiences that the callee receives some form of confirmation as to the nature and authenticity of the call. A variety of responses, then, are given to the callee. And among these responses, a variety of people are found sanctioning the callee's sense of call, therefore influencing his or her final decision.

Only two callees in the entire corpus fail to discuss this aspect of the call.[1] The various people who offer confirmation include pastors, family members, and others. In addition, a significant group of callees place more emphasis on circumstances and providential signs as key to their sense of being validated.

As one would expect, the person who most frequently sanctions the callee's sense of call is the pastor.[2] This is not necessarily due to the pastor going out of his way to help the callee settle his or her struggle. It is more likely due to the fact that ultimately the callee must receive the sanction of the pastor if the callee is to get beyond the liminal state. Without the pastor's confirmation, the callee could remain "betwixt and be-

1. See the following stories in Myers: 20, 39. Two additional callees (61, 69) discuss it in follow-up questions during their interviews.
2. See the following stories in ibid.: 3, 5, 6, 14, 15, 24, 34, 36, 45, 47, 49, 53, 59, 60, 66, 68, 71, 76, 79, 81, 84, 86.

tween."[3] Although the callee goes to the pastor seeking help to get out of the liminal state, his or her desire is not always to move forward in the call process. Some desire to return to a "pre-call" (preliminal) state, and hope to accomplish this by going to the pastor and being denied confirmation. Barbara Essek (UCC) is a perfect example of this liminal state.

> I made an appointment with my pastor. . . . I said to him that I thought I'd been called into the ministry. I was expecting him to ask me a lot of questions. . . . But his response was — the first thing he wanted to do was — to get me into seminary, "and then we'll put you in the in-care process for ordination," and so forth. I had to stop him, because I wanted him to tell me that I really had not been called.[4]

Bishop Adams (AME), however, went to the pastor seeking help resolving his vocational conflict and clarifying his call:

> At that time the Reverend Charles S. Spivey, Sr. was the pastor of St. John. This intense struggle in my life between the call to preach and my decision to go to law school became more than I could handle. So I started talking to him about it, and he helped me considerably to clarify my call.[5]

Family members are the second largest category of people who help to sanction the call.[6] Again, this practice transcends denomination, gender, and age boundaries, as the following quotes illustrate:

3. Ibid., 237. Carey McCreary says, "I had woke up and the Lord hadn't called me. I was a little disappointed, but I was partly glad too, because I felt I wasn't gonna do it. So I was *betwixt and between*" (my emphasis). See part III for a discussion of the liminal state, sometimes referred to in narrative theory circles as a state of being "betwixt and between."

These terms, "liminal state" and "betwixt and between," are used by scholars to refer to a state of instability (uncertainty, confusion). As regards the callees in this study this "instability" may on some occasions mean that they are undecided or ambivalent about what course of action they should take. However, it is that and more. This state is best captured by van Gennep's term ("liminal") and what other scholars refer to as "betwixt and between" which entails a complete state of confusion (mentally) about what's happening and an instability (emotionally) about what to do about it.

4. Ibid., 101. Cf. Leroy McCreary (Baptist), who also went to his pastor: "It was on a Saturday morning, as best as I can recall, and I told him I had been called to preach, and I was shocked at how easily he accepted my confession that I had been called to preach." Ibid., 244.

5. Ibid., 17.

6. See the following stories in ibid.: 3, 4, 6, 9, 13, 14, 22, 28, 30, 31, 34, 36, 44, 63, 65, 78, 80.

Sharon Austin (Baptist), who had some difficulty because she was female, was sanctioned by her father.

> My dad did not have a problem believing [in my call], because he had already gone through his own sort of miraculous call experience as a middle-aged man. He had already dealt with the naysayers and those who sort of wondered if Austin finally had lost it. And so I received his support. . . .[7]

Vivian Bryant (AME) received sanctioning from her husband and daughter.

> I spoke to my daughter and my husband, and my daughter's words were, "What took you so long?" My husband's response was, "I've known you were called all along. You're very different." . . . It was as if the Lord had prepared them for my final acceptance, even though I hadn't accepted at that point.[8]

Often fellow parishioners[9] are key individuals in the sanctioning process. Lucille Abernathy (UCC), Baptist at the time, is a good example:

> When I came home from seminary, there was a little lady, she was very elderly, and had been my teacher when I was three years old. She had been in this church all her life. She said to me, "When you went away to school, I thought that was the worst thing you could have ever done, but now I see what God has done." So, it took all those years, but it was another confirmation that God does call women and that women could finally recognize and appreciate it.[10]

On occasion other preachers help to sanction the call.[11] Yvonne Delk (UCC) says, ". . . All of those seeds began to come together for me at a time that a person came and said to me, 'Yvonne, as you think about what you are going to do with your life, I have often thought that I would like to have you think about seminary.' And suddenly when that person (the Reverend Purcell Austin) named that, all these other pieces seemed to come together."[12]

7. Ibid., 29.
8. Ibid., 62-63.
9. See the following stories in ibid.: 1, 11, 14, 18, 22, 32, 36, 37, 45, 50.
10. Ibid., 6.
11. See the following stories in ibid.: 1, 7, 14, 22, 29, 31.
12. Ibid., 91.

A variety of others received sanctioning from acquaintances and strangers, such as seminary faculty, students, strangers, friends, an employer, and other women.[13]

James Forbes (UCC) tells how a stranger influenced his ultimate acceptance.

> First of all, I got a job over at the Francis Scott Key Hotel. While I was there, a man — I was serving as a bellhop and a man who was at the hotel at that time, I would take him to the seventh floor every-day — would get off the elevator on the seventh floor, turn around and say, "Young man, the Lord has a purpose for your life."[14]

A large group of callees received sanctioning from circumstances and phenomena distinct from individual sanctions.[15]

These concomitant sets of events include aspects of the call experience as follows: visions or dreams, car accidents, crisis situations, lack of fulfillment in doing anything else, getting into seminary as a female and graduating, deficient economic and academic backgrounds, opportunities to preach and fulfillment in preaching, and having all other options turn into dead-end streets. Two examples will suffice.

Agnes Alston (Community Church) recalls:

> These were sanctions to me, because when I stepped on the Wilber-force's campus, Dean Spivey said to me that he thought I should be over on the college side and not seminary because there were no women at the seminary. . . . The only place that would accept me was Wilber-force. . . . Again, that was a sanction to me. I was told when I arrived there that I would never finish. The Lord blessed me and I knew he was sanctioning my ministry, because I finished. In fact, in everything that I have done, I have received a sanction from the Lord.[16]

Marvin McMickle's (Baptist) sanctioning came as a result of encountering a series of dead-end streets:

> What finally began to nail this down for me was that every other thing that I tried to become interested in academically and vocation-

---

13. See the following stories in ibid.: for faculty (6, 38); students (10, 25); strangers (14, 26); friends (29, 36); employer (30); and other women (77, 79).

14. Ibid., 112.

15. See the following stories in ibid.: 1, 5, 12, 14, 16, 17, 19, 21, 22, 24, 28, 33, 35, 38, 40, 41, 42, 43, 46, 47, 48, 50, 51, 52, 55, 56, 57, 58, 61, 64, 67, 69, 73, 74, 78, 80, 82, 83, 84, 85.

16. Ibid., 22.

ally was a dead-end street. The only opportunities that were being afforded me in terms of chances to exercise natural gifts and talents were in relationship to those gifts and talents that could best be applied in this field. What I began to deal with then was a series of confirmations and a series of dead-end streets.[17]

There is another element that emerges during this sanction stage of the call. Some people claim to have known about the callee's call before the callee told them. It is intriguing to observe how the claimant handled this prior knowledge and why he or she handled it that way. Fifteen narratives contain specific assertions of someone claiming knowledge of the callee's call before the callee expressed it. The claimants include pastors and preachers[18] and family members.[19]

One might wish to argue that many of these claims were based on mere conjecture or different behavior and life-style of the callee. In those instances the claim would be similar to the predictions about children becoming preachers because of the shape of their head[20] or some other sign. Furthermore, such a claim might be based on the desire of the claimant, as in the case of PK's whose fathers wanted someone in the family to carry on the family tradition.[21]

Yet the data amassed from these stories seem to militate against these conclusions. When Joseph Blake (Baptist) finally acknowledged his call in the midst of the congregation, the pastor said, "I knew it from the day you came here."[22] Arthur Kemp (Baptist) had a similar encounter sitting in a prayer meeting where he was, for all intents and purposes, a stranger. He was overwhelmed by the burden to preach and started to cry. He says, "And nobody could understand what was going on and the pastor . . . said, 'I know what's wrong with him. I know what's wrong with him, he hasn't told me but I know what's wrong with him.'" When he finished crying he recalls that, "The first words that came out of my mouth was, 'I've got to preach, I've got to preach, I've got to preach.'" And [the pastor] said, "I know it, and you're not going to have any peace until you do."[23] Vivian Bryant (AME) adds that a minister at another church made a similar claim

17. Ibid., 256.
18. See the following stories in ibid.: 8, 14, 15, 24, 29, 36, 45, 49, 53, 66, 83.
19. See the following stories in ibid.: 14, 30, 44, 62, 80.
20. See ibid., story 45.
21. See ibid., story 61.
22. Ibid., 40.
23. Ibid., 209-10.

about her.[24] Similarly, Delores Carpenter (Disciples) explains, "So, when I told [the pastor] that I had this great thing to tell him, after I had struggled and finally I was ready, he looked up and said to me, 'I know.'"[25]

Perhaps the best explanation for this series of events is to be observed in the PK narratives. Sterling Glover (Baptist) says, "Then I told my father. He said, 'I knew it all along.' I said, 'Dad, why didn't you say so?' He said, 'I wanted you to make sure that this is what you are to be about. Only then will you be successful at it.'"[26] And William Jones (Baptist) recalls, "Even though my father noticed what was happening, he played it rather cool; he said later that he would never be personally instrumental in alerting anybody to the call, but he knew that I would come to him eventually to deal with the matter."[27] Unlike any other vocational choice, perhaps, people want to be sure that not only is this the choice of the callee, but more importantly the choice of God.

There is no doubt that sanctioning is a key element in these narratives. It is found without exception throughout the corpus. This is substantiated, of course, by the mere fact that every one of these callees has been ordained.[28] It is also clear that, as with the search stage, one person or event is usually not sufficient confirmation. Sanctioning is a process that may include an admixture of individuals and concomitant circumstances and phenomena, or a variety of individuals. The key individuals are pastors and family members.

Again, as with the search, family members are important because they are often sensitive and, for the most part, safe. Pastors are more

24. Ibid., 62. It could be argued that the claim made by Vivian Bryant's daughter and husband may be an indication of something based merely on observed mannerisms.

25. Ibid., 69. See also ibid., 175-76: Susan Hopkins (UCC) says, "I walked in [the pastor's] office and said, 'Reverend Derm, the Lord has called me to preach and I've accepted the call.' He said, 'Susan, is that all you're bothering me about? I knew that the first day I saw you. Everybody knows it but you."

26. Ibid., 140.

27. Ibid., 202. Ibid., 284. Henry Payden makes a similar statement about his father: "My father had told my mom that when I came out of the service, I would be preaching, but he didn't share it with me. His reason was that he didn't want to call me, he wanted the Lord to do it. I never knew this until after I acknowledged my call to my father."

28. Obviously this is the most direct form of sanctioning. However, it does not have to be the only form. Witness John Calvin and Dwight Lyman Moody, who were "recognized" though never ordained.

important because they can existentially identify with the callee as well as deliver him or her from the liminal state. However, there are other individuals such as preachers, seminary teachers, friends, students, and parishioners who help confirm the call. It is also evident that some people perceive the person's call even before he or she expresses it. However, many of them do not feel it is appropriate for them to share that knowledge until the callee expresses that he or she is wrestling with a sense of call.

The circumstances and phenomena that are part of the validation process are usually a series of concomitant events. There are occasions when a single event may be perceived as the event that pushed the callee into the next phase. However, it seems undeniable that a series of events usually precedes this crisis event. Getting into or out of seminary, visions, voices, a persistent urge that leaves one restless and unfulfilled, a series of dead-ends with all pursuits other than ministry are but a few examples of the phenomena that help sanction the call.

CHAPTER 6

The Surrender

This part of the story describes the callee's acknowledgment, announcement, or acceptance of the call. This is the sixth and final stage. As with the struggle and search stages, surrender is a key part of the narratives. It is absent in only ten (out of eight-six) of them.[1] Surrender is usually described in one of three ways: yield, relief and/or peace, satisfaction, or fulfillment. Occasionally a few overlaps occur; however, one of the three descriptions tends to be dominant.

The state of yielding appears to be neutral and nondescriptive in nature, at least as far as emotions are concerned.[2] This is not to suggest that emotions are not part of yielding; it's simply that the callee gives up the struggle and accepts the new way of orienting his or her life. While this yielding is a kind of submission, sometimes it is not a very humble surrender at all.

Ann Lightner (AME) explains that her surrender came after a long struggle and on a specific occasion after she awakened from yet another dream about preaching. "I was dreaming, here I was preaching again. Preaching in my dreams and I woke up singing. . . . It was like that was the seal for me. Because I actually woke up and it was like I was still in a trance, but I was actually sitting up in my bed singing this song when I came to myself and I just said, 'Well, Lord, I surrender.' "[3]

Joseph Blake (Baptist) describes his surrender before the congre-

---

1. See the following stories in Myers: 5, 18, 35, 39, 43, 58, 60, 61, 67, 76.
2. See the following stories in ibid.: 1, 3, 4, 6, 7, 8, 10, 16, 17, 19, 22, 26, 28, 29, 34, 36, 37, 38, 41, 44, 47, 48, 49, 51, 53, 56, 57, 62, 63, 64, 66, 68, 69, 71, 73, 74, 80, 81, 85.
3. Ibid., 225.

gation with these words, "I can't hold out any longer, the Spirit of the Lord has been on me a long time to preach."[4]

Sometimes when the callee yields to the call, requests are tacked onto the surrender. E. K. Bailey (Baptist), a PK who had resisted from the beginning, says, ". . . it was the 'university of hard knocks' that God used to cause me to submit to the call. Because I was a hard nut to crack." Bailey was living in abandoned cars and on park benches at the time. Correction of that situation was the request tacked onto his surrender. "If you are willing, I need you to do something about this situation. And if preaching is what I have to do, I'll do it. . . . I had been a fair to poor student most of my academic pilgrimage. . . . I tacked onto my surrender, 'If you gonna call me to preach, I gotta go to school.'"[5]

On occasion the callee not only attaches stipulations to the surrender, but the surrender itself is not too humble. Henry Mitchell (Baptist) acknowledges as much. "Well, to make the story no longer, I finally just decided that, well, I can't even sleep, it's gotten this bad. I might as well give up. And in prayer I surrendered. It was not a very humble surrender, it was almost as if I was saying in modern-day terminology, 'Okay, I'll preach your old gospel if you'll get off of my back.' I had also a stipulation: 'But you understand that if I do preach it, I refuse to be a stereotypical chicken-eating, Cadillac-driving, whatever, whatever, preacher. And, I want to do something different and really creative if I'm gonna be a preacher.'"[6]

On some occasions the surrender is described as a sense of relief that the burden that came with the call experience and continued, even heightened, during the struggle is now lifted. Often it manifests itself as peace in the mind and life of the callee.[7] Vivian Bryant (AME) connects her relief to her inability to sleep. After going to her pastor, who was one in a long line of those who confirmed her call, surrender occurred as she left his office. "On my way out, I started singing, 'Have Thine Own Way, Lord.' From that night up until last night, I have slept all night, each night."[8] And sometimes surrender is described as a relief from a sense of burden. Delores Carpenter (Disciples) also connects her

---

4. Ibid., 40.

5. Ibid., 36. Cf. 151-56, E. V. Hill's story (33) for a similar condition tacked onto his surrender.

6. Ibid., 267.

7. See the following stories in ibid.: 9, 11, 12, 14, 15, 24, 27, 31, 42, 45, 46, 52, 54, 55, 57, 59, 65, 79, 82, 83, 86.

8. Ibid., 63.

surrender to her pastor confirming her call. "It was very wonderful to have that burden lifted from me and to just strike out."[9]

Surrender can occur at different places. Johnny Ford's (Baptist) occurred in Israel at the Sea of Galilee. "I just went down by the Sea of Galilee and in a sense I said to God — because all these years I had been fighting it and putting it off — I just finally said to the Lord, 'If you want me to serve you, then that's what I want to do.' I felt so relieved."[10]

Other times surrender is described as a sense of peace. It may come at different points. Barbara Essek (UCC) recalls, "I started the seminary in September of '81. When I walked in the door that morning, there was a sense of peace and confidence that I had never felt before. I knew that that was where I belonged."[11] Walter Kimbrough (UM) felt the same peace when he told his pastor about his call. "Thursday morning I shared with him and from that point it was like a burden just kind of rolled away. So rather than the apprehension, the fear and the rejection, was total acceptance and harmony and peace in my life. Which for me was kind of the affirmation that this is what I wanted to do and had to do and be about."[12]

Perhaps Vashti MacKenzie (AME) sums up the emotional release after one surrenders best: "It was in November that I walked down the aisle and finally told my pastor that I'm accepting my call to preach. . . . Then after that, I experienced such a peace I had never experienced. It seems like for the whole year and a half it was like a fighting and struggling, waking up every morning and saying, 'Who's going to win today? Who's going to win out?' After that I never had such a peace. . . . I mean, it was like, whew! I was just at peace with the world, at peace with God, at peace with myself. . . . Then the turbulence of the past was just the bridge that you came over."[13]

On other occasions the surrender is described as a sense of satisfaction and fulfillment. After the callee has tried other vocations and endeavors, his or her surrender to the vocation of ministry satisfies like

---

9. Ibid., 70.

10. Ibid., 114.

11. Ibid., 103.

12. Ibid., 212. Samuel McKinney's (Baptist) story demonstrates how others receive the same sense of relief and peace when the callee finally surrenders. When he surrendered, he says, "My mother was in the kitchen. She dropped what she was doing and came in there. My mother's oldest sister, who lived there with us, came in. They said, we're glad; we knew you were wrestling with something this summer, now maybe we can get some peace around this house." Ibid., 251.

13. Ibid., 229.

nothing else has been able to do.[14] Cynthia Hale's (Disciples) sense of satisfaction occurred upon entering seminary. "It was during my first week of seminary that it became crystal clear that this was the place for me. I'd never been so happy and so fulfilled."[15] Suzan Johnson (Baptist), who held some lucrative positions in New York City, was not satisfied until she finally surrendered to the call. "[God] has given me, for the first time in my life, the fulfillment that I've been searching for."[16] And McKinley Young (AME) sums it up best: "Perhaps there were a lot of things that would be exciting and meaningful for me in my life, but there would be nothing more fulfilling."[17]

At some point, after struggling with the call experience, callees are brought to the point of surrender. This surrender might be precipitated by one event, such as confirmation of the call by the pastor or God answering a prayer in the form of a sign requested by the callee. However, it is usually the last of a sequence of events that transpires during the struggle stage. The surrender brings the struggle and the search to a close. It is usually the beginning of a new life-style and different understanding for the callee of his or her role and aim in life.

This clear demarcation in the sequence of events subsequent to the call experience is usually described as yielding, finally giving in to what the callee can no longer resist. It manifests itself as fulfillment, satisfaction, peace, and relief, as if a great burden has been lifted from the callee's shoulders. This peace and satisfaction often affect others and on other occasions are observed by others. The surrender may occur privately, between the callee and God or the callee and the pastor, or publicly, before a congregation. Again, because of the rites of passage process, the pastor emerges as an important figure. The surrender is not always done in a humble manner, and on occasion the callee will attach some stipulations to the surrender.

From the analysis of data in the call stories of these six chapters, a theoretical pattern can be observed. The story pattern is a sequential reconstruction of the call events as they actually happened.[18] Analytic

14. See the following stories in ibid.: 13, 20, 21, 25, 30, 31, 32, 33, 40, 50, 77, 78, 84.

15. Ibid., 145.

16. Ibid., 191.

17. Ibid., 386. Cf. ibid., 82: Caesar Clark says, "So you have that inner urge, it haunts you, and you only have a sense — a feeling — of satisfaction when you yield to it."

18. For excellent information on patterns in oral literature, see Heda Jason and Dimitri Segal, eds., *Patterns in Oral Literature* (Paris: Mouton Publishers, 1977). Jason,

narrative theorists such as Genette point out that a narrative is best understood by reconstructing a chronological account of what happened — that is the story.

Toward that end, the analysis of story content in the preceding chapters uncovers six distinct stages with varying frequency throughout the corpus (see Appendix B). Obviously every stage does not appear in the story of every callee. Moreover, there is some obvious overlapping of elements among the stages; thus, all aspects of the sequence are not as linear as the clear demarcation of each stage might lead one to believe. However, six stages can be observed and the theoretical chronology is as follows: (1) early religious exposure, (2) the call experience, (3) the struggle, (4) the search, (5) the sanction, (6) the surrender.

The early religious exposure: Chapter one demonstrated the importance of early religious exposure for each callee. All callees were exposed to religion at an early age, whether at home, in the local church, or in both. Some callees set their actual call experience in a larger life-history narration. Therefore, the first stage in the story pattern is early religious exposure. It must be admitted that a significant number of callees do not include this stage in their narrative. In some instances this stage is observed in the additional biographical data obtained from a callee after he or she had given the narrative. The individual is now prepared for a call experience.

The call experience: This stage consists of an event or sequence of events that forces the callee to face the possibility or probability of a call.[19] Rarely is this element absent from the narrative. Either one event or a series of events in the story leads to the next stage. This stage

---

"A Model for Narrative Structure in Oral Literature," argues that there are four ways oral literature can be structured: wording, texture, narration, and dramatization. Especially significant for this study is his definition of narration as "the organization of the narrative's plot"; John Van Seters, "Oral Patterns or Literary Conventions in Biblical Narrative," in *Oral Tradition and Old Testament Studies,* ed. Robert C. Culley, *Semeia* 5 (Society of Biblical Literature, 1976): 139-63; Joseph Blenkinsopp, "Biographical Patterns in Biblical Narrative," *Journal for the Study of the Old Testament* 20 (1981): 27-46.

19. On the importance and relationship of experience in oral narratives see especially William Labov and Joshua Waletzky, "Narrative Analysis: Oral Versions of Personal Experience," in *Essays on the Verbal and Visual Arts,* ed. June Helm (Seattle: Univ. of Washington Press, 1967), 12-44; Stephen Crites, "The Narrative Quality of Experience," *Journal of the American Academy of Religion* 39 (Sept. 1971): 291-311; William Labov, "The Transformation of Experience in Narrative Syntax," in *Language in the Inner City: Studies in the Black English Vernacular* (Philadelphia: Univ. of Pennsylvania Press, 1972): 354-97.

usually begins a crucial series of stages that influences the callee's understanding of call. That next stage is the struggle.

The struggle: Because of the experiences in the prior stage the callee is forced to struggle with the possibility of a call. He or she starts out wrestling with the experience in an attempt to interpret and understand what it means. Some of the defensive techniques used by the individual in struggling with the call are: to ignore it, deny it, delay it, defy it, or substitute another vocation for it. Some narratives do not contain this stage as a part of their call. On the contrary, some argue that they did not struggle with their call.

The search: Brought face-to-face with the possibility of a call, the callee seeks signs from God. In addition, he or she seeks advice from others about interpreting the call experience. Often one person or one sign is not enough to convince the callee to accept the call. The people sought fall into two basic categories. One group consists of relatives and friends, since many callees consider these people a safe starting point. They believe that these are people with whom they can share such an intimate experience without embarrassment. Usually these are people who can be counted on as a support group during this difficult struggle, although sometimes they are not able to help the callee interpret the experiences. The exception is a PK. The second group consists of people who are in a position to help the callee through the struggle and with the interpretation of his or her experience. This ability is due to either an experiential, theological, and/or political knowledge of the call experience. Ultimately the pastor is the key person in this stage.

The sanction: One could argue that there is some overlapping between this stage and the previous one. Often sanctioning occurs as the callee seeks understanding from various people about his or her experience. However, this stage is distinguished by events that the callee accepts and interprets as sanctions. On some occasions it is one crucial sanctioning event — a meeting with the pastor or a sign from God — and on others it is a series of sanctioning events. Again, the pastor is ultimately the most important person in this stage. Rarely does a narrative exclude this stage.

The surrender: This stage is distinguished from all others by the callee's private and public acknowledgment that the call will determine his or her mission in life. The callee submits to a ritual process that typically starts with informing the pastor, then delivering a "trial sermon," and ultimately concludes with ordination. Although a few narratives do not explicitly include a stage of surrender, it is often self-evident in the additional biographical data; they are ordained.

PART II

THE CALL AS NARRATIVE

CHAPTER 7

The Narratology of Story:
Types, Point of View, Time

Although the call is first and foremost a story, it is equally a narrative. It is a narrative structured with one main purpose: to persuade the hearer of the veracity of the story. Hence, a little known fact is rarely recognized in the ecclesiastical or academic analysis of call — call stories and call narratives are not necessarily the same. They could be, but usually are not. Story and narrative are different for a number of reasons (e.g., elapsed time, retrospection, audience, setting, medium), but mainly one reason is dominant. In order for the narrator to accomplish his or her purpose — persuade the hearer to believe the story — he or she needs to select, arrange, and modify the story. Modification does not mean falsification. It may simply mean a change in sequence of events, length, time, details, interpretation, or emphasis of the story. Usually the call story is longer than the call narrative.

Whereas analysis of the story has led us to examine its contents, analysis of the narrative leads us to examine its structure. Narrative theorists, especially the sequence theorists such as Todorov, Barthes, Chatman, and Genette,[1] have written extensively about the structures and devices of literature.[2] They make a distinction between "story" (the

1. Tzvetan Todorov, *The Poetics of Prose*, Eng. trans. Richard Howard (Ithaca: Cornell Univ. Press, 1977); Roland Barthes, "An Introduction to the Structural Analysis of Narrative," *New Literary History* 6 (Winter 1975): 237-72; Seymour Chatman, "Towards a Theory of Narrative," *New Literary History* 6 (Winter 1975): 295-318. *Idem, Story and Discourse: Narrative Structure in Fiction and Film* (Ithaca: Cornell Univ. Press, 1978); and Gérard Genette, *Narrative Discourse: An Essay in Method*, Eng. trans. Jane E. Lewin (Ithaca: Cornell Univ. Press, 1980).

2. For other interesting perspectives on structure, see also Walter J. Ong, S.J.,

signified, the content, the "what") and "narrative" (the signifier, the discourse/structure, the "how"). As we observed in part one, the call as story is the interpreter's attempt to reconstruct the chronological account of what happened. It is a preverbal view of events in temporal and causal order. The call as narrative, however, is the oral or written words as articulated by the narrator and the interpreter's attempt to flesh out what the narrator wants the narratee to believe.

A simple example from Culpepper's cogent application of narrative theory to the Gospel of John will illustrate the difference between story and narrative:

> John 1:19 states: "All this is the testimony of John (A), when the Jews from Jerusalem sent (B) priests and Levites to ask (C) him, 'Who are you?' John's response follows immediately. From this verse, with its sequence of three events, it is clear that the story order was (B) sending, (C) asking, (A) testifying. Although very simple, this example illustrates how anachronies occur in narrative order. The order in which the narrative tells of the events is not the same as the order in which they occur in the story.[3]

Culpepper goes on to illustrate how this distinction exists throughout the Gospel of John and how the Jesus story can be reconstructed from John's narrative on the basis of internal (the narrative) clues primarily and external (e.g., Matthew, Mark, or Luke) clues secondarily. The seminal work of Genette offers coherent and consistent terminological clarity that is useful as a theoretical framework for the structural analysis of these call stories as narratives.

Narrative theorists are interested in the structural elements of narratives like point of view, narrative time as determined by the order, duration, and frequency of events, and plot. Structural analysis of call narratives necessitates that a few other elements be given attention as well. For the purposes of this study we will examine four structural elements as follows: type, point of view, narrative time, and plot.

"Oral Remembering and Narrative Structures," in *Analyzing Discourse: Text and Talk,* ed. Deborah Tannen (Washington, D.C.: Georgetown Univ. Press, 1982), 12-24; Jean-Marc Blanchard, "Searching for Narrative Structures," *Diacritics* (Mar. 1977): 2-17; William Labov, "Speech Actions and Reactions in Personal Narrative," in *Analyzing Discourse: Text and Talk,* ed. Deborah Tannen (Washington, D.C.: Georgetown Univ. Press, 1982): 219-47; Charles W. Hedrick, "What Is a Gospel? Geography, Time and Narrative Structure," *Perspectives in Religious Studies* 10 (Fall 1983): 255-68.

3. R. Alan Culpepper, *Anatomy of the Fourth Gospel: A Study in Literary Design* (Philadelphia: Fortress, 1983), 54.

It is essential that we start with types in order to classify the eighty-six narratives on which this study is based. This is important both to demonstrate that there is more than one type, and to compare and contrast the types.

Types of Call

Three types of calls are observed in this collection of narratives.[4] There are similarities between the types at both the story level and narrative level. The following descriptions of each type will incorporate both levels. One example from each type will be the focus of further selected analysis of its narrative structure. The goal is to discover how the story differs from the narrative from the perspective of narrative theory. Thus the following offers a view of story through the lens of the narrative.

Type A — Cataclysmic/Reluctant

Cataclysmic in this context means that the callee connects some momentous event/s, open to being interpreted as natural or supernatural, to his or her call. Through the lens of the story the crucial moment of this call type[5] occurs in the second stage, the call experience stage. The third stage (struggle) and sixth stage (surrender) are important because of one element in each — reluctance in the former and relief in the latter. Reluctance completes the dual identity of this type. Persons of this type are reluctant individuals who resist the call of God for a variety of reasons. Reluctance, a crucial aspect of this type (also of type B calls) is primarily part of the the third stage (struggle). However, it may occur as early as stage one (early religious exposure) in some stories of this type. More than any other type, callees of this type refer to the joy, peace, fulfillment, or relief of a burden as a result of having surrendered (stage six) to the call. This may occur at the story level, narrative level, or both.

This is not to say that other stages are not important. Indeed, this type rarely omits any of the six stages. However, it is interpretation and self-understanding at the narrative level where emphasis is placed on

4. A structural analysis of call narratives demonstrates just how limited Glass's sociological and psychological conclusions are in his 1950 study. Although some of these callees claim cataclysmic calls, the three types illustrate that such calls are not the only ones considered "valid" as Glass's study concludes.

5. See Appendix B.

the call experience, reluctance, and relief that make stages two, three, and six pivotal for this type of call.

Through the retrospective lens of the narrative this is a cataclysmic/reluctant type experience. At the story level it may be a series of events, but usually it is a specific event. At the narrative level, in hermeneutical retrospection, the callee usually connects the call to one event. Reluctance, perhaps even active resistance, is the usual response to the call. The individual did not seek the call. On the contrary, it came against his or her will; this callee wanted to or tried to do something else. The key to his or her retrospective understanding of the call is discovered in those portions of the narrative that discuss the experience, struggle, and surrender (stages two, three, and six).

In addition to reluctance, this call is to be distinguished by the inclusion of an extraordinary event or series of events in the stage of the call experience. Usually this is interpreted by the callee as connected in some way with God. Ocular, aural, and sensory phenomena such as visions, dreams, and signs are a part of this type, but do not necessarily occur with every individual. When they do occur, however, these events are greatly emphasized in the callee's narrative as the focal point of his or her continuing conviction that the call came from God.

Although the community of faith plays an important role in the sanctioning of the call, for these callees it appears to hold a secondary role to the cataclysmic event/s, at least in tracing the locus of the call. More than any other type, this call has similarities to the biblical call narrative of the apostle Paul.

Type B — Noncataclysmic/Reluctant

Viewed through the story lens, the keys to understanding this call type[6] occur in stages two, three, and five — experience, struggle, and sanction. Similar to the first type, this type rarely omits any of the six stages. Differently from Type A, this type of call unfolds gradually. There are no cataclysmic moments that are crucial turning points. Reluctance, defined as part of stage three, may begin as active resistance as early as stage one. Sanction in the sense of confirmation occurs as a series of events; usually no one event is viewed as the key to self-understanding of the call.

At the narrative level it is not unusual that these callees show an awareness of type A, so much so that they explicitly reject an interpreta-

6. Ibid.

tion of their call as a single cataclysmic event.[7] On the contrary, they interpret their call as a gradual awareness. However, it should be noted that a few offer the retrospective interpretation that they always knew they were called. The community of faith, especially in its sanctioning rites, is more important for this type. Unlike the first type, in type B the series of sanctions received in the community of faith has importance equal to the experience in tracing the locus of the call. On occasion, but not nearly as frequently as in type A, some callees of this type may express relief and peace at having accepted the call.

Type C — Noncataclysmic/Nonreluctant[8]

At the story level, stage one (early religious exposure) is the critical stage for understanding this type. Unlike type A, no cataclysmic moment occurs; like type B these callees are aware of the cataclysmic type and often assert directly that their call is not that type. This type differs from the reluctance of both type A and B because its individuals were always willing callees. In this sense type C is a different kind of awareness than the sudden or gradual one found in both reluctant types. In comparison with types A and B, this type contains the least number of stages. Beyond stage one other stages are observable only by implication. The second stage that has some importance is stage five (sanction). The community of faith is important for the sanctioning of these callees. Since they are not reluctant, stages three (struggle) and four (search) do not exist.

At the narrative level, these individuals view the call as their destiny, something that they were born, "groomed," and "nurtured" to do. In this sense their call is gradual. In the sense of their consciousness, however, they assert that they have always known. Although there are some in types A and B that assert they always knew, type C is distinguished by the fact that its callees assert that they always saw the call as their destiny, never wanted any other vocation in life, and did not resist it when the time came. This is the perspective at both the story and narrative levels. Certain aspects of the biblical calls of Isaiah and Timothy are observable in this type.

One narrative from each type has been selected for further analysis. Again, the theoretical terminology of Genette will be utilized for

7. For those stories that include an extraordinary event see in Myers numbers 1, 24, 26, and 53. For those that explicitly deny such an event see 3, 22, 32, 35, 47, 50, 54, 55, 65, 67, 79, and 84.

8. See Appendix B.

consistency and clarity. However, there are occasions when the additional conceptual framework of other theorists will enable us to articulate the narrator's point of view more accurately. Although these theorists provide a convenient terminology and structure, the usefulness of their approaches will be tested against the examples.

Point of View

The insights of Genette and Uspensky[9] help us to distinguish between narrator and narrative point of view. Genette argues that most theoretical works on this subject are confused on point of view (or "focalization," the term he prefers).

> . . . [T]o my mind most of the theoretical works on this subject (which are mainly classifications) suffer from a regrettable confusion between what I call here *mood* and *voice*, a confusion between the question *who is the character whose point of view orients the narrative perspective?* and the very different question *who is the narrator?* — or, more simply, the question *who sees?* and the question *who speaks?*"[10]

Genette argues that the distinction is determined by whether the story is told from within ("internal") by the main character or omniscient author, or from without ("external") by a minor character or an author who tells the story as an observer. This conceptual framework makes it possible to identify the narrator by his or her voice. Is it the voice of the author or a character in the story?

It would be inappropriate and artificial to force upon these narratives the distinction between "implied author," "real author," and "narrator" that some theorists have made with other written stories. Since these narratives were recorded in person, there can be no argument over the "real author." In addition, the concept of an "implied author" is in many ways tied to arguments over a "real author."[11] All of this is much more appropriate for written works, especially those

9. Boris Uspensky, *A Poetics of Composition: The Structure of the Artistic Text and Typology of a Compositional Form.* Eng. trans. V. Zavarin and S. Wittig (Los Angeles: Univ. of California Press, 1973).

10. Genette, 186 (Genette's emphasis).

11. Seymour Chatman, *Story and Discourse,* 149, suggests, "There is always an implied author, though there might not be a single real author in the ordinary sense. . . ."

works for which authorship is in question. In this study, the "narrator" is the "real author."

Therefore, Genette's conceptual refinements that focus on the narrator and his situation are those most useful to this study. Genette adopts the following chart from the 1943 study of Cleanth Brooks and Robert Penn Warren to clarify his argument.[12]

	Internal analysis of events	Outside observation of events
Narrator as a character in the story	1. Main character tells his own story	2. Minor character tells main character's story
Narrator not a character in the story	4. Analytic or omniscient author tells story	3. Author tells story as observer

This grid inspires Genette to draw the following conclusion: "Now, it is obvious that only the vertical demarcation relates to 'point of view' (inner or outer), while the horizontal bears on voice (the identity of the narrator), with no real difference in point of view between 1 and 4 . . . and between 2 and 3. . . ."[13]

Some of Uspensky's distinctions as regards point of view are quite helpful. He discusses point of view utilizing five different terms: ideological (evaluative norms), phraseological (speech patterns), spatial (location of the narrator), temporal (time of the narrator), and psychological (internal and external to the characters).[14]

Psychological point of view: On occasion narrators are able to provide us with views that no outside observer would be privy to. They can provide us with inside views of what other characters think and feel. Theorists refer to such narrators as omniscient.

Temporal point of view: This perspective may be juxtaposed to the prior perspective and on occasion may be linked to it. Since these narrators are telling their story retrospectively, they are capable of narrating future events before they occur. Theorists emphasize that speaking retrospectively means that a narrator is not attempting to record history without interpreting it. Yet there are times that narrators, by use

12. Genette, 186, cites Cleanth Brooks and Robert Penn Warren, *Understanding Fiction* (New York: F. S. Crofts & Co., 1943), 589.
13. Ibid., 186-87.
14. Uspensky, 6.

of the historical present, move the narratee into the time of the historical story.[15] The linkage of an omniscient narrator with the retrospective viewpoint allows the narrator to look back to the past and forward into the future in the same story and reconstruct the sequence of events and the psychological state of the characters in the story.

Spatial point of view. Chatman depicts the omnipresent narrator as one who has the "capacity to report from vantage-points not accessible to characters, or to jump from one to another, or to be in two places at once."[16] Such narrators can be any place that is necessary, move great distances in short periods of time, and inform us of events in specific places that no one else could know. Only the narrators know all of the data relevant for the story. On occasion their first-person plural references serve to locate them spatially with others, but in most instances they locate themselves with the first-person singular.

Ideological point of view: These narrators are telling a retrospective story that in some sense legitimates their present self-understanding. Theorists have pointed out that no narrator can be absolutely impartial. In any retrospective account, interpretation is part of the story. As Booth says, the narrator "narrates experiences which took place some time ago, and has since had time to puzzle things out *post factum.*"[17] Therefore, the narrator steers us to what Uspensky calls his "ideological" point of view. This is evaluative in nature. Labov and Waletsky argue that one of the two linguistic functions of narrative is "evaluative." It is that part of the narrative which reveals the attitude of the narrator toward the narrative by emphasizing the relative importance of some narrative units as compared to others.[18]

Understanding the order of events in the narratives is crucial to unlocking the structure of the narratives. Genette argues that order cannot be established until one faces "narrative anachronies," which he defines as "the various types of discordance between the two orderings of story and narrative."[19] This is accomplished by contrasting the order of the events in the narrative with the sequence in which they occur in the story. Two

15. This concept is commonplace in New Testament criticism, especially as regards the Gospel of John. See, e.g., John J. O'Rourke, "The Historic Present in the Gospel of John," *Journal of Biblical Literature* 93 (1974): 585-90, who lists 151 instances of the historic present in John.

16. Chatman, *Story and Discourse,* 103.

17. Wayne C. Booth, *The Rhetoric of Fiction* (Chicago: Univ. of Chicago Press, 1961), 3.

18. Labov and Waletzky, "Narrative Analysis: Oral Versions of Personal Experience," 13.

19. Genette, 35-36.

especially important anachronies are prolepsis and analepsis. Genette designates "as prolepsis any narrative maneuver that consists of narrating or evoking in advance an event that will take place later, designating as analepsis any evocation after the fact of an event that took place earlier than the point in the story where we are at any given moment."[20]

Analytic theorists like Genette are very thorough and detailed in their analysis of the components of narrative time, especially order, because they believe it is crucial to establishing the structure of a narrative. Therefore, in order to critically analyze the structure of these narratives utilizing this approach, the narratives have been reconstructed in segments according to their "narrative time" sequence in the appendixes and will be referred to throughout this analysis.

The examples selected are: Arthur Kemp — type A; Joe Roberts — type B; and Ernest Newman — type C.

Without question, Kemp (Cataclysmic/Reluctant) is the narrator whose voice is heard as a character in the story. His point of view is that of the main character who tells his own story. This is reinforced consistently and continuously throughout the narrative with the first-person singular. Other characters that enter the story are relatives, military officials, a pastor, fellow parishioners, and criminal acquaintances. All of these characters, though minor when compared to Kemp, are crucial for the progress of his story temporally, spatially, and ideologically. Their roles help to clarify, explain, legitimate, or justify certain actions taken by Kemp in the narrative.[21]

A few illustrations will suffice. (See Appendix C.) Kemp received early religious exposure in the church setting and was converted at eight in response to the church superintendent's call for a decision for Christ (1). He delayed his college education fourteen years because he gave the money he had saved to his sister so she could go to college (13). He heard a voice call him while in a military hospital for examination by a military psychiatrist (40-51). He got involved with criminals in an effort to resist the call (58-63). He started attending prayer meetings at the request of his mother. It was in one of those meetings that he responded to the call that he heard seven years earlier (82-95). His call was confirmed in that prayer meeting by the pastor of that church (94).

There is no significant difference between Roberts (Noncataclysmic/Reluctant) and Kemp as narrators. Roberts also is the main character reinforced throughout with the first-person singular. Similar, though

---

20. Ibid., 40.
21. See, e.g., Kemp's statements at 1, 2, 5, 6, 13, 18, 22-25, and 38 in Appendix C.

fewer characters (relatives, fellow parishioners, a pastor) appear in his story to help move the story along. Roberts is a PK who was bothered by the way people in the ecclesiastical structure treated his father and bothered, too, by the lack of freedom in the ministry (5-9). He was persuaded in college by some Presbyterians to try their church (18-20). He talked and had prayer with a Presbyterian pastor about the call (29).

A similar conclusion can be drawn about Newman as narrator. Again, he is the main character telling his story in the first-person singular. His story has the fewest characters (relatives, district superintendent), but they function in roles similar to those in the narratives of Roberts and Kemp — for the purpose of clarity and explanation — in the progress of the story.

There is no evidence to suggest that a distinction can be made between these types on the basis of "narrator." All three types speak through the voice of "narrator as a character in the story."[22] As narrators they always speak in the first-person singular. The narrators are dramatized as characters in their stories. Their presence is always self-evident by the use of the first-person singular. As narrators these callees are quite intrusive. They have no problem interrupting the flow of the narrative if they wish to insert material left out earlier, pick up a point that they started earlier, or clarify points that they are about to make. On occasion, these narrators are self-conscious. Sometimes they are hesitant and cautious. They often grope for the appropriate word, concept, date, or way of explaining an extraordinary event, because they are aware that their story will be put into print.[23]

Since they are narrators, the point of view of these three callees is as the "main character" that tells his own story. No real distinction between the author and narrator exists in these cases. Thus, it would appear that the point of view is the same. To this question we now turn.

Prior comparison at a general level led to the conclusion that there is no significant difference in the voice of these three types. All are "narrators as characters in the story." Moreover, there aren't any significant differences in the points of view. All narrators narrate as the "main character telling his own story." However, a more thorough analysis of point of view is possible than Genette's terminology allows. Uspensky's conceptual framework will be utilized to take a closer look at point of view.

22. This is also true for the entire corpus.
23. See, e.g., statements made by Kemp (115), Roberts (27), and Newman (41) in Appendix C.

Psychological point of view: The dominant psychological point of view in all three types is that of a character with an inside view that is both finite and biased. However, there is one clear occasion when the character offers an omniscient view. Roberts asserts, "They [church trustees] would often feel that it was quite appropriate for them to work for white people and to have white people give us something" (6).[24]

Temporal point of view: It is self-evident that these narrators are telling their story retrospectively. Therefore, they always know more than any of the other characters. They can tell the future before it happens and flash back to a past event from a future point in time. For example, Kemp tells about a future event before it occurs when he says, "I started Ohio State, I moved to Columbus" (14-15). At this point in the narrative this is something that will occur eight years later. In a similar fashion, he is able to flash back when he wants to (17-65). The same is true of Roberts (29) and Newman (4, 35-37).

Theorists argue that such retrospective accounts mean that narrators are not attempting to record history without interpreting it. It is undeniable that these accounts allow the narrator the opportunity to give the narratee "interpreted history."[25] Yet it is a *non sequitur* to argue that a narrator who is giving a retrospective account does not intend for any of the account to be taken as history *qua* history. On the contrary, it might be argued that the numerous historic presents indicate that historical accuracy is important to the narrator though obviously not precision in all instances.[26]

Furthermore, it could be argued that historic presents are not the only way of signaling history in these retrospective accounts. Although no historic presents occur in Newman, it would be ludicrous to argue that he does not intend to be historically accurate in portions of his retrospective account.[27] Should the same data appear on a résumé no one would argue that the person intended anything other than to make an accurate historical statement.[28]

---

24. Newman says, "Of course it's been pretty much understood as far as my entire life up until that time that I was going into the ministry" (7). What is questionable about this statement is whether Newman is referring to himself or his parents, and whether these were his parents' spoken or unspoken thoughts. If the latter, then it is an omniscient statement also. There do not appear to be any omniscient statements in Kemp's narrative.

25. Uspensky, 96.

26. See, e.g., Kemp's statements at 44, 47, 49, 50, 55, 59, 70, 92, 107, and 108.

27. See, e.g., 16-34.

28. Similar data can be observed in both Roberts's (7, 17, 31-33) and Kemp's narratives (4, 6, 7, 14, 15, 17, 18, 102-12). I am often puzzled by how some scholars

Spatial point of view: Each of these narrators exemplifies his omnipresence in the narrative. They can cover great distances in short periods of time. In a couple of sentences, Kemp moves back and forth between Washington, D.C., and North Carolina (4-7) and Washington, Los Angeles, and Columbus (66-67). Roberts covers similar distances between Tennessee, New York, and New Jersey in less than ten words (31-33), and Newman moves around in the South so often and so quickly in his narrative that without the written account one could not keep up (10-34). They inform us of data at certain places and points in time that no other character in the narrative could know. Newman says, "at the age of sixteen when I completed high school I had a sense of call" (5-6). Roberts informs us that prior to his teens, while living in Chicago, he was "bothered by the poverty of ministry" and "found offensive the demeaning nature of the black AME bishopric assistant" (5-8). Kemp asserts that while locked in a room by himself he heard a voice that said to him, "Go feed my sheep." Later, he adds, "I determined that I was not going to do that because preaching was the furthest thing from my mind" (44, 58). All three narrators generally locate themselves spatially with the first-person singular. Kemp says, "I moved to Columbus" (15). Roberts says, "I went from Knoxville College to Union Seminary to Princeton" (31-33). And Newman says, "I entered Clafflin College in Orangeburg, South Carolina" (10). On occasion, they locate themselves spatially with others by the use of the first-person plural.

Ideological point of view: As discussed earlier, these are retrospective accounts, which means that interpretation is to be expected as part of the narratives. Fredriksen captures some of the reasons for the ideological point of view as she discusses the retrospective nature of conversion accounts. "In sum, the conversion account is both anachronistic and apologetic: apologetic personally and publicly, for the convert must explain himself to himself and to his audience. . . . The present is legitimate only to the degree that it rearticulates and reaffirms the past."[29]

For example, Kemp describes his manner of resistance as turning to a sordid life-style in order to make himself unacceptable to God (60-65). Roberts asserts that his going into the Presbyterian church was due to his desire to find a place for a freer ministry (20). Newman attributes his

---

seem to take a somewhat pejorative view about the historicity of an entire narrative because it is a retrospective account. I wonder how they would interpret material of this kind.

29. Paula Fredriksen, "Paul and Augustine: Conversion Narratives, Orthodox Traditions, and the Retrospective Self," *JTS*, n.s. 37 (Apr. 1986), 33.

going into ministry to a personal sense of call which left him with no sense of choice (35). All of these interpretations are ideological in the sense that they fit the narrator's present self-understanding of his mission. Yet each of these events could have been explained in a different and less ideological way. Kemp's action could have been due to anger carried over from his military experience or the desire to recover quickly the money that he had given to his sister. Roberts's decision could have been due to a desire to spite all of his acquaintances in the AME church by going into a predominantly white church. Newman could have been merely yielding to unspoken pressure from a long family history. However, none of these interpretations would tie in as neatly with the overall narrative as retrospectively narrated by each narrator.

Narrative Time

"Narrative is a . . . doubly temporal sequence. . . . There is the time of the thing told and the time of the narrative. . . ."[30] "Narrative time" and "story time" are never the same, although the sequence of events may correspond. "Story time" is the amount of time covered in the actual reconstructed sequence of events. "Narrative time" is determined by the order, duration, and frequency of events in the narrative.[31] *Order.* "Narrative time" is littered with anachronisms. The sequence of events in the story is often not the same as the sequence of events in the narrative. Genette says, "To study the temporal order of a narrative is to compare the order in which events or temporal sections are arranged in the narrative discourse with the order of succession these same events or temporal segments have in the story. . . ."[32] Narrators may tell their story chronologically (abc), *in medias res* (bc) or in flashback (acb). The story sequence may be broken by referring to events in the past (analepses) or events yet future (prolepses).

A reconstruction of Kemp's story validates Genette's point. The

30. Genette, 33, quotes Christian Metz, *Film Language: A Semiotics of the Cinema,* trans. Michael Taylor (New York, 1974), 18.

31. This study is heavily dependent on Genette's elucidation of these elements of narrative time. For additional insights on narrative time, however, see the provocative works of Ricoeur on the subject. Paul Ricoeur, "Narrative Time," *Critical Inquiry* 7 (Autumn 1980), 169-90; *Time and Narrative,* vols. 1 and 2, Eng. trans. McLaughlin and David Pellauer, vol. 3, trans. Kathleen Blamey and David Pellauer, 3 vols. (Chicago: Univ. of Chicago Press, 1985-88).

32. Genette, 35. See also Chatman, "Towards a Theory of Narrative."

sequence of events that one observes in the story differs from the sequence in the narrative. Using the chronological numbers from the narrative sequence in Appendix C, the reconstructed story would appear as follows:

8-59-4-5-1-3-2-6-7-9-11-10-12-13-16-17-18-19-20-26-21-22-27-23-24-25-28-29-30-31-32-33-36-37-35-38-39-34-40-41-42-52-43-44-55-56-45-46-47-48-49-50-51-53-54-57-58-60-61-62-63-64-65-69-66-67-68-71-70-15-73-74-72-75-76-77-78-79-80-81-82-83-84-85-87-86-88-89-90-91-92-93-94-95-96-14-97-98-100-101-102-99-103-104-105-106-107-108-110-111-112-113-109-114-115.

It is obvious by the way that Kemp begins his narrative that his intent is to narrate his story chronologically. The narrative has three sections: 1-16 (chronological); 17-65 (flashback); 66-115 (chronological). Each of these sections has its own anachronisms that break the story sequence.

Section one (1-16) begins with the following element as regards order:

"From a child of about eight years old." (1)

Kemp's call is set in what appears to be a larger life-history account which begins with his childhood conversion. This part of the narrative occurs some fifteen years (1937) before his first call experience (1952).

However, the story sequence numbers shown above demonstrate how quickly and totally the narrator has rearranged the sequence of the story. The actual beginning of Kemp's story is better reconstructed as follows:

As one of seven children ours was a sheltered life in a religious home where my mother and father was [sic] very active in church. (8)

I had been taught that if you are going to be a vessel for God you've got to be a fit vessel and you got to have good behavior, good morals, good ethics. (59)

We were living in Washington, D.C. [at this time]. (4)

But, I had moved back to North Carolina with my family when I accepted Christ as my Saviour. (5)

About eight years old I accepted Christ as my Saviour in response to [the] superintendent's call for a decision [while we were living in North Carolina]. (1)

I guess [thereafter] I had spent a lot of time reading the Sunday School books. (3)

Then my family predicted that I was going to be a preacher. (2)

We moved back to Washington, D.C. (6)

Where I was raised on up through the public school system and through high school. (7)

The narrator has an important retrospective reason for constructing the narrative time differently than the story time:

I guess to get at the very rudiments of my call experience I have to tell you what it was not.

This statement reveals that Kemp wants to do more than set his call in a larger life-history. In fact, the larger life-history merely serves the purpose of Kemp's retrospective interpretation, which in turn serves his present self-understanding of call. Although he does not explicitly articulate his reasons, the reasons could be paraphrased as follows: My call experience is distinct from my conversion experience and I did not go into the ministry because people predicted that I would be a preacher. The retrospective desire to give a proper interpretation of his call affects Kemp's ability to keep the story in chronological sequence.

We also observe that the narrator breaks the story sequence by a prolepsis in this section. It is clear that the first section should take us up to 1952, as is made evident by the beginning of the next section (17). Yet Kemp refers to two events yet future in this section.

I started Ohio State in 1960. I moved to Columbus Ohio. (14-15)[33]

Kemp has structured narrative time in such a way that it alters the story time and advances the story into the future. As a result, he finds it necessary to structure the next section as a very large analepsis.

Section two (17-65) functions as a flashback. Kemp says:

Now remember I brought you up to 1960 where I'm started at Ohio State as a thirty-year-old freshman. But an odd thing happened in 1952, eight years earlier. (17)

33. Item 15 follows 70 and item 14 follows 96.

The narrator has brought the story up to the year 1960 (14-15) only to flash back to 1952. This section is self-contained and the narrator will again attempt to be chronological without success. It covers the period from 1952 through 1959. There are numerous anachronisms within this section. A reconstruction of the beginning of the section will illustrate the anachronies.

> An odd thing happened in 1952, eight years earlier. I was in a special signal corp unit of twenty-six men in the United States Army in Fort Monmouth, New Jersey. (17)
>
> Then my mother had a heart attack. (18)
>
> The Red Cross arranged for me to come home to be with her while she was recovering. (19)
>
> Meanwhile this special outfit that I was in shipped out to Canada on a field trip and they would be gone for six months. (20)
>
> I had just re-enlisted for a six-year period. (26)
>
> I went back to [the] Army after looking after my mother. (21)
>
> My slot had been filled by my backup man and I couldn't join the team. (22)
>
> I was really bent out of shape by being pulled off that team and not allowed to join it in Canada. (27)
>
> They put me in the supply room handing out fatigues. (23)
>
> I became really really embittered with the Army. (24)
>
> I started to rebel against them. (25)

We observe one proleptic event (20)[34] and two occasions of analeptic events (26, 27).[35] The reconstruction above clearly shows the appropriate story sequence of these two events. However, the difference in the chronology of the story sequence necessitates that Kemp narrate them as events in the past.

---

34. See two additional prolepsis events at 34 and 35.
35. Three additional analepsis events are located at 52, 55 and 56.

Section three (66-115) picks up where section two ends, and is the most chronologically consistent section in the narrative. It covers a period of thirty years (1959-1989) with only minor changes in story time.

In 1959 I left Washington, D.C., and moved to Columbus, Ohio. (66)

This opening statement represents a significant turning point in story time for the narrator. It is a clear demarcation in his life. There is one analepsis (69) in this section and one prolepsis (99).

I had really hit the pits. I had lost self-respect. I was really in the gutter, a street person sleeping in fourth-rate hotels. (69).

I took the bachelor of religion in nearly fourteen years of on and off. (99)

The prolesis is a minor matter, a case of the narrator getting ahead of himself. However, clearly the analepsis is more significant. It is not just a matter of sequence. The analeptical event belongs to that part of Kemp's life covered in section two. In the final section he abandons that life, therefore it is out of chronological sequence, hence the anachronism.

A reconstruction of Roberts's story reveals that, contrary to the sequence of events that one observes in the narrative, the story order is as follows:

2-1-3-7-5-6-8-9-10-15-4-11-12-13-14-24-25-26-27-28-29-30-16-17-31-18-19-20-21-32-33-34-35-36-22-23

Similar to Kemp, Roberts begins his narrative in a manner that suggests his intent is to narrate his story chronologically also. Roberts's narrative order also has three sections: 1-11; 12-30 (27-30 is a polemical digression within section two); 31-36. Each of these sections contains anachronies that break the story sequence. Roberts's narrative does not have clear dates as markers like Kemp's narrative, and Roberts's story sequence is rearranged even more than Kemp's.

Section one (1-11) contains the following elements as regards order:

I grew up in an AME minister's and his wife's home. (1)

Coming out of three generations of AME folk. (2)

As with Kemp, Roberts sets his call in what appears to be a life-history account. However, he traces it back to generations of religious people in his family that were AME and to the fact that he was a PK himself.

The actual beginning of Roberts's story is better reconstructed as follows:

Coming out of three generations of AME folk. (2)

I grew up in an AME minister's and his wife's home. (1)

So there was a certain extent in which I feel that I was almost always in part a child of the church. I knew nothing other than that. (3)

I lived in Chicago, Illinois. (7)

I was bothered by the poverty of ministry, the lack of material acquisitions as was evident in my father's life. (5)

I was bothered by the solicitous nature and stance which I felt was demeaning as he had to deal with trustees. They would often feel that it was quite appropriate for them to pass on third-hand things to us. (6)

The third thing I found offensive was the demeaning nature of the black AME bishopric assistant which was definitely a plantation sort of pecking order. (8)

So I just didn't like the lack of freedom that one had in all of that. (9)

And really I thought that I would have very little to do with the ministry. (10)

But I fought it because I thought the political trappings and the infrastructure of my denomination mitigated against fulfilling the kind of ministry I wanted to fulfill. (15)

I went through the natural rebellion that a person will go through in my teenage years feeling that if I wanted to do anything it would not be in the ministry. (4)

I was talking about law and dentistry and all the rest. (11)

It is self-evident that this section includes *prolepsis* (4) and *analepsis* (7).

Section two (12-30) also includes breaks in the story as a result of considerable changes in chronology. As with Kemp there is a distinct break between section one and two in Roberts's narrative.

> But I found that after I was really honest there was a love for the people shown of all of these entrapments that I have already talked about that made me feel that I wanted to do my ministerial role. (12)

> But I was not sure just where. (13)

In contrast to Kemp, however, Roberts gives no clear time breaks either in the story or the narrative to indicate when this shift occurred. On the contrary, he argues that there was no specific time.[36] This section, like the prior section, also includes an analepsis (15). The prolepsis (16-23) in this section covers a considerable amount of the story that belongs to the last section.

Certain events from section three illustrate how the analepsis in section three (31-36) is a prolepsis from section two. A clear break in the story actually occurs in section two of the narrative, as the following events demonstrate:

> The next thing that I really knew was that I wanted to have a ministry that was broad. . . . (16)

> So I went looking . . . I went to college. . . . (17)

> I went to Knoxville College. (31)

> Then I went to Union Seminary. (32)

> Then to Princeton. (33)

> These perfected the ministry. (34)

A reconstruction of Newman's story reveals that, contrary to the sequence of events that one observes in the narrative, the story order is as follows:

> 35-36-37-38-1-2-3-4-5-6-7-8-9-10-12-11-13-15-14-16-17-20-18-19-21-22-23-24-25-26-27-28-29-30-31-32-33-34-39-40-41-42-43-44-45-46

---

36. This important point will be addressed under plot (93ff.).

Similar to Kemp and Roberts, Newman begins his narrative in a manner that suggests his intent is to narrate his story chronologically. The narrative order has three sections: 1-8; 9-34; 35-46. Each of these sections contains anachronies that break the story sequence. Newman's narrative is a combination of Kemp's and Roberts's as regards date markers. Newman's markers are not as explicit as Kemp's, but they are much clearer than Roberts's.

Section one (1-8) contains the following elements as regards order:

I am from a large family of preachers. (1)

It is seemingly a kind of family tradition. (2)

My father was a Methodist preacher. My grandfather was a Methodist preacher. (3)

Newman also appears to set his call in a larger life-history. Like Roberts, he traces his religious influence back for several generations. He places special emphasis on the assertion that many Methodist preachers emerged from his family. Also like Roberts, Newman is a PK.

When Newman's story is reconstructed, it is even more evident that he is narrating it in the context of a religious family.

My call to the ministry was almost a kind of thing that I considered I had no choice. (35)

I had been born and brought up in the Methodist church and the family of preachers. (36)

I just assumed that on the day of my own knowledge of ministry that this would be my calling. (37)

So my call to some extent comes out I guess of a family tradition. (38)

I am from a large family of preachers. (1)

It is seemingly a kind of family tradition. (2)

My father was a Methodist preacher. My grandfather was a Methodist preacher. I am one of seven boys and six of us went into the ministry. (3)

Newman is far more consistent than Kemp or Roberts in his efforts to narrate a chronological story. However, he is not totally successful either. There are only a few anachronies in Newman's narrative. The following are proleptic events that occur in sections one and two:

I am one of seven boys and six of us went into the ministry. (3)

I did not find it possible to continue my education on to seminary. (14)

Obviously, the narrator is informing the narratee of events to come. In like fashion one discovers analepses in all three sections as follows:

Now going back my father was a Methodist preacher. (4)

Even during the time I was in college I preached. (12)

In each of these instances the narrator is looking back on the past from a point in the future. A larger analepsis occurs in section three (35-38). Although the former analepses are minor, the latter is much more significant. It is evident that this part of the story belongs in section one. In fact, as the reconstructed story sequence demonstrates, it belongs at the beginning of the section.

Duration. Duration is the length of the narrative compared to the length of the story. Genette defines duration in terms of "speed." He says, "By 'speed' we mean the relationship between a temporal dimension and a spatial dimension . . . : the speed of a narrative will be defined by the relationship between a duration (that of the story, measured in seconds, minutes, hours, days, months, and years) and a length (that of the text, measured in lines and in pages)."[37] Attention to duration reflects the "movement" of the narrative, how parts of a story are told more quickly than other parts.

Genette describes four basic forms of narrative movement. "Scenes" provide more than minimal details about story events, while "summaries" provide only the essential facts. In the former, "narrative time" and "story time" converge, while in the latter the gap expands. "Ellipsis" describes the sections in the narrative where there are gaps. "Descriptive pauses" are extended descriptions with no advance in story time.[38]

The narratives are in two types of media: oral tape-recordings and transcribed text. Therefore, the "speed" can be tested in two ways. A comparison of the "speed" of all three types is as follows:[39]

---

37. Genette, 87-88.
38. Genette, 86-112, esp. 94-95.
39. Kemp covers approximately 1.6 years per minute to Roberts's 4 years per

Type	Duration of story	Length (tape)	Length (text)
Kemp (A)	49 years	30 minutes	4¼ pages
Roberts (B)	32 years	8 minutes	2 pages
Newman (C)	61 years	9 minutes	1¼ pages

The duration of Kemp's story begins when he was eight years old (1937) and ends at the time of the interview (1986). The duration of Roberts's story is much more difficult to calculate. The way he begins his story, it appears necessary to measure it from birth (1935) and end it at his graduation from Princeton (1967). Newman's story also begins at birth (1928) but ends at the time of the interview (1989). Whether calculating speed on the basis of years covered per minute or per page, the speed is slowest with Kemp, faster with Roberts, and fastest with Newman. The speed is so different with each that no two of them are really comparable.

The movement in Kemp's narrative is based on a good mixture of all four forms. He covers many events that took hours, days, and years with summaries, often in one sentence. A few examples will suffice.

1. Many hours are necessary for relocation from one state to another (4, 5, 6, 15, 66, 70, 71).

2. It takes years for him and his sister to complete the public school system (7, 13).

3. Days or weeks are necessary to leave the military, come home to stay with a mother who had a heart attack, and then return to the military after she recovered (18, 19, 21).

4. Many years are necessary for ministerial training under Pastor Johnson (96).

5. It takes years to complete college degrees (99, 102, 111, 112).

6. Pastoring a church (103) and obtaining another church cover a period of years (107-8).

However, he is also capable of narrating more extensively scenes that are important to him. For example:

1. The significance of his conversion experience to his call utilizes much more text, although it covers less story time than all of the summary events (1).

2. His reaction to what he considers to be mistreatment in the military covers an extensive amount of text (28-42).

---

minute and Newman's 7 years per minute. Kemp covers approximately 10 years per page to Roberts's 16 years to Newman's 53 years.

3. His call experience (43-51).

4. His resistance to the call (57-65).

5. His surrender to the call (85-95).

A few ellipses as follows are evident in his narrative also:

1. The period of time from eight years old to eighteen years old (1, 8, 9).

2. The period of time from starting college to getting married and having a son (97, 100).

There are also a few occasions on which he uses descriptive pauses.

1. Predictions about his becoming a preacher and his not taking it seriously (2, 16).

2. Summary about his sheltered life (8).

3. His embitterment with the Army (24).

4. His condition while resisting the call (69).

The movement in Roberts's narrative is due to his lack of scenes, few summaries, and extensive descriptive pauses. He has only seven summaries:

1. He grows up as a PK (1).

2. He resists the call in his teen years because of the lack of freedom in his denomination (4, 15).

3. He talks with a pastor about the call (29).

4. He goes to college and seminary (31, 32, 33).

He has only one scene; his search for a place that fits with his desire for a broader understanding and freedom of ministry (17-21). Roberts's descriptive pauses are too numerous to list. With the exception of the one scene and the seven summaries, virtually all else is descriptive pauses.[40] There appear to be no ellipses in this narrative.

Newman's narrative looks more like Roberts's than Kemp's. Its movement is faster because it contains no scenes, only summaries and descriptive pauses. It has far more summaries than Roberts's, although it is equal in length; and more than Kemp's, although it is barely one-fourth the size. The summaries include a variety of events covering hours, days, and even years. A few will suffice:

1. Completion of high school (5).

2. Licensure as a preacher (9).

3. Completion of college (10).

4. Preaching across an entire state (11).

5. Father's death and fulfilling his tenure (15-17).

---

40. See, e.g., items 5-14, 16, 22-28, 30, 34-36.

6. Pastoring two churches for two years (18-19).

7. Serving as district superintendent for seven years (27).

8. Serving as bishop for five years (32-34).

The descriptive pauses are numerous. All sentences that are not summaries are descriptive pauses.[41] There appear to be no ellipses in this narrative.

In summary, Genette's framework and Uspensky's conceptual refinements provide no reason to suggest that there are any significant differences between these three narrators' points of view. Each point of view is from the perspective of the main character telling his own story, and each is psychologically, temporally, spatially, and ideologically like the other in structure.

Although some similiarities exist in "narrative time," they are minor compared to the differences. There are differences in all three components of "narrative time." Order is handled in a similar manner by each narrator. All three narrators attempt to narrate chronologically but fail. As a result "story time" is changed significantly. Kemp uses date markers to locate temporally a number of key themes. Newman uses date markers also, but not nearly as many as Kemp, and they all are related to one theme. Roberts does not use date markers.

Among the three components of "narrative time," duration brings about the greatest differences. It appears that all three narrators attempt to set their call in a larger life-history, but the speed of each narrative makes it evident that they have covered only those events relevant to their purpose. All three select carefully those events that help move their narrative along. However, besides the fact that they all begin early — Roberts and Newman at birth and Kemp at age eight — there are few similarities. The speed is vastly different among the three; Kemp is the slowest and Newman the fastest. Kemp uses all four forms (scenes, summaries, descriptive pauses, ellipses). Roberts has only one scene, a few summaries and extensive descriptive pauses. Newman's narrative contains no scenes, numerous summaries, and frequent descriptive pauses.

The reasons for the similarities and dissimilarities between the narrative structures of these three types will emerge when we explore the plot of each in the next section.

---

41. See, e.g., items 1-3, 4, 7-8, 12, 20, 23, 26, 35, and 37-46.

CHAPTER 8

The Narratology of Story: Plot

Plot, like many other terms in narrative theory, is not an easy term to define because theorists define it in so many ways, and in the process they often use technical terms differently.[1] A comparison of three significant theorists will illustrate this point. In their classic book *Understanding Fiction*, Brooks and Warren write, "Plot may be said to be what happens in a story. It is the string of events. . . . Plot, we may say, is the structure of an action. . . ."[2] Chatman asserts, "This book may be taken as a standard of accepted opinion of what is thought and taught about narration in American universities."[3] Chatman also quotes from Aristotle's *Poetics* as follows: "Plot is defined as the arrangement of the

1. See, e.g., M. H. Abrams, *A Glossary of Literary Terms*, 3d ed. (New York: Holt, Reinhart and Winston, 1971), 127, which says, "The plot in a dramatic or narrative work is the structure of its actions, as these are ordered and rendered toward achieving particular emotional and artistic effects."

R. S. Crane, "The Concept of Plot," in *Approaches to the Novel*, ed. Robert Scholes (San Francisco: Chandler Publishing Co., 1966), 241, asserts that plot is "the final end which everything in the work . . . must be made, directly or indirectly, to serve."

E. M. Forster, *Aspects of the Novel* (New York: Penguin Books, 1962), 470, says, "A plot is also a narrative of events, the emphasis falling on causality. . . . The time-sequence is preserved, but the sense of causality overshadows it."

Frank Kermode, *The Sense of an Ending: Studies in the Theory of Fiction* (New York: Oxford Univ. Press, 1967), 45, describes plot in the following way, "The clock's tick-tock I take to be a model of what we call a plot. . . ."

Robert Scholes and Robert Kellogg, *The Nature of Narrative* (New York: Oxford Univ. Press, 1966), 12, 207, describe plot as "an outline of events" and "the dynamic, sequential element in narratives."

2. Cleanth Brooks and Robert Penn Warren, *Understanding Fiction*, 77.

3. Chatman, "Towards a Theory of Narrative," 311 n. 16.

93

incidents. . . ."[4] Given that he has read the classic works on the subject, it is interesting to observe how Chatman uses some of these same terms. For him, "events" consists of "actions" and "happenings." Events are one-half of the ingredient for a "story" — *histoire* for the French, *fabula* for the Russian formalists — which is a series of "events."[5] Note, however, that these terms do not lead us by definition to plot. If the story is *what* happened, then plot is *how* it happened (*discours* and *sjuzet*, French and Russian respectively). More basically, the differences might be put this way. For Brooks and Warren the progression is as follows: events are subsets of actions and actions are subsets of plot. For Chatman the progression is: actions, events, then story. Thus, not only are similar terms used differently, they do not even lead to the same result.

The confusion is even greater today, because narrative theory has become respectable in so many different disciplines, and each discipline gives key terms another twist. Thus, from Aristotle and Quintilian to present-day literary critics as well as New Testament rhetorical and literary critics, plot is a crucial concept in narrative theory. Although it must be granted that there is a lack of terminological consistency among theorists, some degree of conceptual consistency exists. Brooks and Warren help us to understand the concept of plot.

> We see . . . plot does not use all of the facts of the action and that the chronological order has been scrambled. The plot, then, is the structure of the action as presented in a piece of fiction. It represents the treatment the story-teller makes of the events of his action. . . . When we say 'a novel,' 'a story,' or 'a plot,' we instinctively imply the idea of a unity. We imply that the parts, the various individual events, hang together. There is the matter of cause and effect. In any story we expect to find one thing bringing on another. . . . Every story must indicate some basis for the relation among its parts, for the story itself is a particular writer's way of saying how you can make sense of human experience. Cause and effect constitute one of the ways of

4. Ibid., 311. Whereas Chatman quotes from Leon Golden's translation of Aristotle's *Poetics*, any other quotations in this study of Aristotle's *Poetics* are taken from D. A. Russell and M. Winterbottom, eds., *Ancient Literary Criticism: The Principal Texts in New Translations* (Oxford: Clarendon Press, 1972).

5. Chatman basically follows the formalist-structuralist theory of narrative, which can be described simply as follows: Narrative text consists of story and discourse; story consists of events and existents; events consist of actions (character as the subject — he does something) and happenings (character as the object — something happens to him). Existents consist of characters and setting. See Chatman's "Towards a Theory of Narrative" for further details.

saying this. . . . Logic, including the logic of motivation, binds the events of a plot together into a unity. This unity is, of course, a dynamic unity. It is a unity involving change: no change, no story. At the beginning of a story we find a situation with some element of instability in it. At the end of the story, we find that things have become stable once more. Something has been settled. . . . This movement from instability toward stability involves, as we have said, certain natural stages — the beginning, the middle, and the end.[6]

Therefore, it should be self-evident that plot is thematic. It has a beginning, a middle and an end.[7] Its central features are the sequence, causality, unity, and affective power of the narrative. We learn from other theorists that plot seeks to bring the narratee to an emotional response; for example, relief, outrage, or belief.[8] Plot highlights the narrator's points of interpretation. Repetition highlights themes that the narrator wants the narratee to pay attention to.

In order to get through this maze of terminology, it will be necessary to explain how certain key terms will be used in this section. An "action" is a circumstance in which a character acts or is acted upon. "Action" merges Chatman's *action* (subject) and *happenings* (object). "Episode" is a series of actions having unity. Chatman considers it to be equivalent to the term he prefers — *event*.

The argument that follows will demonstrate that Kemp, Roberts, and Newman, who represent three different types, utilize their call narratives to legitimate their call. Moreover, the narratives are stuctured in a way that allows each callee to develop in his distinctive way the theme that is appropriate to his type.

An understanding of Kemp's plot starts with the observation — detailed in the "narrative time" section — that he has rearranged the order for thematic purposes. The modifications are crucial to the sequence and causality that Kemp establishes as three distinct sections (1-16; 17-65; 66-115). In section one Kemp begins his narrative with an episode that describes his conversion experience. The purpose of the first episode appears at first glance to be twofold: First, Kemp wants to define call by defining what it isn't. It is not his conversion. Second, he describes his earliest recollections about call discussions in his life.

6. Brooks and Warren, 80. What is one theorist's "action" is another's "event," another's "episode," yet another's "incident," and still another's "function."

7. Aristotle, *Poetics*, 1450b-51b, says, "Order requires that the plot have a beginning, a middle and an end."

8. For example, Crane, 239, and Chatman, *Story and Discourse*, 85.

Thus, Kemp appears to be setting his call in a larger life-history. However, this episode is but one of many causal factors that prepares Kemp for a later call experience.

A second episode, prior even to the conversion experience, is the influence that a religious home had on him in childhood. Under strict religious parents, he lives a life sheltered from worldly activities. This assertion receives further development in section two. In order to assert in section two that his later sordid life is a new departure for him, he needs to establish beforehand that he had no prior exposure to worldly activities.

This assertion emerges as an example of structural retrospective interpretation in Kemp's narrative. He could have attributed his later sordid life to repressed anger or desire due to an overly strict religious childhood. He doesn't because that does not support the claim he wants to make. In addition to the influence that a religious home has on Kemp, it is obvious that church attendance also shapes his life. It is in this overall atmosphere that he learns biblical rhetoric and what it means to be a preacher. While it appears that Kemp starts the narrative at this early age in order to narrate his life-history, it soon becomes evident that such is not the case. Both episodes are causally and sequentially related to his plot.

A third episode addresses the early family predictions that one day he would be a preacher. Kemp is not particularly fond of the idea even at this early age. Therefore, this episode helps to set the stage for his discussion of resistance in section two and his further development of this theme.

A fourth episode is Kemp's rejection of a four-year scholarship. After graduating in 1948 from high school at eighteen in Washington, D.C., Kemp rejects a scholarship to Howard University because he doesn't want to go to a black school. In order to go to a white school of his choice, he has to work and save money. He takes a job with the federal government in Washington with the intention of earning the money to go to Ohio State University and major in sociology or medicine. It is interesting to note that this last bit of data is irrelevant to the episode. The inclusion of the major, however, supports further the notion that being a preacher was not one of his goals in life.

The final episode in this section is related to his sister's graduation from Dunbar High School in Washington. She needs money to go to college. Kemp had saved his money to go to Ohio State, but there isn't enough for both of them. Therefore, he gives his money to her so that she can go, and this delays his entrance into Ohio State for twelve years.

The manner in which this episode ends requires that Kemp disturb his sequence and thus set up the anachronism of the next section. He gets ahead of himself by tacking on the descriptive pause about how this episode delays his college entrance. The unity of his theme necessitates that he correct the sequential and causal disruption. He does so by making section two a flashback. It is clear, however, that we are in an ellipsis somewhere between 1948 and 1952 (the starting point of the next section).

A matter that is of the utmost significance in this section is Kemp's frequent use of spatio-temporal "actions." The concrete activities and settings, in terms of both places and dates, may suggest that at times Kemp is interested in narrating history.

Kemp's second section is the middle of Kemp's plot. In terms of plot development this is the key section of the narrative. This section also contains a number of episodes. Kemp's first episode places him in an elite group of twenty-six signal corps men in the United States Army stationed at Fort Monmouth, New Jersey. They master the latest communication equipment and go all over the world to military establishments demonstrating it.

We are told neither when nor why during the 1948-1952 *ellipsis* Kemp leaves his job and goes into the military. A change in direction since he no longer has the money to pursue his college dreams, a draft, and a loss of job are but a few speculations. Perhaps his reference to a high aptitude score on a test given by the military is the only connection to that period. This might be an apologia against the suggestion that he goes into the military because he isn't college material. However, for Kemp it is irrelevant. Such is the advantage of plot development.

Now that Kemp has completed the opening scene of the plot he increases the speed of the narrative. He quickly moves the narratee to the middle scene where the crucial episode unfolds.

The second episode in this section revolves around the heart attack his mother has in 1952. "The Red Cross arranged for me to come home to be with her while she was recovering." The causal connection in this episode is that while at home aiding his mother, Kemp's outfit leaves for Canada on a field trip and will be gone for six months.

The third episode is Kemp's return and discovery that the Army has filled his slot with his backup man and he is not allowed to join the outfit. He is given a lower job in the supply division.

The fourth episode is Kemp's response to what he considers unfair treatment. He is embittered with the Army. It is made all the more difficult by the fact that he has re-enlisted for six years. He rebels by refusing to wear military clothes and take orders, and being unwilling to accept punishment or court martial, as well as writing a letter to the Communist Youth Party seeking admission.

The fifth episode is the Army's reaction to Kemp's rebellion, particularly the letter to the Communist Party. The highly sensitive nature of the unit that he served in necessitates further action in this matter. Kemp is interrogated to determine if he is a Communist. When it is determined that he is not a Communist, it is concluded that he must be crazy. Therefore, he is sent to the military hospital for examination by a psychiatrist.

The sixth episode is the examination during the period of the hospitalization. The psychiatrist discovers that Kemp is not crazy, but, like himself, bitter with the Army. He promises to work toward Kemp's discharge. These episodes are both sequential and causal in design. The intent of all six is to set the stage for the call experience which appears in the episodes that follow.

The seventh episode is Kemp's call experience. While in a hospital room Kemp hears a male voice three times tell him to "Go feed my sheep." He recognizes the words from his early religious training as coming from a biblical episode between Jesus and Peter. He is in a single room that is locked because it is the psychiatric ward. At the same time he feels a heaviness on his mind that leaves him with the sense that he has to respond with obedience to this voice.

The only glass in the room is a glass peephole in the door. There are no people in the rooms on either side of him, and the halls are padded with carpet and soundproof tiles on the ceiling. There are no radios in the wing. The interval between the first and second occasion of the voice is about five minutes and between the second and third occasion it is about one-half hour. Kemp goes to the door and looks out the peephole after the first two occasions to see if there is anyone in the hallways talking to him. This whole matter leaves him "restless all of that night."

Kemp wants the narratee to accept this as an historical event and not the work of a psychologically disturbed mind. Therefore, his narration at this point is more detailed. Furthermore, he addresses beforehand certain challenges that the narratee might raise. There are no radios, no windows, and no people in adjacent rooms.

This conclusion is supported by the eighth episode. Kemp is already scheduled to see Dr. Freeman, the psychiatrist. He "was quick to share with him what had happened." Freeman reviews his files for any history of hallucination and determines that there isn't any. This episode helps to counter the psychological objection that Kemp anticipates the narratee may have with his experience. A psychiatrist concludes that Kemp is not hallucinating. The frequent insertion of Kemp's own words in this episode as opposed to the doctor's words is another illustration of the retrospective interpretation in this narrative. Would Kemp have discussed hallucination if his experience had not occurred in the psychiatric ward of a hospital?

The ninth episode addresses Kemp's resistance to the call. "At some later point it dawned on me that that would have been a call for me to go into a preaching ministry, then I determined that I was not going to do that, because preaching was the furthest thing from my mind." "Now this is still 1952. So I determined that I was going to be the worst possible human being that you could be, to make myself unfit to be a minister of the gospel. And then I started, I wasn't drinking then, but I started drinking. I had been gambling occasionally, but I became an avid gambler. And subsequently drove getaway cars for thieves." Kemp also became involved in narcotics and prostitution.

A number of interesting points emerge in this episode. Kemp had an extraordinary experience with the divine. This is suggested by his connecting the words he heard to the biblical episode between Jesus and Peter. In addition, Kemp recognized the voice well enough to specify its gender as well as the exact words spoken to him. Yet with all of these incredible supernatural phenomena engulfing him, he does not recognize the experience at that time as his call. It is the retrospective interpretation of the event — "sometime later" — that brings him to the conclusion that this must have been his call.

It is also interesting that he does not specify how long it takes him to come to this decision nor what leads him to draw this conclusion. The omission is understandable, however, in view of his plot. A better causal connection can be put in the form of questions. What was the response, and why that particular response? Hence, this "later" revelation sets up the explanation that will follow for why Kemp — this individual who was reared in a sheltered, strict, religious setting and converted at an early age — turned to such a sordid life. Kemp had to make himself so unfit that even God would have to renounce the call because he was not a "fit vessel." How else does one explain the excessiveness of the resistance in both the story and the narrative?

Recognition that the earlier experience was his call to the preaching ministry causes him to turn to such a life because he does not want this call. In addition, tnis episode serves as a further connection to episode two and three in section one regarding the sheltered life and resistance to the call. This is retrospective interpretation at its best and it is crucial to the unity of his theme.

The fact that this middle section is the heart of the narrative is evident from the following observations. (1) The section is self-contained and represents nearly half of the narrative. (2) It outlines the backdrop for the call experience. (3) It contains the call experience. (4) It contains the description of the resistance to the call. (5) It contains the largest number of historic presents[9] in the narrative, as well as significant spatio-temporal activities and settings which demonstrate that the narrator is interested in history. (6) Yet at the same time it contains significant retrospective interpretation which demonstrates that the narrator is not interested in uninterpreted "history."[10] (7) It contains as many episodes as the other two sections combined.

Kemp's final section (66-115) brings the plot to a close. This section also contains numerous episodes. Kemp's first episode locates him spatio-temporally in Washington, D.C., January 10-11, 1959. He is about to leave that city to visit his parents in Columbus, Ohio, for ten days with the further intention of continuing on to Los Angeles to make a new life for himself. Kemp's resistance and running from the call have caused him to "hit the pits," and he has "lost self-respect." He is "really in the gutter," has become a "street person," and is "sleeping in fourth-rate hotels." He "had run out" in Washington and thought he could "go out to Los Angeles and make a new life for myself."

This opening episode is an excellent transition between the final episode in the prior section and the episodes to follow in this section. It begins the motion that locates Kemp spatio-temporally for the end of the plot and explains why this particular setting is necessary. His resisting the call has led him into the "gutter" and he has "played out" in Washington. A change of location and life is necessary. However, before going to a new location he visits his parents.

Again, Kemp's retrospective interpretation of this episode is connected to his theme. One might wish to speculate about other motives — latent or overt — for Kemp's return home. Kemp ends his last section by saying, "I made a lot of money. I spent it as fast as I made it and had a good time." Is it possible that Kemp's return home is due to the fact that he is broke and can't really go to Los Angeles without first going home to borrow money from his parents? That could be a state that Kemp not only wanted to conceal from the narratee, but from his

9. See, e.g., 44, 47, 49, 50, and 55.
10. See, e.g., 57 and 61.

parents as well. A son reared with Christian values who has sacrificed his own goals in favor of his sister's needs but has turned to a wasteful life that leaves him penniless is not so easy to convey to very devout parents. Yet it is also possible that Kemp felt so guilty about the sordid life that he had led, especially the excessive nature of that life, that he needs to return home for forgiveness and cleansing. This is the setting in which his religious convictions are instilled and, therefore, the most appropriate place for absolution. Obviously Kemp remembers the Jesus and Peter episode. Perhaps he also remembers the parable of the prodigal son. However, he does not make an association with these biblical narratives because the goal of the plot at this point is to place him in the orbit of his parents' influence — the same people that influenced and helped shape his life earlier — so that they can influence and help shape his life once again.

This episode signals a clear turn in Kemp's plot and narrative. He makes this connection clear by observing that he has his "final drunk" on January 10, 1959. He sets the stage for his new life by observing that he "sobered up enough" on January 11, 1959, to leave Washington and "come" (historical present) to Columbus, Ohio. The final drunk, January 10, and Washington are symbolic of the old life. The sobering, January 11, and Columbus are symbolic of the new life. This reminds one of the Pauline old man-new man dichotomy. Is this yet another example of Kemp's latent or overt retrospective use of biblical rhetoric?

At the same time, Kemp signals by the addition of "enough" that this is not the new life but that it sets the stage for the new life. It makes a new beginning possible and imminent. The historical present again emphasizes that Kemp intends this to be taken as history. In addition, it may also indicate that to some degree Kemp is reliving the experience while he is narrating it, at least vicariously.

The second episode deals with the response of Kemp's arrival. His parents barely recognize him. After cleaning up he is again recognizable. They have a "good reunion" and his parents ask him to stay longer than the ten days he has intended to stay. They are getting older and would like him to look after them. Furthermore, "I didn't know anybody in Los Angeles." Therefore, he stays.

Kemp consistently narrates the retrospective angle that develops his plot best and avoids the irrelevant. The causal relationship in Kemp's plot necessitates that Kemp's conduct be attributed to others and not to himself. He doesn't stay because he is broke, has no job, has nowhere else to go, and doesn't know anyone in L.A. The fact that he doesn't know anyone in L.A. is an after-the-fact observation. He stays because "they put that kind of parental beg on me." It is at his parents' insistence and for their benefit that he stays, not his own. Thus again he returns to a familiar sphere of influence, the religious setting of his parents' home. The next episode supports this conclusion.

The third episode brings Kemp back into the influencing orbit of the church via the religious setting of his parents' home. He has truly come full circle. Repetition here emphasizes the importance of this "episode" to his theme. His parents attend church and his mother requests that he attend with her on occasion. He does. For the first month or so he attends only on Sundays. About that time she asks him to attend Wednesday night prayer meeting. "And I did."

Again, there are questions that Kemp does not address for the narratee. Why does his mother ask him to attend church, then prayer meeting? Is it because that is merely her way; the way she dealt with his religious training when he was a child? However, he is an adult now. Has he told her about the sordid life he had led so that she feels that he needs to repent and be cleansed? Better yet, has Kemp told her about his call experience? Though important to the narratee, these questions are irrelevant to Kemp. Answers to them could to some degree have shifted the spotlight for his actions onto himself. Kemp needs to keep it on others. He goes to church and prayer meeting because "she asked" him to. The significance of these actions is causally connected to the final episode.

The final episode addresses Kemp's surrender and the sanctioning of his call. "In the third month that I was there, in March of 1959, I was sitting in prayer meeting." Kemp is in prayer meeting with about twenty to twenty-five others. Just before the pastor is about to pronounce the benediction Kemp feels a "sudden flush of heaviness as though I were carrying the weight of the world." He breaks into "uncontrollable sobbing." No one understands what is happening, but Pastor Johnson says (although Kemp had not told him his problem), "I know what's wrong with him." Johnson repeats this statement three times. When Kemp finally gets control of himself he says three times, "I've got to preach." The pastor responds, "I know it, and you're not going to have any peace until you do." Kemp concludes this episode by saying, "It was at that point that I made the determination that I would not ever again spend a moment of my life outside of the call of Christ to be a preacher of the gospel."

All of the episodes in this section are causally structured to get the narratee to this point. Again Kemp's conduct is dictated by forces external to himself. It is this "heaviness," this "impacting" (sic) that is beyond his control, that forces him to lose control of his emotions. This retrospective observation makes the obvious connection with the initial call experience in the hospital room. He felt a similar "impacting on his heart" at that time. By the use of repetition Kemp highlights how this episode is important to his theme.

Therefore, the two experiences are to be taken as confirmations of each other and further evidence that this is Kemp's call and time for him to surrender. Additional confirmation is offered by the pastor. Retrospectively, this implies sanction from the community of faith. The pastor's acceptance is crucial to the rites of passage in this particular community of faith. The insertion, however, that Kemp had not discussed this matter beforehand with the pastor, but that he knew anyway, implies divine confirmation.

Now the spotlight can shift to Kemp and he can acknowledge the call. The pastor's final words — that he will not have peace until he surrenders — make it possible for Kemp to surrender. Kemp gives this episode a spatio-temporal setting also. It is in a church, in a prayer meeting which includes his mother, a pastor, and twenty to twenty-five other witnesses. It occurs in March of 1959, in the third month after he has returned home. It occurs after everyone has prayed, just prior to the pastor's final words before benediction. A clear, understandable dialogue between the callee and an authorized mediator takes place among numerous witnesses in the community of faith. The latter neutralizes the retrospective insertion that the key witness is now deceased.

The repetition observed in the dialogue between the pastor and Kemp further emphasizes the importance of this episode to theme development. The tripling of statements recalls the tripling in the initial call experience in a manner that allows them to serve as further divine confirmation. The initial call, the affirmation from the authorized mediator in the community of faith, as well as the surrender of the callee all come as tripling communication.

What follows this episode is not another episode, but a list of actions. These actions update the narratee on what Kemp has been doing since he surrendered, and how it relates to the perfecting of his ministry in response to acceptance of the call.

Kemp's plot has a beginning, a middle, and an end. Episodes are the primary units used to structure his plot. All four features of plot (the narrative's sequence, causality, unity, and affective power) are present in Kemp's narrative and each is made to serve Kemp's theme. As a result of sequence each episode has a significant place in the narrative.

Causality, though not as important as thematic development, is the most important of the four features of plot. It connects the episodes and the sections together, thereby contributing to the overall unity of the story. Like the author of the Fourth Gospel, Kemp utilizes affective power with great effect, because he wants the narratee to believe him.

Throughout the narrative the narratee is led to believe that Kemp's actions are influenced by external forces and characters. He appeals to the emotions of the narratee when he denies himself college in favor of his sister. Then he receives an injustice at the hands of the Army while attending to a mother who has had a heart attack. In a similar fashion his embittered response, his call experience while in the military psychiatric ward, and his sordid life-style are but a few of the actions that are sequentially and causally related in Kemp's plot. This use of affective power helps him to develop a theme that is believable.

That theme is as follows: *Although I was reared in a religious setting where many in my childhood predicted that I would be a preacher, I neither wanted it nor sought it. However, the call came upon me in a catastrophic manner. When I later understood that this experience was a call I resisted it to the point of excess. Ultimately it forced itself upon me in a manner that overwhelmed me to the point of surrender. It was witnessed and confirmed in the community of faith.*

The goal of Kemp's plot all along is to get the narratee to believe this theme. He has carefully selected actions and interwoven them into "episodes" to construct a plot in order to accomplish his goal. He uses all four aspects of plot, but clearly causality is the dominant feature. He uses repetition throughout to give further unity to the plot. Although the beginning and ending of the plot are significant, the middle of the plot holds the key to Kemp's retrospective self-understanding of his call.

The structure of the plot and the numerous retrospective insertions make it clear that Kemp is not attempting to record history without interpreting it, for to do so would mean that the narratee would miss the theme that Kemp wants him or her to believe. Yet at the same time, Kemp's retrospective interpretation should not be understood as fiction or created history. The constant and consistent spatio-temporal activities and settings, as well as the use of the historic present, make it undeniably clear that Kemp wants to record certain aspects of history. He wants the narratee to believe that his theme is true in a spatio-temporal sense. In other words, this is a true story. It actually happened. Yes, he has retrospectively interpreted it. His narrative structure, which differs significantly from the story, unmasks the retrospective interpretation. Yet it is history juxtaposed to retrospective interpretation. Occasionally, historical actions are used to develop further the narrator's theme. Moreover, the pointed use of historic presents gives the narratee the impression that Kemp is reliving the experience as he narrates it.

It was observed in the "narrative time" section that Roberts also rearranges the order of events for thematic purposes. Furthermore, these modifications are crucial to the sequence and causality that Roberts establishes in three sections (1-11; 12-30; 31-36). Roberts uses episodes also to develop his theme. However, only two episodes appear in his narrative; the remainder is a combination of actions and descriptive pauses set in a polemical apologia.

The first episode describes why Roberts resists the call. Roberts comes out of "generations" of religious AME's and is reared as a PK. He "knew nothing other than that." However, he "rebelled" during his "teenage years" against any thought of going into "the ministry." He was "bothered" and found "offensive" the "demeaning" situation of "the poverty of ministry," lack of freedom in their "house," hand-me-downs from "white people," and the "pressure" and "plantation sort of pecking order" of the "bishop" which leads to an overall "lack of freedom."

The importance of causality in Roberts's plot is evident in his opening episode. What at first appears to be an attempt to set his call in a larger life-history, upon closer examination turns out to be thematically directed. Although he has early religious exposure from a long family tradition, the setting does not influence Roberts in a positive way. On the contrary, the lack of freedom as a PK influences Roberts in a negative way to the point of rejecting ministry as an option for his life.

The narratee may wonder why Roberts restricts the episode to the influence all of this had on his feelings about ministry as a profession and does not discuss other aspects of his life and thoughts as a PK. What was the influence on his secular life as a child? When was he converted? How frequently did he go to church? Were there any positive consequences of being a PK? Did Roberts have any freedom as a PK? Perhaps we receive a hint in the summary statements that "there was a certain extent in which I feel that I was almost always in part a child of the church," and "I knew nothing other than that."

Yet the answers to these questions do not in any way serve the causal purpose of Roberts's plot. Therefore, if Roberts answers at all, he does so with the two aforementioned summary statements. Roberts's overarching theme demands that he connect all of this in a causal sequence to ministry as a profession. He does it skillfully by making a connection with his father, who was in the ministry. He asserts that all of the things that he was bothered by and found offensive and demeaning "were evident in my father's life" and "laid upon him." The causality and sequence are now made clear. Roberts is a close observer — a PK nonetheless — of what happens to one in the ministry, and he wants no part of that profession. He rebels. He ends the episode by asserting that he thought he would have nothing to do with ministry and was considering a host of other vocations, among them law and dentistry.

The enormous repetition of words and situations in this one episode emphasizes its importance to the development of Roberts's plot and theme. For example, "demeaning," "bothered," "offensive," "white people," "pressure," "their house not our house," "bishop," and "poverty of ministry" (cf., e.g., "lack of material acquisitions") are the primary ones. "Bishop," "white people," "pressure," and "their house not our house" serve symbolically or metaphorically as "lack of freedom."

The absence of any spatio-temporal grounding in this episode is noteworthy. This narrator has a theme that he wants the narratee to believe. Obviously, by narrating retrospectively he has concluded that his interpretation of history develops his theme better than merely recording history.

The second section (12-29) is also the second episode. It describes how and why Roberts changes his mind about ministry as a profession and surrenders to the call. He says,

> But I found that after I was really honest there was a love for the people shown of all of these entrapments. . . . I wanted to do my ministerial role, but I was not sure just where. So I think the call was not a traumatic thing that came to me, but something that I yearned to do but that I fought, because I thought that the political trappings and the infrastructure of my denomination mitigated against fulfilling the kind of ministry I want to fulfill. The next thing that I really knew was that I wanted to have a ministry that was broad enough to let me address some political, social and economic problems and would not be so narrow. . . . So I was looking. . . . I went on to college and while in college had opportunity to meet some Presbyterian folk . . . they encouraged me to consider going into the Presbyterian church. And it was for political reasons that I went into the Presbyterian church because I saw that it gave me more freedom to be unencumbered . . . to do the kind of ministry that I wanted to do.

When that opportunity for education really came on to me, then I think that the call was really sort of authenticated. . . . The Presbyterian Church made me feel like I could take that tradition and blend it into whatever I wanted it to be so that my call was not a catastrophic, vertical thing that suddenly came upon me. It was rather the accumulation of a number of experiences that nudged me on toward ministry. . . . So it is not something that I can date in terms of a Tuesday at one o'clock when anything happened, but rather something . . . gradual. . . . I believe when people stop lying most of them will admit that it was a gradual thing that they were nudged to and not a catastrophic, one day piece . . . but the pinnacle of a long series of God's prodding and nudging us toward decision.

The core of Roberts's plot and theme is located in this episode. Roberts comes to the conclusion that, despite all of the entrapments that he dislikes, he has to admit that the service of people can be observed in these entrapments. Again in this episode, we see Roberts's lack of interest in spatio-temporal grounding. Roberts tell us nothing about when, where, or what caused him to change his mind from law or dentistry to ministry.

However, what he does tell us that is interesting is that the call is upon him even before this point. "I wanted to do my ministerial role." In other words, Roberts has been aware of a call for some time. However, he has led the narratee to believe from the beginning that call was something that he never considered, either as a profession or as an experience. Why?

Again, this use of narration serves his causal and thematic purposes. Roberts sets up the reasons for this at the beginning of this episode and interestingly he picks it up again at the close of this episode. The "call was not a traumatic thing that came to me." Roberts does not want the narratee to get the impression that he has had some type of "traumatic" call experience that can be spatio-temporally located. That is one of the reasons he avoids all historical grounding in the first episode, and does so in this one as well.

The call for Roberts is something he "yearned to do" but "fought" because he felt the "political trappings" and "infrastructure" militated against his "fulfilling" the "ministry" he wanted to "fulfill." For how long, we do not know. One might guess that it was at least as early as his teens when he rebelled against the ministry. By use of repetition we see a causal connection with the first episode.

Perhaps another reason for Roberts's resistance to spatio-temporally locating his call experience is that he was still in a *liminal* state at this point. Although he "wanted to do my ministerial role" and "knew" that he "wanted to have a ministry that was broad," he "was not sure just where" he could do it and be comfortable. He is aware of the call upon his life, "yearns" to do it, but resists it because he doesn't know where he can do it the way he wants to do it.

Therefore, he goes "looking" for such a "camp." He goes to "college" and meets "Presbyterian folk" who suggest that he should consider the "Presbyterian church." He does and finds that it is the "camp" that he has been looking for that will allow him more "freedom" to do the "kind of ministry" that he wants to do. The "educational opportunity" "authenticated the call" for him. "The Presbyterian church made me feel like I could take that tradition and blend it into whatever I wanted it to be."

Again the narratee is not told information that would be helpful. Did he discuss call with these people? Did he tell them he already had a call? Did they suggest that he join their church because of their understanding of how the call is viewed there or for some other reason? These questions are irrelevant to the development of his theme. He seeks a denomination with greater freedom for ministry than his own. Again the repetition causally connects this episode with the first episode. He has to go to another denomination because his denomination defines ministry too narrowly. Furthermore, the political trappings militate against his fulfilling a concept of ministry like the one he has.

Once again this scene is not historically located. Although we know that he went to college, he does not say when, where, or how. In addition, we know that he joined the Presbyterian church, but again we do not know when, what church, or how. All of this is irrelevant to the development of his theme.

Roberts ends this episode with a polemical apologia. His call is not "catastrophic," but "gradual" — the result of "a long series of God's prodding and nudging" him to a decision. When others who were called "stop lying" he thinks they will admit the same. He could say that "my call was confirmed" when he "talked" and "prayed" with the pastor of the "Shiloh Presbyterian Church," "but that would be a lie" and he is not going to do that.

It is interesting to observe that Roberts, while narrating his own retrospective story, asserts that other callees are lying when they claim a one-day catastrophic call. Roberts's confusion on this matter is due to a failure to distinguish between the story and the narrative. He may be correct about the story. Perhaps all call stories are — after further investigation — gradual. However, it is the narrative — not the story — that the narrator wants the narratee to understand. Furthermore, it would be a great injustice to assert that these narrators lie because their story and their narrative do not agree. They do not lie any more than the Gospel writers lied when each offered his narrative of the Jesus story. All of these narrators offer their retrospective interpretation of a story that can be spatio-temporally located. Maybe the call experience in the story did not occur with one catastrophic event, but it does in the narrative. When viewed from the proper perspective, this is not lying, but hermeneutics. Weems understands this quite well: "One of the interesting things about being asked to talk about your call ten years afterwards, you know, you can interpret it the way you want to. It's one thing to ask someone about their call a week afterwards, but after ten years, you get prosaic and philosophical about it and so profound."[11]

Interestingly, Roberts closes the episode the way he opened it. His call is not "traumatic," but "gradual," and he responds after a long series of "nudgings." He thinks all calls, when fully explored, are this way. As was the case earlier, the repetition emphasizes the importance that he attaches to this point. The one "action" — talking with the pastor — that has some degree of spatio-temporal location turns out to be a foil. He will not even use it as a point of confirmation for his call. Certainly he cannot. This would be counter to the whole point of this episode that his call was "gradual" and "authenticated" in the education rite of this particular community of faith.

Roberts's final section (31-35) concludes this plot not with another episode, but with a number of actions given as descriptive pauses. His call is "perfected" at Knoxville College, Union Seminary, and Princeton Seminary. He finally has found a denomination in which he can "reconcile" his desire for a "broad," "free," and "political" ministry with their "system of governance." He thinks that "a connectional church that has bishops who are not sensitive can be demeaning to the sacredness of human personality. It can almost be another form of slavery." Although he feels that there are "some good bishops," to have remained in the "AME church" would have always meant "a rugged and unhappy relationship between myself and the bishop."

Although he does not use an episode to end his plot, it is connected to the prior episodes by the overarching theme. The educational activities and settings connect this section to the prior episode. The

11. Myers, 341-42.

repetition also connects it. In the prior episode it is education that "authenticated" the call; here it is education that "perfect[s]" that ministry. This also demonstrates how the specific settings are still at the service of theme development as opposed to history. He does not temporally fix the attendance or graduation from the three schools; it is irrelevant to his theme.

He connects the ending with the opening by repetition. The terms "bishop," "demeaning," and "another form of slavery" (cf. "plantation") recall the first episode. The terms "broad ministry" and "free ministry" connect this section to similar usages of those terms in the prior episode while juxtaposing them to "lack of freedom," "plantation sort of order," and "political trappings" in the opening episode. He has come full circle. Although the narrator does not end his plot with an episode, he successfully connects it to the opening and middle by a strict adherence to his theme.

Although Roberts's plot has a beginning, a middle, and an end, it is not wholly dependent on episodes. The opening and middle have only one episode each, while the end has none. All four features of plot are present in Roberts's narrative, and each advances the development of his theme. Causality, though not as important as thematic development, is the most important feature of the four. Sequence is made subservient to causality, especially since there are a limited number of episodes held together by causality. Causality dictates the unity of the narrative and holds the two episodes together, but development of theme gives unity to all three parts of the narrative. Roberts wants the narratee to believe him, but he does not draw upon the emotive aspect of affective power frequently to accomplish this goal. Clear use of it is seen in the opening section only.

Roberts's theme can be expressed as follows. *I was reared as a PK in a denomination that made ministry so unattractive to me that although I had the yearning to go into ministry I started resisting it at an early age. I wanted a broader and freer ministry, but I did not know where to find it. I went searching for a camp that would give me freedom in ministry to be myself. When I discovered that option in another denomination I surrendered to the call. It was not a catastrophic vertical [divine] experience. It was gradual and both horizontal [community of faith] and vertical. It came as a long series of nudgings and proddings; the educational process was the pinnacle of authentication.*

The development of his theme has determined the structure of Roberts's narrative. He speaks retrospectively, and by the absence of spatio-temporal markers he demonstrates that he is interested only in narrating interpreted history. He uses repetition throughout to signal how the theme holds together. Although the beginning and ending of the plot are significant, the middle of the plot holds the key to Roberts's retrospective understanding of his call. It is here that one discovers that Roberts has a call even during the time of the first episode. One also learns how Roberts resolves his conflict with ministry, as well as his retrospective understanding of call.

As with Kemp and Roberts, analysis of Newman's "narrative time" demonstrates that he alters the order of his story for thematic purposes. The modifications are also crucial to the sequence that he establishes in three sections (1-8; 9-34; 35-46). Newman's plot depends not on episodes, but on a variety of actions and descriptive pauses.

Newman's first section opens his plot with an array of actions and descriptive pauses. He is "from a large family of preachers." It is kind of a "family tradition." His "father" and "grandfather" and six of the seven boys, his brothers, all "went into the ministry." When he finished high school at age sixteen he "had a sense of call." It had been "pretty much understood" until that time that he was "going into the ministry." He "did not see any other profession or calling as to what would be my life's commitment."

At first glance it looks as if Newman is establishing the backdrop for a larger life-history story of another PK. However, it soon becomes evident that what we have here is the beginning of a theme. Newman comes from an area and a family that produces preachers "seemingly" as a tradition. At least three generations of Newmans have followed this path. However, Newman does not want the narratee to get the impression that this is a matter of mindless clones. Therefore, he retrospectively includes the point that, "I had a sense of call." This assertion is temporally fixed at age sixteen when he graduates from high school.

The narratee wants to ask Newman a series of questions. What do you mean by sense? What was its content? What is the relationship between age sixteen and high school graduation? What was it like growing up as a PK? All of these questions are irrelevant to Newman, and the answers would merely confuse the retrospective theme that he wants to develop. He graduates from high school at sixteen, and it is at this time that he comes to grips with what he has understood about his life's direction for quite some time.

Again the narratee wants to ask: understood by whom and for how long? Although he does not answer these questions specifically, one gets the impression from what he has said so far that it was probably a combination of family "tradition" and individual "sense."

Additional development of Newman's theme is captured in his assertion that he saw no other "profession" or "calling" that would be "my life's commitment." These terms are crucial to Newman's theme. It is evident that he is using "profession" and "calling" synonymously. What is not clear, however, is how he is defining them. Part of the answer may lie in his last phrase — "life commitment." All of this may suggest that Newman believes that a "calling" is something to which you commit your life, and in this sense it is similar to a profession.

Newman's second section, also the middle, supports this thesis. It is connected to the first section sequentially and causally in order to develop his theme further. At "age sixteen" he "received a local preacher's license." "Then, after completing high school, at the age of sixteen, I entered Clafflin College in Orangeburg, South Carolina." This was a "black college" supported by the "United Methodist church." These actions are followed sequentially by numerous other actions, mostly ministerial assignments, but also educational achievements.

By temporal repetition, Newman connects this section with the prior section. Age sixteen is when he graduates from high school, has a sense of call, receives a preacher's license, and enters college. Newman is interested in spatio-temporally grounding his claims, but offers retrospectively interpreted history. In all of the other actions, he does the same thing. In each instance he tells us where he went (South Carolina, Florida, Tennessee), and what "action" he performed (pastor, district superintendent, associate director, bishop). All of these actions are intended to demonstrate historically what Newman has been doing from the time he graduates from high school at age sixteen until the present.

The narratee might wonder how these actions are any different from what one would find on Newman's résumé. The difference is that these spatio-temporal actions are selectively and sequentially utilized retrospectively to develop Newman's theme. If we are correct in our assumption that Newman defines "calling" as "life commitment," then it is these sequential actions that attest to Newman's "life commitment." To list only one is to allow the narratee an unacceptable challenge — "You call that life commitment?" Newman anticipates that challenge and addresses it with such a mass of actions that it looks like overkill.

Newman's final section and close of his plot give ample support to our assumptions. Newman closes this section, not with actions, but with a string of descriptive pauses. "My call to ministry" was a matter of "no choice." I was "born" and "brought up in the Methodist church" from a "family of preachers." It was a "family tradition." There was never a time that I considered that I would "do anything else." It was a "life commitment." There is "the call and you make the commitment to it and dedicate your life to it." "I did not see any spectacular vision of some kind or some unknown mysterious voice that came to me." "I saw mine as a family tradition, heritage." It was a "desire" to work on the behalf of people "developing a ministry" to "respond to their concerns." "It was a commitment, and out of this commitment, a dedication." "This has been my response to the call to the ministry."

Without episode or action, Newman has connected this final section to the previous two sections. It is connected to the first section by use of repetition. It is now self-evident that Newman defines "calling" by the term "commitment," especially "life commitment." In this way the final section is connected to the spatio-temporal actions in section two that demonstrate that Newman qualifies as one who has been called. Thus all three sections are unified. Newman locates his understanding of call in the response to the call, especially a lifelong commitment. Therefore, Newman needs to make it clear that he has had no "spectacular" experience. To discern whether a call is upon one's life one must look at the lifelong response to it. Obviously, this is done retrospectively.

Newman's plot has a beginning, a middle, and an end. However, it has no episodes. It is totally a combination of actions and descriptive pauses. All four features of plot are evident in Newman's narrative. Causality contributes to the story's unity and is the most important of the four features, though obviously not as important as thematic development. Sequence enhances thematic development by appeal to an array of actions that illustrate Newman's life commitment. The use of affective power is weak. However, if it exists at all it is located primarily in section two. A key aspect of theme, lifelong commitment, is captured in the array of actions offered as support in section two.

Newman's theme can be expressed as follows: *My call comes out of a family tradition. There has never been a time when I considered any other direction for my life. However, when I graduated from high school at age sixteen I sensed it more fully. At that point I responded to it by committing myself to a life of ministry that I have not relinquished to this day.*

The development of his theme determines the structure of Newman's narrative. He uses numerous spatio-temporal markers. Although each of these actions is given as history, the whole makes it self-evident that they are used to serve his retrospective purposes, namely, development of his theme. He uses repetition and causality to unify the story. Although the beginning and middle of the plot are significant, the ending of the plot holds the key to Newman's retrospective understanding of call. It is here that Newman defines what call is in his understanding. His theme receives its fullest development here. It is as the plot closes that the narratee can look back with the narrator and better appreciate how the beginning and middle support the theme.

When the three types are compared in terms of narrative plot, a number of similarities emerge. All of these narrators' plots have a beginning, a middle, and an end. The narrator's plot is controlled by thematic development. Theme unifies the entire narrative. All four features (sequence, causality, unity, affective power) of plot are present in all types. Causality is the most important feature of the four for all types. Each narrator's use of causality and repetition contributes to the unity of the narrative.

However, some significant differences emerge as well. The kind of plot differs for each type. Kemp uses numerous episodes. Roberts uses a limited number of episodes. Newman does not use episodes; he prefers actions. The most important part of the plot is the middle for Kemp and Roberts, but the end for Newman. Although each one narrates retrospectively, indicating that he is recording interpreted history, they all do it differently. Kemp uses frequent spatio-temporal activities and settings to fix his episodes in history. Newman does the same but with actions. The three narrators all have a different theme. Kemp's theme is that his call was catastrophic. He didn't want it, and he resisted it. It was forced upon him until he had no choice but to surrender. Roberts's experience as a PK made him reject the call. He didn't want it. He accepted it when he found the right denomination. His call was gradual, not catastrophic. Newman's experience as a PK conditioned him to accept the call from the very beginning as a lifelong commitment; he never resisted it. It was a family tradition. Like Roberts's, then, his call was gradual, not catastrophic.

The analysis of these narratives has led to these conclusions about their narrative structure:

1. The voice of the narrator is a character in the story.

2. The point of view of the narrator is that of the main character telling his or her own story.

3. The narrators rearrange the order of their "story time" to reflect their theme and type.

4. The duration of the narrative is modified by how each narrator selects that history which is relevant to their theme and type.

5. The frequency in the narrative is dictated by the necessary repetition that reinforces the theme of the narrative.

6. Causality is the key feature of plot. It controls the unity of the narrative and dictates the sequence.

7. Theme development unifies the entire narrative and controls the plot as well as the framework of the plot.

These features represent the common core of story content and narrative structure that will allow us to formulate a comprehensive definition of an African-American call story. *The story of an African-American call is a first-person narrative of the revelation to an individual that he or she has been chosen by God for ministry. In the retrospect of those who later become ministers, this revelation is discerned as an urge that cannot be successfully resisted. The individual's subsequent acceptance of this revelation is then sanctioned by the pastor and, after, by the community of faith, and finds further confirmation in the ensuing mission of the individual called. All these sanctions are represented retrospectively as evidence of the sanction of God. Causality, sequence, and repetition are interwoven to construct a theme designed to demonstrate that the narrator made the correct vocational choice and therefore is an instrument of God.*

We observed earlier in the chapter that a call story is transformed into a call narrative with the distinct purpose of getting the narratee to believe the callee's story. Moreover, it is clear that the narrative is structured to accomplish the larger purpose of getting the callee validated and legitimated as an instrument of God among the community of believers. We further observed that this is done by the selected use of parts of the story. This chapter helps us to understand how the callee has structured that selected material to accomplish this objective. The callee develops an overall theme throughout the narrative, depending on which of the three types of call he or she wants to convey to the narratee. The causal linkage of key events, selected emphasis of terms, phrases, or events, and modification of chronology are narrative techniques used by the callee to create a narrative that helps to legitimate his or her claim to be an instrument of God.

PART III

THE CALL AS RITES OF PASSAGE

CHAPTER 9

The Liminality of the Call to Ministry

In his classic work, Arnold Van Gennep[1] laid the foundation for discussion of rites of passage that has gone virtually unchallenged until recent times. He argues that there are three phases of the rites of passage which he called separation (preliminal), margin (liminal — from the Latin *limen,* meaning threshold), and aggregation (postliminal). Transition is the key point in Van Gennep's theory. An individual (e.g., girl to woman, layperson to clergy) moves from one social status or "state" to another. He argues that an individual "cannot pass from one [phase or state] without going through an intermediate stage."[2] Victor Turner elaborates on the process:

> The first phase of separation comprises symbolic behavior signifying the detachment of the individual or group either from an earlier fixed point in the social structure or a set of cultural conditions (a "state"); during the intervening liminal period, the state of the ritual subject (the "passenger") is ambiguous; he passes through a realm that has few or none of the attributes of the past or coming state; in the third phase the passage is consummated. The ritual subject, individual or

1. Arnold Van Gennep, *The Rites of Passage* (Chicago: The Univ. of Chicago Press, 1960). See also Victor Turner, *The Forest of Symbols: Aspects of Ndembu Ritual* (Ithaca: Cornell Univ. Press, 1967), esp. ch. 4; Louise Mahdi, Steven Foster, and Meredith Little, eds., *Betwixt & Between: Patterns of Masculine and Feminine Initiation* (LaSalle, Ill.: Open Court, 1987), esp. ch. 28; Mark Searle, "The Rites of Christian Initiation," ch. 29; and Thomas Patrick Lavin, "Psychological Reflections on the Rites of Christian Initiation." Most recently, see the splendid and provocative Tom F. Driver, *The Magic of Ritual: Our Need for Liberating Rites That Transform Our Lives & Our Communities* (San Francisco: HarperCollins Publishers, 1991).

2. Van Gennep, 1.

corporate, is in a stable state once more and, by virtue of this, has rights and obligations of a clearly defined and "structural" type, and is expected to behave in accordance with certain customary norms and ethical standards.[3]

The state that gets the greatest amount of attention is the second, because unlike the first and last state the liminal state is a state of instability. It is the state of transition within which the state of the passenger is ambiguous. Mark Searle equates it to being caught "between two worlds."[4]

Rites of passage, especially initiation as part of ritual process, occur during various parts of life in all cultures throughout time. Tom Driver argues that it is part of the life-style of both animals and humans[5] and that it can be found in political and social life just as well as in religious life.[6] Ronald Grimes argues that we should see ourselves as "ritualizing animals."[7]

One of the images that Driver uses when discussing rituals is a "pathway." He says, "To ritualize is to make (or utilize) a pathway through what would otherwise be uncharted terrritory."[8] In Van Gennep's theory the uncharted pathway is the liminal state. In an attempt to move from one relatively stable state (preliminal) to another state of relative stability (postliminal), one must venture out into this uncharted territory. Most often this creates an unsettling feeling that in turn engenders internal and external struggle, doubt, fear, resistance, and a request for a guide to help one negotiate the pathway.

We have already argued that it is possible to view call as story and call as narrative. A series of rites of passage is yet another way to view the call to ministry: being separated from a former life and set apart to carry out a special mission for God. On the way one gets caught "betwixt and between," both in status and state of mind. Negotiating this uncharted pathway is not always as easy as it appears in retrospect. It is possible to view the liminal phase (state) as a much longer period that begins with the preliminal period and ends with the postliminal period. A close view of Driver's description of his call in the context of his discussion of ritual suggests that he views his call this way:

3. Turner, 94.
4. Searle, 460-61.
5. Driver, 12-31.
6. Ibid., 5-6.
7. Ronald L. Grimes, *Beginnings in Ritual Studies* (Lanham, Md.: University Press of America, 1982): 36.
8. Driver, 16.

In the southern Protestantism in which I grew up, much emphasis was placed upon a preacher's "call." If you were going to enter the ministry, you were supposed to have received a "call to preach." I myself received such a call when I was in high school. It came to me during a period of struggle within my soul, which lasted for many months and had its roots in early childhood, when I felt very attracted to what went on in the pulpit of the Methodist church I attended regularly with my parents. My months of agony during high school culminated in a clear awareness of divine calling, which came to a climax one afternoon after school. I was in the basement of my home, shoveling coal into the furnace fire and feeling very angry that a mark of some sort had been put upon me so that I would have to become a preacher in spite of myself and be the laughingstock of all my friends. On this particular afternoon, an inner voice whispered, "Would that be so bad?" and I knew that the struggle was over. I had the call, and there was nothing to be done about it.[9]

Biblical call narratives contain elements of rites of passage also; the liminal state is especially evident in these narratives. Liminality is observed primarily in the initial and subsequent response to the call. Most, if not all (Isaiah, especially, may be an exception) Old Testament callees manifest some level of reluctance, confusion, doubt, and instability in understanding and/or accepting the call. Youth, poor speech, lack of a family tradition, and the resistance of people to the message are but a few reasons given for the callees' reluctance. The desire for some kind of sign (e.g., either God's name or person, the wetting or non-wetting of a fleece) is sought in an effort to gain greater clarity about the experience.

The most prominent example, however, is the New Testament call narrative of Paul recorded by Luke, especially since there are three different accounts of the story.[10] Paul's preliminal state is that of a persecutor of the Jesus movement within Judaism. Contrary to past opinion, Paul is not unstable at this point in his life about whether he should accept Jesus for who he claims to be and join the movement. At the story and narrative level, both Paul and Luke make it abundantly clear that Paul adamantly believes this movement is blasphemous and a threat to genuine Judaism.

Up to the point of his call experience on the Damascus road, Paul, who was "still breathing threats and murder against the disciples of

9. Driver, 70.
10. Acts 9, 22, 26.

the Lord, went to the high priest and asked him for letters to the synagogues at Damascus, so that if he found any who belonged to the Way, men or women, he might bring them bound to Jerusalem" (Acts 9:1-2). This does not sound like an unstable man, unsure of whether he should join this movement.

It is at this point, however, that uncertainty, lack of understanding, and ambiguity are observed, and Paul moves into the liminal state. The reason is the call experience. Paul's call is sudden and cataclysmic; it includes voices and lights from heaven. There is not enough light in this transcendent event, however, to make all things clear for Paul. On two later occasions when Paul needs to give an apologia for his apostleship, he retrospectively reinterprets this experience with such great certainty as to eliminate any ambiguity about what he knew. God revealed his Son Jesus Christ to him is Paul's unambiguous assertion to the Galatians (1:11-17), and "Have I not seen Jesus our Lord?" is his rhetorical question that demands an affirmative response from the Corinthians (1 Cor. 9:1). Yet at the story level Paul's very ambiguous response to all the voices and lights is filled with darkness — "Who are you, Lord?" (Acts 9:5)

On another occasion when Paul is depicted as telling his story in a different context it is evident that ambiguity also existed. In all of his subsequent letters Paul speaks retrospectively about the certainty of his call as well as his mission. That God has set him apart before he is born and has called him to proclaim Jesus among the Gentiles is one way he defines his call (Gal. 1:15), and "Paul, called to be an apostle of Christ Jesus" is another way (e.g., 1 Cor. 1:1; cf. Rom. 1:1; 2 Cor. 1:1; and his other letters). However, when telling his story on this occasion Paul's question, "What am I to do, Lord?", makes clear that he understands neither the purpose nor mission of his call at this time. Moreover, coupled with the earlier question, "Who are you, Lord?", it is clear that Paul doesn't even know who he is asking to respond to the question. More confusion abounds in this telling of the story because Paul asserts that even those with him cannot corroborate his experience. In this instance only he hears the voice, although he claims that the witnesses saw the light. This account is even more confusing because the earlier narrative says just the opposite — the witnesses did hear the voice, though they saw no one, and there is no mention about whether they saw the light (Acts 22).

In the final account, which is yet another occasion, the ambiguity continues. In the first two instances Paul is depicted as the one falling to the ground, whereas on this occasion everybody falls to the ground.

Moreover, in this instance he asserts that he knows more about the specificity of his call and mission (Acts 26).

The narratives in this study also suggest that the call can be viewed as a series of rites of passage. However, it is beyond the scope of this book to argue this fully. This preliminary analysis will address three components of the call as rites of passage: the preliminal, liminal and postliminal elements of call; the liminality of the call as story-narrative; and the pastor as the primary portal through the rites of passage.

The Preliminal, Liminal, and Postliminal Phases of Call

In order to examine the preliminal, liminal and postliminal elements of call, it is necessary to look at call as story. Based on the discussion in part one, stage one — early religious exposure is viewed as the preliminal stage. Callees are being prepared, perhaps unconsciously, to ultimately accept the call. As we saw in chapter one, the home and the church are key places where this nurturing process unfolds. This tends to be a relatively stable stage.

The liminal phase encompasses stage two — call experience, stage three — struggle, and stage four — search. This is a period of ambiguity, confusion, doubt, fear, and perhaps internal and external resistance; basically, it is a very unstable period of time for the callee. Callees often do not understand what is happening to them even when the experiences include supernatural elements. Ambiguity engenders reluctance and a search for answers.

The liminal phase is the key phase because the call experience sets callees on a course from which they will emerge as different people. They cannot go back to the preliminal state remaining the same, and they certainly will not be the same when they emerge in the postliminal phase. In the preliminal phase they were not legitimated spokespersons for God, but they will be in the postliminal state.

However, they aren't sure that they want that role for a variety of reasons. Like Amos they might not come from a family of preachers; like Moses they might feel that they are unqualified to speak for God; like Jeremiah they might feel that they are too young, or like Samuel and Paul they just might be totally overwhelmed and confused about who this is that is calling their name. Whatever the reason, they find themselves in limbo, betwixt and between. Carey McCreary describes two separate occasions when this liminality manifested itself during his call:

When I got to that place downtown I walked inside, and I turned blind, but not completely blind. I could see folks, you know, moving around, but I felt like I was about to fall. A fellow came over to me and asked me if I was a preacher. I don't know what made him do that. And I didn't know what to say. Man, I hated to say yes and I hated to say no. So I said, "Yes and no." That man said, "What kind of talk is that?" . . . I got on my knees that night, and I asked the Lord if he had called me to the ministry. I wanted to know. . . . I had woke up and the Lord hadn't called me. I was a little disappointed, but I was partly glad too, because I felt I wasn't gonna do it. So I was betwixt and between.[11]

As discussed in chapter three, the struggle may also be due to a number of external factors such as gender pressures for females, or resistance by family, clergy, and friends. The struggle begins as the callee tries to find the pathway out of this phase.

This leads to a search (as described in chapter four) for an advocate, not just a guide, nor merely someone who can help the callee understand what is happening. Rather, someone is needed who knows the pathway and can unlock doors. Ultimately, this individual is the pastor, the one who will usually perform the ritual of ordination that ends this rites-of-passage process.

Sanction and surrender of the callee to this new task both ends the liminal state and begins the postliminal state. Although a variety of phenomena, events, and individuals may help the callee to surrender as well as sanction him or her, the pastor is the key person in this stage as well.

At this juncture we must raise a question about the linear assumptions of Van Gennep's three phases. Whereas stability might be the dominant aspect of the first and third phase and instability the dominant characteristic of the middle phase, it could be argued that there is some circularity as well as overlapping of these three phases in call stories.

Instability may begin in what appears to be primarily a preliminal stage because of childhood predictions or pressures, as well as certain nudgings, but may not manifest itself overtly until later. Gardner Taylor may be an example:

I was a pastor's son. I had, growing out of some of my family member's attitudes, some antipathy toward the ministry. I came by it in

---

11. Myers, 234-35, 237.

that atmosphere. My father was a pastor, a rather well-known pastor, and I greatly admired him. . . . But together with that family influence, my own, I guess, inclinations and schooling, I became very scornful of the ministry and wanted absolutely no part of it.[12]

It was observed in chapter one that, whether PK's or not, these callees are exposed to religious environments early in life. This exposure influences their vocational decisions. In some instances, although negative feelings begin early on, ultimately the callee still chooses ministry as his or her life vocation. However, these early negative reactions, as in Taylor's story, may be an indication that incipient liminality has already begun in this so-called preliminal phase. The seeds of instability in terms of resistance, tension, doubt, and uneasiness are observed even at this early stage. Raised in a religious atmosphere Taylor comes to greatly admire his father the pastor; yet, that same environment engenders in him "some antipathy toward the ministry," and he "became very scornful of the ministry and wanted absolutely no part of it." It should be noted that Taylor represents one of the two reluctant-type calls that have obvious elements of liminality contained in the stories.

However, the one nonreluctant type may not be so easily described, because these callees deny ever being betwixt and between. Newman and Scott's narratives, for example, suggest that they always wanted ministry as their vocation, were not reluctant, and negotiated the pathway with ease. If this is the case, then only in the broadest sense of rites of passage (i.e., movement from laypersons to clergy) could it be argued that this type of call should be seen as a series of rites of passage. It would not contain the liminal phase in the same sense (e.g., ambiguity — limited understanding, clarity, and certainty) as the other types. Further investigation will be necessary to determine whether in fact this is the case. It may be that it is yet again an example of the different perspective of story that a callee can offer when he or she recounts it through the lens of narrative.

Call as rites of passage is also part of a larger ritualizing process. In fact, it is an ongoing process. Whereas the ordination ritual may be a key portal that transforms one from layperson to clergy, it is not necessarily the end of liminality, rites of passage, or the ritualization process of call to ministry. For example, the call to a church as pastor, whether it is the callee's first appointment or a change in assignment, starts the rites-of-passage phases anew, thus continuing them in a circular fashion,

12. Ibid., 328.

engendering a new set of rituals (e.g., installation of the new pastor) and furthering the call process. Hence, liminality may continue in what can be viewed as primarily postliminal phases (e.g., surrender).

The call may unfold in a multiplicity of different ways (e.g., with the help of a layperson, clergy, pastor, professor, ecclesiastical administrator, college or seminary president, author, or retired volunteer) throughout the lifetime of the callee. This may be due to new opportunities that did not exist earlier because of traditions at the time (e.g., gender), inadequacies of the callee (e.g., lack of experience, education, maturity), new revelations, or a different self-understanding of call and mission. As all of these new understandings break forth, both in the individual and in religious communities, the circular, almost spiral, nature of the call as a series of rites of passage continues to unfold as a ritualizing process.

One of the most unfortunate consequences of not understanding call as a process that may continue to unfold differently throughout one's life is getting frozen into one aspect of ministry, sometimes merely one function, even when a callee would like to do something different. Prevalent in many churches is the idea that one can never retire from a "call to preach." This has the misfortune of misunderstanding the call, preaching ministry, and retirement. When the call to ministry is seen as a process that may unfold differently throughout one's life, then one can continuously move on (i.e., retire) from one understanding of ministerial function to another, especially when one has the gifts and desire to do so. Any narrower understanding of ministry may keep one in a liminal state for life.

The Liminality of the Call as Story

The liminality that exists in the call to ministry is best observed at the story level, especially when it is juxtaposed to call as narrative. Since call as narrative is the callee's retrospective interpretation of story, a slightly different perspective often emerges when story and narrative are compared. For instance, a closer examination of call stories reveals that there is less understanding and more uncertainty, less clarity and more ambiguity in the call at the story level than the callee's narrative often suggests.

Many callees assert that they have always known without any doubt that they were called to preach. This is an assertion, however, from the perspective of the present looking back over a series of past events and tying them together. However, at every critical moment in the past ambiguity abounds.

Carey McCreary asserts in his story that he "knew" all of his life as sure as he could look at the sun, "without a shadow of a doubt," that he was called to preach. Yet doubt prevails at every critical turn in his life, even after having numerous supernaturally confirming experiences. As with Paul, the supernatural aspect of the experience is not enough to eliminate all the questions. Charles Adams makes a similar claim when he says: "There has never been a moment in my consciousness of being alive and being a person that I have not understood myself as having been called and commissioned to preach." Later, however, he encounters tension over whether he should be a doctor or preacher in order to please his mother, and he tries to leave the decision up to her. Her shifting the decision back to him forces him to choose preaching. In addition, women like Lucille Abernathy, Cynthia Hale, Delores Carpenter and Ann Lightner, among others who assert at the narrative level a certainty that God had called them, subsequently have much doubt and many questions and challenges for God because of their gender.

As we pick up Gardner Taylor's story where we left off earlier, we observe how much liminality is resident there:

> As a matter of fact, I had been admitted in my senior year of college to the University of Michigan Law School. . . . And I wanted to be a criminal lawyer. But in the spring of my senior year in college, I had a traumatic experience with an automobile accident. I was chauffeur for the college president, and there was an accident on the highway driving his car. Three men, White, cut across me in an old Model T Ford. One was killed on the spot, one other died later. That experience — and this was a rural Louisiana highway in 1937 — the only people who gathered were Whites. Now, I did not associate this directly with my call, with any call. But I would guess that this was the culmination of some disquiet that had been going on in me for some time. Within the next week or two, I went into the president's office and, I suppose to his surprise, told him that I felt called to the ministry. I would guess that this was something that had been going on inside of me for some time. But this accident brought it to the fore. . . . The call grew out of this. I would not want to say that that was the cause of it. I would not want to say that I would have surrendered to this without it. I can't disentangle these things. I cannot untangle these things. I just don't know. More than what I've said, I just don't know. I know I wasn't comfortable, I was going to the University of Michigan Law School, but I wasn't comfortable. I guess something was going on inside of me.[13]

13. Ibid., 328-29.

The ambiguity of this experience and its relationship to Taylor's call are arresting. First, there appears to be both an internal and an external struggle over the direction of Taylor's vocational choice. He is set against becoming a preacher, an "antipathy" arising "out of some . . . family members' attitudes," although his father is a pastor, a rather well-known pastor, whom Taylor admires. Therefore, he decides to become a criminal lawyer. Before he can launch out on that vocational choice, however, a traumatic accident occurs, and it becomes the stimulus for his acknowledgment of his call.

Although Taylor did not "associate this directly" with his call at the time, he does interpret it as "the culmination of some disquiet that had been going on in me for some time." The ambiguity about this experience and its relationship to Taylor's call are self-evident. Taylor did not associate it with the call at the time, but does connect it now as the culmination of an internal struggle. We are not told how long "some time" represents. However, this may be additional data that supports our earlier argument that incipient liminality in the sense of a struggle was going on in Taylor even in the preliminal phase.

At the narrative level Taylor asserts an even stronger connection between the accident and his call. Unlike many, however, Taylor is cautious and sensitive about maintaining the ambiguity that he experienced in the story for the narratee in the narrative. He says, "The call grew out of this. I would not want to say that that was the cause of it. I would not want to say that I would have surrendered to this without it. I can't disentangle these things. I cannot untangle these things. I just don't know."

This may be one of the best examples of how much liminality exists at the story level for the callee, how all of it may not be totally understood by the callee many years later, and how ultimately even the story transformed as narrative cannot hide all of the ambiguity. Some narratives, as has already been demonstrated, give the narratee the impression that knowledge of the call is complete, clear, and certain, without a hint of doubt or ambiguity. That, if it obtains at all, is retrospective interpretation at the narrative level; it is highly questionable whether that is the case at the story level. Taylor, on the other hand, doesn't eliminate it, either in the story or in the narrative. "I just don't know. More than what I've said, I just don't know. I know I wasn't comfortable. . . ." He does know some things, but his knowledge is limited; thus ambiguity, at least hermeneutically, continues.

The Pastor as the Primary Portal

The pastor is the primary pathway through the rites of passage. He sets in motion a series of events that culminates in the ultimate ritual of the call to ministry — ordination. Pastors can be involved in events as diverse as setting up a time for the callee to present his or her story to the congregation, a time to deliver a "trial sermon," convening an ordination council, as well as coaching the callee for the ordination exams. Recognized as the primary doorkeeper through the rites of passage from layperson to clergy, the pastor is among the first people, often the very first, that callees inform of their call. In many instances, the pastor comes before family and friends; family members as well as others are aware of the pastor's primary role and will often advise, and on occasion escort the callee to the pastor. Leroy McCreary is an example of the former:

> And it was some time after that, and it was a short time after that I went to my aunt with whom I was living. And I said to her that God has called me to preach. She expressed some surprise and shock, and I told her he had and she said to me, "Well you better go and see Rev. Carey McCreary," who was my cousin, [of] whose church she and I were both members. . . . However, I do need to backtrack for a minute. Just before going to her, my aunt, I believe . . . I spoke to a minister. . . . And he told me the first step in getting started is to go see my pastor. It was after that I met with him after having talked with my aunt I went to Rev. McCreary and I told him.[14]

In Charles Booth's story we observe the result of his mother's advice:

> I recall at the age of fourteen announcing to my mother that I knew that I was to preach, at which point she quickly halted me. . . . She felt that I was a bit young to be talking about preaching and a call to preach. She said, "If it's of God and for real, you'll come to a point and place where you will not be able to contain yourself. At that point, I think we should move ahead with some kind of public acknowledgment. It was not until three years later . . . that I reached that point. She instructed me to go and talk with my pastor. . . . He scheduled me to preach my initial or trial sermon. . . .[15]

The reservation expressed by Booth's mother that the callee needs to be certain about the call before moving forward with any public

14. Ibid., 243-44.
15. Ibid., 42-43.

acknowledgment is one reason that callees are hesitant about going to the pastor. However, Ronald Williams reveals the primary reason. In his case the pastor also happens to be his father:

> I came home and I told . . . my father and I said, "Dad, don't tell anybody, but I've decided to enter the ministry. I'm tired of fighting." He did not honor my word. . . . He got up in front of eight hundred people the next Sunday and told all of them that I had entered the ministry. Then I was caught. I couldn't get out. Not only did he do that, but he set a date for me to accomplish my trial.[16]

"Then I was caught. I couldn't get out." This is the greatest fear of the callee in going to the pastor — getting fenced in before you are certain, before you are ready. Once the callees go to the pastor, they have gone through the first portal that sets into motion a momentum that takes on a life of itself. Rarely is there a turning back at this point. Some callees go to their pastor hoping that this will be the doorway that closes the pathway completely, only to discover that momentum takes over. Ann Lightner gives us an example of how quickly the callee can lose control once the pastor is informed:

> So, after that, I called Reverend Bryant up and I told him, "I need to make an appointment to come talk with you." So when I went, I told him, "I think the Lord is calling me to preach. . . ." So, he said, "Have you accepted it?" And I said, "Well, at this point I realize that that's what's happening but I don't know what to do." "Well, you either say yes or no. . . ." "Reverend Bryant, I never wanted to be a preacher." "Well, I'll tell you what. I'll give you a trial sermon date if you want it." "Right now?" "Yes." "But you make people wait." "Not when I already know."[17]

Without the pastor it is virtually impossible for the callee to negotiate the liminal state and move through the rites of passage. Although the community of faith helps to validate the callee, without a sponsor like the pastor the individual could be left in the liminal state for a very long time. Lacking legitimating credentials the callee is a claimant without a home. Without the pastor's sanction the ultimate ritualization — ordination — will be very difficult indeed to obtain.

The power of this office to help end or prolong the liminality of

16. Ibid., 361.
17. Ibid., 223.

a callee is enormous. No one should approach it lightly. Much sensitivity and understanding are needed if the pastor is to help move the callee into a postliminal state. Callees who come seeking advice may come manifesting limited clarity, certainty, and knowledge; they may be confused, fearful, resistant, and in great pain. Such is the nature of the call; callees need a pathfinder, whatever it may be and whoever they may be. Show them the path and help them along the way and leave the rest to God. The path will be different for each one.

We have observed in this chapter that the call to ministry can be viewed as a rite of passage in a much larger ongoing process. The call at the story level is best suited for categorizing the content as preliminal, liminal, and postliminal. The early religious exposure stage is primarily preliminal; the call experience, struggle, and search stages are primarily liminal, and the sanction and surrender stages are primarily postliminal. However, we also observed that the linear assumption of Van Gennep's phases is to be questioned because of the circularity of the call as rites of passage and the overlapping of the phases. Moreover, it may be that the nonreluctant-type call does not include liminality in the same sense as the reluctant types do. Yet this needs further investigation, because it may be only an example of the difference between story and narrative.

In addition, we observed that the liminality in the call to ministry is evident when the call as story is juxtaposed to the call as narrative. There is less understanding and more uncertainty and ambiguity at the story level than at the narrative level. This is due primarily to the fact that the narrative is a retrospective hermeneutical retelling of the story.

Finally, the pastor is the primary portal through which callees must pass if they expect to successfully negotiate this uncharted territory and emerge out of the liminal state.

PART IV

THE CALL AS HERMENEUTICAL RETROSPECTION

CHAPTER 10

The Call as Hermeneutical Retrospection

Up to now these calls have been analyzed in an effort to understand them as a whole. Moreover, the primary methodologies used to analyze the data have been narrative and ritual theory. This chapter will look at individual narratives of each type. The primary goal is to compare the call as story to the call as narrative in order to demonstrate the prevalence and significance of hermeneutical retrospection in the narratives. Six stories have been selected, two from each type. The stories represent a mixture of gender, as well as denominational, generational, and educational backgrounds. Some observations and hermeneutical implications useful in our goal to rethink call to ministry will conclude the analysis.

Carey McCreary: Betwixt and Between:
Blinded at High Noon

Carey McCreary, although reared in Pensacola, Florida, was born in McWilliams, Alabama, in 1917 to parents also born in Alabama. He later "stopped off" in Cleveland, Ohio, where he accepted the call and was ordained a Baptist minister in 1957. Though lacking formal theological degrees, he is viewed as a model pastor among ministers in the Cleveland area, pastoring the New Mount Zion Baptist Church of Cleveland. His story is an example of type A (cataclysmic/reluctant).

> Well, Doc, I knew that I was going to preach all of my life. From the time — you hear me say — that I preached my little sermon out there around five years old. . . . I knew that I was going to preach the gospel

135

just as sure as I could look at the sun. But I didn't know when. I didn't have anybody to guide me. But I knew it. Now this was before I became a Christian. Deep down in my heart I knew it, and I don't know how I knew it. But I did. Without a shadow of a doubt, I knew I was going to preach one day. I think the reason that I got much older before I started preaching, I guess, was because I didn't have anyone to guide me. I was by myself and most of the folks around me were doing a lot of sinning, like dancing, and I was in the bunch with them, but this never left me — that feeling of preaching the gospel. When I was about twelve, maybe thirteen years old, we went to a party. . . . I started singing the blues that night and something told me not to never sing the blues like that anymore. And I never did. . . . And I don't know why, I never understood why, but I felt sorry that I did it. You know, singing the blues with those guys, because I knew I had to preach one day.

Immediately one is seized by the retrospective hermeneutics in this narrative. McCreary asserts that he "knew," "without a shadow of a doubt," all of his life that he was "going to preach." He admits that he doesn't know how he knew. Such is often the case with the existential moment, the person doesn't really know — better, understand — much about what is happening. In this case it is even more evident because of his age. How much can one really understand about such a complex matter at age five? However, given the opportunity to speak about it decades later, his retrospective interpretation is that he knew without a shadow of doubt. The hearer is left with the impression, at least on the basis of the narrative, that the callee understood his call quite well at this early age. A closer examination of the hermeneutics of the story, however, might reveal something quite different.

A second interpretative point that emerges early in this narrative relates to why McCreary delayed accepting the call: "I didn't have anyone to guide me." The impact of the cultural-religious beliefs of that community of faith contributed to his interpretation of the delay. Moreover, it also subtly contributes to his understanding of what it means to be called (e.g., what you can or cannot do). He was surrounded by sinners and sinning, interpreted in this instance as dancing, singing the blues, and the like, and it influenced him and caused the delay. Perhaps, however, it was too much — both in terms of understanding and behavior — to expect of someone so young, guidance or no guidance.[1]

1. See, e.g., in Myers the problems and responses created for callees at an early age in the stories of Odell Jones (43) and Wheeler (78), among others.

Well, I was preaching all the time after that. I just started preaching. I'd go off to myself and get in my car and just drive along and preach. The last time I preached that way was just before I left home to come to Cleveland. . . . I was in my twenties then. But I had been preaching all the time and having visions all of my life. Like I said earlier, all of my life I knew one day I was going to preach the gospel. I don't know how I knew it. I knew just as good as I'm riding in this car with you. But after I preached that sermon, every now and then it would come to me that the Lord didn't want me. After I got older I went to thinking about money, cars and land. I was saying inside myself I have made it over, I won't have to do it now. Now that's when God is about to get you. Yessir, when I came to Cleveland it worked so fast. I came to Cleveland in April or May, 1956 and I started preaching in September.

There is an interesting juxtaposition of McCreary's interpretation of preaching at the beginning and end of this quotation. He interprets what he was doing at an earlier age at home and later in Cleveland as preaching. However, the juxtaposition of the opening phrase, "Well, I was preaching all the time after that. I just started preaching" with the ending phrase, "I came to Cleveland in April or May, 1956 and I started preaching in September" may suggest some tension in his interpretation of what is preaching. He had already started preaching before he came to Cleveland, so how could he start after he gets to Cleveland? Perhaps this merely refers to his preaching after being ordained over against preaching before being ordained. However, it is also possible that he now retrospectively reinterprets and understands what he was doing before he came to Cleveland as preaching just as much as the ordained preaching afterwards. This would suggest an evolving understanding of the concept that he would not have been able to articulate before ordination in his religious community because the cultural norms of what preaching is and who can do it would not have allowed such an interpretation. It may be that this is an example of the kind of tension that exists in similar religious communities today about what preaching is and who can do it.

The idea that he always knew he was going to preach emerges again. His repetition of this assertion signals its importance and should not be taken lightly. We should admit that at minimum he was aware of an inclination in this direction. Since he also repeats the notion that he didn't know how he knew, it is probably safe to conclude that he didn't understand much more at the time than that he felt motivated in that direction.

He doesn't tell us why he felt "every now and then" that the Lord didn't want him. His connection of this idea to a desire for more material things in life might suggest that he really didn't want to pursue this career for fear that he couldn't have both this ordained life and material comforts. Perhaps it was that he didn't want the Lord, at least not in this way. Again, his cultural pre-understandings of what it means to accept a call influenced his behavior.

> Now, this is what happened. I got to the place that I didn't want to be around anybody doing or saying anything wrong. . . . I started reading and praying. I started having visions at night. . . . Then I got a job in the building trades. One day I finished one job and left to go downtown. . . . When I got to that place downtown I walked inside, and I turned blind, but not completely blind. . . . A fellow came over to me and asked me if I was a preacher. I don't know what made him do that. And I didn't know what to say. Man, I hated to say yes and I hated to say no. So I said, "Yes and no." That man said, "What kind of talk is that?" Then I tried to explain it to him to the best of my knowledge. Doc, I heard a voice saying, "I want you to leave here and go tell your pastor that you have been called to preach." I went home, pulled those clothes off, and I went on down to the church and knocked on the back door. Rev. Fuller opened that door and a voice said to me, "Look at the clock." And that's something I've never understood yet: why that voice told me to look at the clock. But when he opened that door and the Spirit said to me, "Look at the clock," that clock was straight up twelve o'clock.

The cataclysmic nature of this call story is made evident by reference to visions and voices. However, these phenomena do not bring as much interpretative understanding to the callee as one might think. Was he blind or is this merely the way he interprets what was happening to him? His assertion that he felt like he was about to fall may suggest that he was dizzy. Nonetheless, his interpretation is that he was "blind, but not completely blind." Further, though he had been preaching for quite some time at home, it is clear that he didn't at this moment interpret it as such, nor did he consider himself a minister. This is what causes the liminality for him as he tries to answer a direct question about his status. Whether the appearance of the man as well as his question are providential or not is not nearly as important as the effect they had on McCreary. He was truly betwixt and between at this point. As much as he claims to have known, it is clear that at this point in time he didn't really know very much.

Again, we see the difference in his actual knowledge in the story over against his retrospective knowledge in the narrative. Moreover, the yes-and-no liminal answer in the story might be a conflict between his own call experience and his attempt at the moment to interpret and fit what was happening to him into his religious community's understanding of call. Hence, the answer might be interpreted this way: "Yes, I am called according to how I interpret what has been happening to me, but no I am not according to how my religious community allows that question to be answered." How many people get caught in this liminal state for a variety of different reasons (e.g., gender)?

One of the most interesting aspects of this part of the narrative is the way the voice and the message of the voice are interpreted and not interpreted by McCreary. On the one hand he heard a voice and interpreted that voice to be that of the Spirit, but on the other hand he didn't understand — and still doesn't — "why that voice told me to look at the clock." His religious community had given him the language to name the voice, but it did not in this instance translate into an obvious biblical analogy for the whole. For example, the blinding at noon and being sent to a specific person in the religious community (Rev. Fuller) are so similar to elements of the Paul and Ananias story that one would have expected that connection to be made. Again, there is much that the callee neither knew at the time nor chose to interpret in certain ways later.

> I told him with tears in my eyes what happened. . . . He said, "Well that's one thing you got to be sure of." Then I said, "Well, maybe I won't have to do it," because he didn't seem to believe me. . . . I said, "Rev. Fuller, I want to ask you to do something for me. Will you pray for me?" He said, "Yes." He laid his hand on my head and he prayed. And I said then, since that man prayed for me I won't have to do it. . . . He's close to the Lord and the Lord will hear him and I won't have to do it.

Again, for someone who has "known" so much "without doubt" for so long there is an eager yielding of that knowledge. This may be due, as was stated earlier, to a desire not to accept the call in the first place. Then again, it may also be a recognition of the rites-of-passage process in that religious community. Without the pastor, or someone similar, it is not possible to get out of this liminal state. Moreover, this quotation demonstrates how much McCreary is dependent on those in his religious community, especially its leaders' hermeneutical beliefs about call. The fact that his pastor didn't believe him and prayed for him is enough to negate all of the phenomenological events and certain knowledge about his understanding of the call. It should be evident how dominant is the community's perspective on call for anyone asserting a call in that community.

> But, Doc, that thing looked like it was getting tighter and tighter, And it got so tight my plate would talk to me, my pillow would talk to me . . . and it would tell me, "You got to preach, you got to preach." And when I'd lay down at night, my pillow would tell me, "You got to preach." Sometimes it would say, "You must preach." Boy, you talking about being sick. Then I started having visions. . . . I've had plenty dreams about my calling. . . . Sometimes those dreams would last two and three hours, and when I'd wake up I'd be so tired. . . . And when I'd wake up, it would be so clear. I can see the day when God handed me that Bible, just like it was done this morning. . . . Rev. Fuller told me to meet him a couple times, but we didn't get together. So, finally, he asked me to come to his house. He told me, "Now you got to be sure that the Lord called you to preach." In the way he talked to me and what the folks had told me about him, I felt like whatever he told me, that would be what God wanted. So I talked with him and he carried me through some scripture that I didn't know too much about. Then he said, if I had been called I would have known that scripture. So I said to myself, all right, maybe it's not so.

The conflict between what's known versus what's really known, and personal interpretation of call versus community interpretation continues. The cataclysmic events continue in a variety of ways: dreams, plates talking, pillows talking. It is self-evident that McCreary uses the terms "dreams" and "visions" synonymously. Although Fuller has left McCreary in doubt about his personal interpretation of these events as a call, more phenomenological events occur to give him more certainty.

His visions are incredibly detailed, specifically tied to a call to preach. He was called upon to rescue "God's children trapped in that river" in one dream, and "God gave [him a] Bible" in another dream and told him that the people were waiting on him. We are not told how and why he determined that the person in the dream was God, but all of the dreams were sufficiently detailed and linked enough in his mind to interpret them as evidence that he had been called. At least this is the case retrospectively.

Upon closer examination, it is not the case at the time the dreams were happening. Again, in the face of all of this transcendent evidence

— at minimum retrospectively transcendent — he yields to Fuller's interpretation of events in his life. Fuller's interpretation was God's interpretation. Fuller's test, not these cataclysmic events, was what mattered. "Then he said, if I had been called I would have known that Scripture. So I said to myself, all right, maybe it's not so." We don't know what Scripture is being referenced, what question was posed about it, nor whether it was relevant to a call. It doesn't matter; what matters is that he didn't pass Fuller's test. That is sufficient for the moment to negate all that he has claimed to have known up to that moment. Again the community's perspective, as represented in this instance by Fuller, prevails.

> Well, I felt kind of good because I thought I didn't have to preach. He told me to "Get on your knees and talk to the Lord about it." I got on my knees that night, and I asked the Lord if he had called me to the ministry. I wanted to know. And, Doc, I woke up; I think it was about the crack of day and I felt pretty nice about it because I hadn't felt anything and I didn't see anything in a dream. I don't know whether I went halfway back to sleep or what. But the Holy Spirit jumped on me and it felt like to me it was going to choke me to death. It was so hard until I scared my wife. I scared her so that she jumped out of the bed, and it grabbed me and held me down and it almost killed me. I had woke up and the Lord hadn't called me. I was a little disappointed, but I was partly glad too, because I felt I wasn't gonna do it. So I was *betwixt and between.* I was kind of worried that I misled myself. Then I said, well, I won't have to do it now nor what I had gone through with hearing these voices talking about "preach the gospel, preach the gospel." Then I said, well, it could have just been something else.

The liminality of McCreary's call is seen in its full force at this point. Fuller's understanding of call and his examination of McCreary create doubt as well as a temporary respite. It is evident in this quotation, as has been suggested earlier, that part of McCreary's liminality is attributable to the fact that he didn't want this commission in the first place. He "felt good" when he thought that he wouldn't "have to preach." Perhaps the "have to" suggests a lack of choice in the decision. The doubt engendered by Fuller's response to McCreary has offered him what appeared to be an out. The temporary respite was not enough, however, because he wanted to "know." Here is clear evidence that most of what McCreary claims to have known is retrospective interpretation.

However, even at this point in the story, after all of the supernatural events that he has interpreted as evidence of his call, he still doesn't
"know" if "the Lord" "had called me to the ministry." The past tense
— "had called" — is striking in view of his repetitive claims throughout
the narrative to this point that he always knew. From a narrative perspective that may be the case; however, at this late point in the story
he is still unclear about how he should interpret all of these events in
his life.

On the advice of Fuller he returned to the Lord for confirmation.
Another dream and another supernatural event occur. The Holy Spirit
— left undefined — almost killed him by choking him to death. We are
told neither how he knew it was the Holy Spirit nor why the Spirit
wanted to kill him. We are left to assume that it was because he had
not yet accepted the call.

Here is the one place in the narrative that McCreary acknowledges
— even retrospectively — how little he really knew at the time: "I was
betwixt and between." Although he doesn't use "betwixt and between"
as a technical term like narrative theorists, it functions in the same way.
He was in a liminal state, confused and not knowing what to do. Part of
this is due to the fact that he didn't want to accept the call anyway, and
part is due to the doubt that Fuller had created in his mind. "I was kind
of worried that I misled myself." He was worried that he had misinter-
preted events in his life as evidence of a call to ministry that "could have
just been something else." It should be evident that the clarity and
certainty about his call to ministry is retrospectively interpreted and
understood. While it is captured that way in the narrative, an entirely
different picture emerges in the story — liminality continues.

> But, man, after that experience . . . , I said then, and I've said to
> everybody else, "If the Lord told you to do something, you do it and
> don't ask anybody else nothing. But be sure the Lord told you." That
> man [Rev. Fuller] almost messed me up, you know, with doubt. But
> the Spirit of the Lord got on me and gave me confidence to know not
> to fool with nobody when the Lord tells you to do something. Go
> ahead on and do it. . . . I just want to be sure the Lord said so and
> ain't nobody can tell me nothing. And I'm not going to man for any
> advice. I'll do what the Lord says. Of course, I was young, you know,
> and I didn't have nobody to guide me. That's why I was trying to
> get someone to guide me and tell me what to do. But I found out if
> God tells you to do, just go ahead on and do. He will fix a way for
> you to do it if he tells you to do it.

This is the turning point for McCreary. He attributes it to this particular experience. One wants to ask whether his turn toward the ministry is this single event or the series of all the previous events culminating with this one. At minimum we must conclude that he retrospectively attributes it to this single event. What was it about this experience that sealed it for him? Was it the dream, or the presence of the Holy Spirit in the dream? Neither was new to him. Was it the near-death experience? We are not told. It is sufficient for him to say, however: don't let any human being place doubt in your mind about your call when God has made it certain in supernatural ways. One can't help note that again this is hermeneutical retrospection. Such certainty emerges out of the opportunity to see it from a distance after many years have passed.

The advice McCreary offers is contrary to what he did. "If the Lord told you to do something, you do it and don't ask anybody else nothing." At the same time, however, he raises the greatest difficulty of all. "Be sure the Lord told you." How one is to know this we aren't told. His story is told after years of looking back on the events. His reason for not following his own retrospective advice is that he was young and needed advice. Of course, youth, among many other concerns (e.g., gender), may be the reason for the liminality of others caught in this situation.

McCreary's final advice is that "if God tells you to do, just go ahead on and do it. He will fix a way for you to do it if he tells you to do it." Again, we are left to determine for ourselves how one discerns that it is God who is speaking. Yet the suggestion that one should move forward because God will "fix a way" is deeply rooted in the religious community out of which McCreary comes. Thus we see once again the appeal to both the beliefs of his religious community and his own interpretation.

> Now, this is the next thing I thought. I would try to get out of it because, you know, dedicating your life and living the type of life expected of a minister, you wonder if you will make it with all you have to give up. But at the same time, it looks like the clock keeps rolling for you to get going. And with me, I was in a strange place and fooling with these old preachers up here. I didn't get any encouragement and it was a hard thing. But that spirit will keep rolling inside of you, and then you've got to do it.

The resistance theme emerges again. The reason given in this instance is the perceived expectations of one who accepts the call. We are not told how these expectations were derived; we can only conclude that they are another example of where the interpretation of call that McCreary's religious community holds emerges yet again. What you have "to give up" is part of a tradition passed on to each person who acknowledges a call. Naturally this varies from one religious tradition to another; it is a part of each community's interpretation of what it means to be called. In spite of the resistance to accepting the call, due at least partly to what the community expects of a claimant, the call is ultimately an irresistible "spirit" inside that "will keep rolling inside of you, and then you've got to do it." This is indeed a hermeneutical retrospection, because throughout the call story one wonders whether McCreary would ever accept the call.

Another thought that emerges out of this quotation focuses on how other preachers treat those claiming a call to the ministry. McCreary attributes his delayed acceptance to the fact that he "didn't get any encouragement" from other preachers. At minimum this refers to his pastor (Rev. Fuller), who raised questions about whether in fact he was called, as well as others who did not receive him with open arms and opportunities in their churches. From the era out of which McCreary comes, many older pastors and preachers did not believe that one should interfere with God's call. If God was going to call, God would make it sufficiently known to the person, and they didn't want to be responsible for encouraging someone to go into the ministry that God had not called.

> After that, it looked like I was gonna preach, because this pastor I was under set up a time for me to deliver my first sermon; then I started getting sick. My stomach got to the place I couldn't eat. And I was so sick at the stomach that medicine didn't do me any good. But when I preached my trial sermon, all that left me. That left me. I felt better than I ever did in my life.

In the narrative McCreary is finally "gonna preach," but in the story he still doesn't "know"; it only "looked like" it might happen. What should his sickness be attributed to? Is it butterflies from the thought of having to preach his "first sermon," or the finality of accepting the call that he must now prove he has in his "first sermon," which he later refers to as his "trial sermon"? In what sense is his call placed on trial by a trial sermon? Then again, maybe his sickness is not about finality at all; maybe even at this late point some liminality remained and that's why he got "sick at the stomach that medicine didn't do me any good." Maybe you don't really "know" until it finally happens; it just "looks like" it might happen.

Another fact that we discover is that McCreary had to leave his home church in order to have his call validated in the community of faith. The pastor that "set up a time" for him to deliver his first sermon was not Fuller. Sometimes people who have been called and cannot get support and validation in their home church find it necessary to go to another church, in some instances even another denomination.

The final thought that emerges from this quotation is relief and fulfillment, a common element in type A calls — "I felt better than I ever did in my life." The burden of the call and the liminal state is removed as McCreary moves into the postliminal state upon preaching his "trial sermon."

> I figure that's the reason I always try to treat everybody so kind in the ministry, because I was treated so badly. A man in the ministry needs a lot of encouragement. Someone needs to tell him what he's got to go through and how he ought to be schooled. Because if he is not schooled, brother, he's got to go through the pits of hell. You need that schooling to help you, and you need somebody behind you to tell you to go ahead. But you know a lot of guys, especially if he's got a good voice, he thinks he's got it made. But, you see, from now on you got to study. And right now I study more than I ever studied in my life.

This is another occasion on which McCreary justifies his present action by his past. His interpretation of the reason he treats kindly people called to the ministry is that he "was treated so badly." Obviously he includes his doubting pastor in this category. The context would suggest that what McCreary means by "kind" is that he is more accepting of people's claim to be called and does everything he can to help move them out of the liminal state.

However, one wonders what McCreary means by "everybody." One must wonder whether the gender-specific nature of a number of following statements necessitates that one interpret this initial statement differently than McCreary does. He says a "*man* [my emphasis] in ministry needs a lot of encouragement." Moreover, all of the pronouns that follow this statement in the remainder of the quotation refer to the male gender (e.g., he, guys). It would appear that what McCreary means is that he helps every male that he comes in contact with that professes a call to the ministry.[2] This raises the issue of women in ministry and what they must go through to gain acceptance. If men

2. McCreary is adamant and immovable in his belief that God does not call women to preach.

who have had difficult times because someone doubted their call cannot bring themselves to encourage women who have had similar experiences, then who will encourage women?

Another important issue that McCreary raises is that of the necessity of education for those who have been called. For one who did not receive formal seminary training, it is evident that he looks at what problems that creates today for someone going into the ministry — "he's got to go through the pits of hell." We are not told what that means and can only assume that serious limitations are placed upon one as a result of lack of education. McCreary seems to be juxtaposing the era from which he comes, where one could get by with "a good voice," to the present era in which he lives, when he recognizes that things are much more complex, and suggests that "from now on you got to study." He has made that transition himself, because "I study more than I ever studied in my life."

The remainder of McCreary's narrative is devoted to giving detailed examples of a specific gift that God gave him, which he claims came with his call — "a gift of seeing things." He is able to see death and sickness before they happen. He doesn't understand it, doesn't know how to fully interpret it, but knows it when he sees it and is never wrong. He keeps a lot of it to himself because he doesn't want to "frighten anybody," and sometimes he just wants to "watch it" himself to be sure he is right. Hence, even as the story ends on an element not directly related to the call, we observe once again retrospective certainty in the narrative that has a sliver of doubt in the story.

It is evident that McCreary has structured his narrative so as to emphasize and locate his call in the cataclysmic moment/s of the call experience. Although he claims to have always known that he was called, he nonetheless locates his call in this phase, especially that cataclysmic frame when the Holy Spirit tries to "kill" him. Careful analysis of the story has demonstrated, however, how this is McCreary's retrospective interpretation of his call. The story suggests that this particular frame was not the only one of its kind, and that this series of cataclysmic events was but a moment — the culminating moment, the decisive turning point, no doubt — in a sequence of events that started long before it.

The fact that McCreary's hermeneutical retrospection, given more than thirty years later, can be interpreted quite differently when viewed through the lens of story is not cause for alarm. It does, however, have implications for how we interpret call to ministry that may be quite significant. It should be self-evident that one individual's hermeneutical retrospection of his or her call to ministry cannot be the paradigm for all others, but an analysis of call to ministry through the lens of story may serve as a useful heuristic device for broadening our understanding as well as our appreciation of this phenomenon. When story is juxtaposed to what happens to story when it becomes narrative, we may learn even more.

Joseph L. Roberts: Rebellion of an AME Preacher's Kid

Joseph Roberts was born in Chicago, Illinois, in 1935 to parents born in Georgia and Illinois. He was reared African Methodist Episcopal, ordained Presbyterian in 1959, and now serves as pastor of the historic Ebenezer Baptist Church in Atlanta. He received his formal seminary training at Union Theological Seminary (N.Y.) and Princeton Theological Seminary, earning a Th.M. from the latter. Roberts's story is an excellent one to analyze not only because of his intriguing background (having been exposed to three quite different religious communities), but because he is so adamantly set against call stories being interpreted as only the cataclysmic type. His story is an example of type B (non-cataclysmic/reluctant).

> I grew up in an African Methodist Episcopal minister and his wife's home, coming out of three generations of African Methodist Episcopal folk. So there was a certain extent in which, I feel, that I was almost always, in part, a child of the church. I knew nothing other than that. I went through the natural rebellion that a person will go through in my teenage years, feeling that if I wanted to do anything, it would not be in the ministry.

Like McCreary's story, this narrative immediately unveils its retrospective hermeneutics. However, it has a different point of departure. One gets the impression that everything that follows will in some way be connected to this religious setting in his early childhood. Roberts is a preacher's kid (PK), one who "grew up" in the context of "three generations of African Methodist Episcopal folk."

One senses the liminality in Roberts's situation even at this early point. This setting serves as a double-edged sword. He felt like he was "a child of the church," but "went through the natural rebellion" period during his "teenage years" and came to the conclusion that if there was anything he wanted to do "it would not be in the ministry."

This religious setting at home and church both drew Roberts to the ministry and drove him away from it. Although he retrospectively interprets his rebellion as natural teenage rebellion, it is far more than that. It is not just a rebellion against going to church or the restriction of freedoms that children of the church, especially PK's, go through; it is a determination to reject anything to do with a career in ministry. What is interesting is that nothing is mentioned about a sense of call at this point or prior to it that would even make him consider ministry as an option. That is a part of the story that we are not privy to at this point. It has been left out in his retrospective emphasis to make clear from the very beginning why resistance to a career in ministry was dominant in his mind. One may speculate that the generations of religious people in his family as well as the influence of being a PK were key factors. His resistance to ministry, however, appears to be very specific, passionate, and driven by some particular dynamics at a very early age. What those dynamics are obviously shapes his view of call to ministry; they are seen in what follows.

> I was bothered by the poverty of ministry, the lack of material acquisitions, as was evident in my father's life. I was bothered by the solicitous nature and stance (which I felt was demeaning) that was laid upon him not only as he had to deal with trustees who would determine what kind of furniture we had in "their house," not our house but the house that was theirs — the parsonage. They would often feel that it was quite appropriate for them to work for white people and to have white people give me something. Then they'd use it and pass it on to the preacher, so that it had gone through three hands. That I found very offensive. . . . The third thing that I found offensive was the demeaning nature of the black African Methodist Episcopal bishopric assistant, which was definitely a plantation, sort of, pecking order. . . . I just didn't like the lack of freedom that one had in all of that, and really thought that I would probably have very little to do with the ministry. I was talking about law and dentistry and the rest.

Roberts makes clear what were the driving forces behind his determination to "have very little to do with the ministry." Basically it is the "poverty of ministry" that he observed in his "father's life," the "demeaning" nature in which his family was treated by "trustees" of the church as well as the demeaning nature of the ecclesiastical structure of the church, especially the "bishopric assistant." A lack of material possessions and freedom is at the heart of Roberts's anger. Obviously there is the impact that all of this had on Roberts as he observed his father being treated in this way, but one can't help but wonder how many of his feelings are to be traced to what things he was denied as a child because of this setting.

It is here that we observe just how much of this is hermeneutical retrospection interpretation and how much story is still missing. We are being told as Roberts looks back on all of this why he responded the way he did. It is doubtful that at this early age he had so organized his thoughts about why he didn't want to go into the ministry. The driving force may have been simply that from the perspective of a child who is a PK it is no fun to be a preacher's kid; there is too little freedom and too few possessions. This conclusion may be supported in two ways: the vividness in which he remembers hand-me-downs, especially things that were given to him personally ("have white people give me something"), and the careers that he considered as options ("I was talking about law and dentistry . . .").

One wonders what things (e.g., clothes, toys) were passed on to Roberts as a child due to being a PK in a poverty setting and what impact this had on his interest in other careers that appeared to him at the time to be much more lucrative (law and dentistry).

> But I found that after I was really honest, there was a love for the people shown (through all of these entrapments that I have already talked about) and a love for God . . . that made me feel that I wanted to do my ministerial role. I was not sure just where. So I think the call was not a traumatic thing that came to me. It was something that I yearned to do, but that I fought, because I thought that the political trappings and the infrastructure of my denomination mitigated against fulfilling the kind of ministry I wanted to fulfill.

The liminality of Roberts's situation emerges again. All of his negative feelings about his denomination and ministry were held in check by the positive things he observed ("there was a love for the people"). The negative "entrapments," "political trappings," and denominational "infrastructure" drove him to reject ministry, while the "love for the people" and "love for God" shown even with these trappings drew him to ministry.

He was yet in a liminal state. He felt that he wanted to "do my ministerial role," but he was "not sure just where," nor was he sure that he could fulfill the "kind of ministry that I wanted to fulfill" in his denomination. How do we get to the point of doing a "ministerial role" without discussion of a call? It is not until this point that we hear about call, and even here the first words are a negation as opposed to an affirmation.

"So I think the call was not a traumatic thing that came to me." Roberts's interpretation of his call is an assertion that it was not sudden and cataclysmic. "It was something that I yearned to do, but that I fought. . . ." We are not told how long he yearned to do this, nor what experiences set the yearnings in motion. We may assume that family history and religious exposure — home and church — contributed greatly to this yearning. It is clear that Roberts is interpreting his call in one sense by observing the good that could be done in this setting in spite of the negative forces that "mitigated against" it. It was the negative forces resident in his own denomination that kept him in the liminal state of resisting doing the very thing he wanted to do, because he didn't think that he could fulfill the kind of ministry he "wanted to fulfill."

> The next thing that I really knew was that I wanted to have a ministry that was broad enough to let me address some political, social, and economic problems and would not be so narrow in its confines that I would have to be wedded to a particular parochial situation. I was looking for some sort of a quasi-political, theological bridge that would allow me to be comfortable in both camps, as I took the theology and tried to apply it to all these other areas. I went on to college and while in college had opportunity to meet some Presbyterian folk. In the process of meeting them, they encouraged me to consider going into the Presbyterian church. It was for political reasons that I went into the Presbyterian church, because I saw that it gave me more freedom to be unencumbered by a number of folk, to be independent and to be able to do the kind of ministry that I wanted to do.

What drove Roberts in the pursuit of authentic self-understanding of his call was the freedom to do the kind of ministry he wanted. This theme is carried over from the prior paragraph, indeed from the very beginning of the narrative. Roberts's interpretation of these events is that he was trying to find a place to do ministry as God had called him to do it. He tried to reinterpret ministry in a way that he perceived his denomination wouldn't allow. This then becomes the justification for his action. He left his church and went to the Presbyterian church for "political" reasons. Political in this case obviously refers to ecclesiastical polity. Of course one could offer a number of other alternative or collateral reasons for why Roberts may have left his church, but all of them would fail to appreciate that they would be possible only at the story level, not the narrative. The freedom to do ministry as he desired is Roberts's interpretation of his actions.

> When that opportunity for education really came on to me, then I think that the call was really sort of authenticated; because I felt that I would be able to exercise ministry in a way that would allow me to honor who I was. At heart, I was an AME. I enjoyed everything that the church was about. . . . The Presbyterian church made me feel like I could take that tradition and blend it into whatever I wanted it to be; so that my call was not a catastrophic, vertical thing that suddenly came upon me. It was rather the accumulation of a number of experiences that nudged me on toward a ministry that was unencumbered by some political problems of infrastructure.

Roberts returns again to discuss call specifically. First, the call was "authenticated" for him in the context of education and in another church. This is because it allowed him to "exercise ministry in a way that would allow me to honor who I was." Perhaps this is one of the most important reasons why people leave their churches — whether local or denominational — to fulfill their call to ministry elsewhere. They want to fulfill their calls as the unique individuals they are, and not be limited to one traditional view of what that should be. It is also noteworthy that Roberts attributes this further self-understanding of call to his educational experience.

There is a sense in which Roberts did not really leave the AME church, because "at heart" he was an AME in the Presbyterian church. He saw this as a place where he could carry on the AME tradition of the eighteenth and nineteenth centuries when he couldn't do it in the AME church. Whether or not this was the case we do not know; we do know, however, that this is Roberts's hermeneutical twist on why he left the AME church.

This leads Roberts to interpret how all of these events relate to his call. Unlike McCreary he denies any "catastrophic, vertical" elements in his call. It is not something that "suddenly" came upon him. Rather, it was "the accumulation of a number of experiences that nudged me on toward ministry." We are not told what all of those experiences are, but can assume that they include family history and early childhood church experiences mentioned previously as well as the educational experiences in seminary with the Presbyterians.

> It is not, therefore, something that I can date in terms of a Tuesday at one o'clock when anything happened but, rather, something that

I think was rather gradual. And not to sound defensive, but I believe when people stop lying, most of them will admit that it was a gradual thing that they were nudged to and not a catastrophic, one-day piece that suddenly came and hit them like a bolt of lightning out of the air. Notwithstanding what Martin Luther said about what happened to him, I think all of those stories, if we looked them up, are but the pinnacle of a long series of God's prodding and nudging us toward decision. Then we talk about one that was critical, and that was it. I can remember the day when Frank Gordon, who was pastor of Shiloh Presbyterian Church, talked to me. I could say it was on that day, after we had that talk and that prayer, that my call was confirmed, I came out of the darkness. But that would be a lie, so I'm not going [to] do that.

Roberts continues the description and interpretation of his call. However, he does so by continuing to describe what it was not. Obviously Roberts is aware of the sudden cataclysmic-type call that can be dated to the hour by some people, because he spends a considerable amount of time to make it clear that his was not that type. He cannot date his call on the calendar or clock, because his was "gradual." What is interesting about Roberts's attempt to define his own call and not be defensive about anyone else's is that he ends up in a sense defining all other calls just like his own.

His call was "gradual" and "when people stop lying, most of them will admit" that theirs was "gradual" also and not a "catastrophic, one-day piece that suddenly came and hit them like a bolt of lightning." One can only guess at why Roberts uses such strong language here as he juxtaposes his gradual call to that of others who claim a more sudden call.[3] Perhaps he has had to endure too many instances in which all discussion of call was reduced to this type. In an effort to argue that his type is different, however, there is a sense in which he reduces all others to his type — a gradual series of confirming events.

Still, it may be that he offers an angle on the truth that is most important; an insight that needs to be considered by all of us who are attempting to broaden our understanding of call. When compared to McCreary's story and others like it, Roberts's story is self-evidently different. McCreary's story has obvious sudden cataclysmic events in it. Yet, Roberts is partially correct in his observation, as was demonstrated in the analysis of McCreary's story, that the cataclysmic event

3. Myers, 202. William A. Jones says, "It 'came upon me' — I was never aware of any gradual urge to do it. It was an overwhelming thing."

that was the turning point for McCreary was but "the pinnacle of a long series of God's prodding and nudging" McCreary "toward decision." Both of them remained in a liminal state before some specific event — in McCreary's case cataclysmic, and Roberts's case noncataclysmic — settled it for them.

Roberts, however, misses a crucial point. He completely misunderstands call, as have most of us, when he says that "when people stop lying, most of them will admit that it was a gradual thing that they were nudged to and not a catastrophic, one-day piece that suddenly came and hit them like a bolt of lightning out of the air." This is a failure to distinguish between the story, which attempts to report as accurately as possible what happened, and the narrative, which is a retrospective interpretation of what happened. Hence, the people should not be viewed as "lying." In the narrative they are reporting their subjective retrospective view of history.

Although statements in the narrative may be nonverifiable, that does not mean the narrators are lying; they are merely reporting what they experienced and believe happened. This is no different from what Roberts does in reporting about his noncataclysmic experiences. Moreover, a retrospective interpretation of the call in narrative as something datable on the calendar and clock is not lying either; it is the difference between story and narrative. In the story the call may come across as a gradual series of events culminating in one specific crowning event, as Roberts suggests; however, in the narrative a callee gives us a hermeneutical restrospection of those events. As with texts, so with human experiences — they receive a different interpretation based on one's perspective.

Roberts's insight that all calls are a series of gradual nudgings by God that culminate in a pinnacle event that nudges one into ministry is valuable. It remains to be seen whether all calls are to be described in that way. What is more important, however, is that such a view addresses only call as story, but fails to appreciate the equally important view of call as narrative.

The final point that gives further support to this distinction is also made by Roberts. Roberts refers to an event when he discussed and prayed about his call to ministry with a Presbyterian pastor. The context makes it clear that this is a story event — a spatio-temporal event. What is intriguing, however, is Roberts's interpretation of the event. Roberts refuses to claim that this was a confirmation of his call; to make that claim "would be a lie." Here again a distinction between story and narrative is helpful. The fact that the event happened (story) is truth and not a "lie"; Roberts's refusal to interpret it (narrative) as confirmation is also truth and not a "lie." However, as this corpus demonstrates, story events similar to this one do serve as confirmation for many, both at the story level and the narrative level. To make such a claim would only be a lie for the person for whom the event did not serve in that way.

> My pilgrimage since then has been a long one. But if you ask specifically about how that call came into being and how I went in from Knoxville College to Union Seminary to Princeton to perfect that ministry and what happened in the ministry, that's another story. But that is how I actually was drawn to it. I was able finally to reconcile myself with a system of governance in a denomination that would not impede my view of a broad ministry and my view of a free ministry, where I would not be controlled by a people who might take personal vendettas against me, because they either didn't like my political stance or they didn't like the fact that I was not going to acquiesce to their supreme authority they thought they had because they were a part of the Episcopal ranks. I think there is a certain extent as to which a connectional church that has bishops who are not sensitive can be demeaning to the sacredness of human personality. It can almost be another form of slavery.

Like McCreary, Roberts emphasizes the important role of education in the call to ministry. Unlike McCreary, however, who came to grips with his call in the context of a cataclysmic experience, it was in the academic setting that Roberts went on "to perfect that ministry" and "was drawn to it." It would appear that what Roberts means by perfection is that he "was able finally to reconcile myself with a system of governance in a denomination that would not impede my view of a broad ministry and my view of a free ministry."

The narrative closes in the way it opens — freedom in ministry; we also return to a point of tension that we saw throughout McCreary's story — a callee's self-understanding of the call over against that of the tradition of his or her religious community's understanding. It is interesting that in Roberts's case, the third part of the trio — education — is the place where the tension gets worked out. In this setting he was able to better understand his call, his present religious context, and the type of context he needed to fulfill his call as he understood it. In an important sense, he did not leave his religious community; he merely found the one that "would not impede" his view of the broader ministry to which he had been called.

Perhaps this is a lesson that many religious communities should learn: sometimes their traditional views of call to ministry are too restrictive and are in need of updating to keep up with who, how, and to what God is calling lately. A failure to do so can create an environment in which the church is "demeaning to the sacredness of human personality." Instead of freedom to serve God as one is called to do, "It can almost be another form of slavery."

Ernest W. Newman: "I Had No Choice"

Ernest Newman was born in Kingstree, South Carolina, in 1928 to parents also born in South Carolina. He was called from birth and ordained a United Methodist elder in 1956. His formal education was at Clafflin College, and he earned the advanced seminary degree from Gammon Theological Seminary. He serves as a bishop of the United Methodist church in the Nashville district. Newman's story is an example of type C (noncataclysmic/nonreluctant).

> I am from a large family of preachers. There seems to be — especially in South Carolina, which is my home state — a number of clergy families to a large degree responsible for replenishing preachers in South Carolina. Kind of a family conference tradition, seemingly. My father was a Methodist preacher. My grandfather was a Methodist preacher. I am one of seven boys and out of the seven boys, six of us went into the ministry.

Like Roberts, Newman is a PK, comes from generations of preachers, and the significance of a religious context during childhood is self-evident. Newman's interpretation of the South Carolina setting, however, is quite different from Roberts's setting. He claims that "a number of clergy families" provided most of the preachers. He attributes this to tradition, which would seem to suggest that perhaps some choose the profession as a vocation because this is the tradition of the family. This type of influence existed in Newman's family as well since his grandfather, father, and five other brothers also chose that profession.

> Now going back, my father was a Methodist preacher and at the age of sixteen when I completed high school, I had a sense of call. Of course, it's been pretty much understood as far as my entire life up until that time, that I was going into the ministry. I did not see any other profession or calling as to what would be my life's commitment.

So, at the age of sixteen, I received a local preacher's license by the charge conference that my father was pastor of at that time.

Newman returns to the theme of family tradition in a less direct manner. He connects his "sense of call" to a specific historical moment — "when I completed high school" — as well as to the family tradition — "my father was a Methodist preacher." We are not given any specifics about his recognition of call other than that it was an inclination. No experiences are mentioned. What is mentioned, however, is that "it's been pretty much understood as far as my entire life up until that time, that I was going into the ministry." One can't help but ask, "whose understanding was this?" Was this Newman's understanding or his father's or his entire family's or some combination thereof. One gets the impression that this is in some sense what is meant by family tradition, that there was a strong expectation that the "boys" would choose ministry as their vocation. Perhaps this is why Newman "did not see any other profession or calling as to what would be my life's commitment." Maybe sixteen is significant not because he had a sense of call at that time — he has had this sense all of his life — but because it is when he both graduated from high school and received his license. It is noteworthy that this occurred "by the charge conference that my father was pastor of at that time."

After this opening Newman goes on to list, almost in résumé fashion, all of the places that he has served in his career and how long he served in them.

My call to the ministry was almost a kind of thing that I considered I had no choice. I had been born and brought up in the Methodist church and the family of preachers. I just assumed that on the day of my own knowledge of ministry that this would be my calling. So, my call to some extent comes out, I guess, of a family tradition. And it was not a matter of any time that I considered I wouldn't do anything else. It was a life commitment.

Like Roberts, Newman was a child of the church, "born and brought up" in it surrounded by this "family of preachers." Unlike Roberts, Newman was not caused to rebel by the church; on the contrary, he felt he "had no choice." The important question is whether this feeling of no choice was vertical or horizontal. Newman seems to interpret it, at least in part, as horizontal. "So, my call to some extent comes out, I guess, of a family tradition." This seems to be confirmed when he asserts, "I just assumed that on the day of my own knowledge of ministry that this would be my calling." This interpretation seems to suggest that the expectation coming out of the family tradition was there first and Newman merely assumed that when he reached the point of understanding what it all meant, he would choose that vocation. He never considered that he would "do anything else." "It was a life commitment."

However one wishes to arrange the chronology and interpret these events at the story level, Newman's interpretation is that he chose this vocation as a result of an environment that nurtured him in this direction. He was never conscious of another direction, and he later came to a sense that this was the vocation that he should choose. Although other narratives are similar at the story level, what makes Newman's different is that he interprets his that way at the narrative level as well.

> So, my call, I don't think is any unique. . . . it's not unique to any extent of any other person's call, call and a commitment. I feel that there is the call and you make the commitment to it and dedicate your life to it. I did not see any spectacular vision of some kind or some unknown mysterious voice that came to me. I did not see that. I saw mine as a family tradition, heritage. A desire to be a participant in working with people, looking at their concerns, developing a ministry that would respond to their concerns. Let's say it was social and at the same time it was a commitment, and out of this commitment a dedication. I tie the call and history together. And this has been my response to the call to the ministry.

Three times the term "commitment" is repeated in this very short narrative. The narrative opens and closes on it. It may give us the best insight to Newman's self-understanding of call. Call to ministry for Newman is as follows: "I feel that there is the call and you make the commitment to it and dedicate your life to it." If this is the case, then whether one has been called must be measured to a great degree by his or her life. This is why Newman's narrative reads like a résumé, because he wants to demonstrate in retrospect that he did commit and dedicate his life to the call.

He is aware of the cataclysmic-type calls that include visions and voices, but that was not his. He saw his call "as a family tradition, heritage." Newman closes his narrative where it began, with his interpretation of his call arising out of a family tradition. It is both social action and commitment, because he wanted to help people by "developing a ministry that would respond to their concerns."

The way Newman closes his narrative makes it clear that it is interpretation, because this is his "response to the call to the ministry." He ties "the call and history together." That is in fact what hermeneutical restrospection is — justifying your present in light of your past.

Lucille Abernathy: "We Would Rather Have an Unqualified Man than a Qualified Woman"

Lucille Abernathy was born in Hattisburg, Mississippi, in 1944 to parents also born in Mississippi. She received her call in 1978 and was ordained American Baptist in 1985. She earned the master of divinity degree from Princeton Theological Seminary and now pastors the Hough Avenue United Church of Christ in Cleveland, Ohio. Abernathy's story is an excellent one to examine for a number of reasons. First, it contains all of the elements of the type A call (cataclysmic/reluctant) usually attributed only to males. In addition, she is from a younger generation which demonstrates that the tradition continues from one generation to another. Most importantly, the narrative is ideal because it contains most, if not all, of the unique elements found in the other female call stories.

> If you are in communication with God, there is a voice within you that you hear. The only thing I can equate it with is where in the Scriptures it says, "My sheep will know my voice." When God speaks to you, you are in conversation with God. I used to be in conversation with God all the time when getting direction for my life and what I was doing. As a young person, I remember at sixteen or seventeen, I was a Cub Scout leader. I was a den mother at this age because none of the mothers would take the troop. So I became a den mother with the kids, and secretary of the Sunday school. I was always doing something in the church. I've always done that as long as I can remember.

At the very beginning of the narrative Abernathy emphasizes the importance of the cataclysmic, supernatural element in her call — "there is a voice within you that you hear." As in McCreary's story, hearing God speak to her is an important aspect of Abernathy's call. Hermeneutical retrospection emerges quickly as she utilizes some biblical rhetoric to give further meaning to her statement. The nature of this voice is not clear to the narratee at this point. Are we talking merely about theological reflection on the Scriptures being applied in the life of a Christian, or are we talking about the hearing of an actual voice that she believes to be the voice of God and later associates with a certain Scripture? Abernathy gives the impression that she speaks of the latter because she was "in conversation with God all the time."

The other important point that comes out in this part of the narrative is early religious exposure. Like McCreary, Roberts, and Newman before her, Abernathy is a child of the church. "I was always doing something in the church. I've always done that as long as I can remember." Even as a young adolescent she held leadership roles in church and the Cub Scouts. The importance of early religious exposure both in the story and the narrative is the most consistent element in call stories irrespective of denomination, generation, or gender.

> It was around age thirty-four when I started to deal with this thing about a call to the ordained ministry. It was a thing where I heard a voice. A voice spoke to me as I was leaving prayer meeting. I remember that we had noonday prayer service. I had taken my lunch break to come to noonday prayer service, and I was teaching school down on 30th Street. I was getting ready to rush back to school for my afternoon class and the voice said, "You can't do what I want you to do and keep teaching school." I didn't understand it. But it came back again. And it was as if going back to school was robbing me from doing whatever God wanted me to do.

The parallels between Abernathy's and McCreary's narratives are striking. Both were children of the church that heard the call of God as a voice speaking to them at early ages, but did not finally accept it until much later in life, almost at the exact same age (thirty-four, thirty-five respectively); they are from two different generations and two different genders. Abernathy makes clear what was ambiguous before — she is talking about an actual voice. "A voice spoke to me as I was leaving prayer meeting." The voice said, "You can't do what I want you to do and keep teaching school." Abernathy is certain about the voice as well what the voice said. Nonetheless she is not clear enough to keep herself from entering a liminal state. "I didn't understand it. But it came back again. And it was as if going back to school was robbing me from doing whatever God wanted me to do."

Abernathy's response to this supernatural phenomenon is similar to McCreary's — confusion. Although she has been in conversation with God throughout her life up to this point and suggests that God converses with followers of God in a clear and understandable manner, when she hears the voice in a manner that she can repeat verbatim, her response is "I didn't understand it." Moreover, her liminality is exacerbated because although she returns to school, contrary to the voice's direction, she feels that it "was robbing me from doing whatever God wanted me to do."

Like McCreary she does not know as much as she thinks she knows at the time; only in retrospect does she know a little more. In other words, cataclysmic, supernatural phenomena in the call do not necessarily bring more light; on the contrary, they may bring more darkness (liminality, ambiguity, confusion).

> So after that I can't tell you exactly how the call came, but it was to the ordained ministry. It was like, "You are to go into the ordained ministry." I didn't know what ordination meant. I kept seeking after people to tell me what it meant to be ordained. They would want to know why, and I kept saying, "Because I feel like God is saying I'm to be ordained." But they would not tell me. The way I finally found out about ordination was through the executive minister of the Cleveland Baptist Association (CBA). Our church was dually aligned with the National Baptist and American Baptist. I don't even remember how that took place.

Both the liminal state and retrospective interpretation continue. Some things are remembered, others are not; some things are known, others are not. Abernathy knew that she was called to the "ordained ministry," but she cannot tell us "exactly how the call came" (narrative), and she "didn't know what ordination meant" (story) at the time. This implies that she knows only now, retrospectively. However, in the story she "kept seeking after people to tell me what it meant to be ordained." For whatever reasons they left her in her liminal state — "they would not tell me." She remembers where she got the definition — "the executive minister of the CBA" — but she does not "remember how that took place."

Such is the case with both memory and knowledge when story and narrative are compared. Some things are remembered, others are not; sometimes it is intentional, as when the narrator doesn't think it important, other times it is just a matter of a memory fading as the years passed. These omissions should not be viewed as deceitful, erroneous, or misleading; it's a matter of understanding the difference between story and narrative, as well as understanding the significance and importance of subjective hermeneutical retrospection.

I remember my pastor saying, "Well, you had better be quiet about this, because you don't know what you are talking about and you can't tell anybody." I was trying to be obedient because I respect pastors, and our pastor was our friend and everything. So, every time I would go to prayer meeting I felt like I needed to tell people, especially at the testimony period. I could never do it because the pastor would say, "No, don't do it." And finally, one day: It was like it was burning; it was driving me crazy. Inside me was like this overwhelming thing to just tell them. It was like, if you tell them you will have peace inside. So, finally I just told them. Everybody got real quiet, and nobody said anything. I remember talking to the pastor again and him saying, "Well, you can be a teacher or a counselor, but God didn't call you to preach." I said, "I never said God called me to preach." That was my whole thing throughout the process. God never called me to preach. He didn't. He said, "Ordained ministry," and I said, "Whatever that means, that's what I have to do."

Abernathy's retrospective memory is evident again as she "remembers" what must have been a very difficult part of her call experience. When the time came for her to tell someone, she went to the right person, her pastor. This is the person who, more than anyone else, could help her to move out of her liminal state. Instead, he helped to keep her there by calling into question her "knowledge." "Well, you had better be quiet about this, because you don't *know* [my emphasis] what you are talking about and you can't tell anybody." We encounter the first clash between the individual's self-understanding of call and that of her church's tradition, at least as it's represented by the community's leader.

Again, Abernathy's story is remarkably like McCreary's. His pastor also questioned whether he knew what he was talking about. The differences are twofold. The pastor questioned McCreary's call because McCreary didn't know certain Scriptures, but the pastor did not forbid him to tell people about his call. In Abernathy's case she is confronted with a direct assertion that she doesn't know what she is talking about and that she "had better be quiet" and not "tell anybody." Either she is not told or we are not told what is the foundation for the pastor's position.

However, like McCreary who had a high regard for pastors and his pastor in particular, so did Abernathy. Thus, she "was trying to be obedient." Hence, both of these people's liminality and doubt were increased initially as a result of going to their pastors rather than diminished.

Although Abernathy, like McCreary, was trying to be obedient, neither of them could do so because of the irresistible urge of the call. Abernathy "needed to tell people," because it was "burning" inside and driving her "crazy." She felt that the only way she could get some "peace" was to tell someone. Her pastor insisted, however, "No, don't do it." We still don't know why. Finally, despite her pastor, she told of her call in "prayer meeting," during the "testimony period."

Abernathy remembers "talking to the pastor again." This time he insisted, "Well, you can be a teacher or a counselor, but God didn't call you to preach." Again, the denial comes, this time with the assertion that God didn't call her to preach. He will allow her to be a teacher or counselor, but not a preacher. Does he think she is qualified for the former roles and not the latter? What is his understanding of a preacher? The narratee wants to guess that it has something to do with her gender, but either the pastor, the narrator, or both are silent as to the reason up to this point.

Abernathy's response is intriguing; she does not protest because her interpretation of her call is that "God never called me to preach." Her understanding of her call at that time was that it was a call to the "ordained ministry, whatever that means." Hence, it is self-evident in the story that Abernathy is still in a liminal state, understanding some things about her call but in the dark about many other things.

Abernathy is not concerned about the appropriate story sequence because her hermeneutical retrospection at the narrative level is of greater importance.

> So when I went down to CBA [Cleveland Baptist Association], I asked, "What does it mean to be ordained? What do you have to do, and what do you do after you get ordained?" Then they told me about school. Then I went through the whole struggle that if I have to go back to school, where do I go to school? My daughter said, "You know where you have to go." So I went to Bishop College. When we were at the National Baptist Congress my pastor took me to Bishop, and I met the dean of the religion department. It was like, "Oh God, I know I have to be there. . . ." I was so ill at ease that I left before the Congress was over. . . . I cried all the way to the airport, because I knew I was gonna have to be there. Yet I thought that by leaving I wouldn't have to be there.

Abernathy went on a search seeking a better understanding of her call and got some help from the "CBA." It is unfortunate that in many cases callees are pressed into going beyond their pastors, sometimes their churches, and other times their own denominations to get help in understanding their call. An internal "struggle" emerged for Abernathy because she was told that ordination requires "school." Yet the struggle was centered around "where do I go," as opposed to not wanting to go. The narratee wants to know whether the emphasis is on "I" ("Where do *I* go?") or on "go" ("Where do I *go?*"). The former might speak of a limited choice (e.g., because of gender or finances), whereas the latter would speak of too many choices (e.g., which one of the many schools should I choose?).

For some reason which we are not told, her daughter knows what the choice should be, "Bishop College." The fact that it is a Baptist school and that her pastor took her there (perhaps he went there) might be the reasons. On a visit to the college where she met the "dean of the religion department," she knew she had to be there. How she knew we do not know. The story would suggest that it was that internal communication with God that she spoke of earlier.

As with McCreary, resistance set in for Abernathy so much so that she "left before the Congress was over," and "cried all the way to the airport"; "because I knew I was gonna have to be there. Yet, I thought that by leaving I wouldn't have to be there." Her liminal state, as well as what she thought she knew yet didn't know, continues to be self-evident. She knows that she is destined to follow this path, but she thinks that she can avoid it. Both McCreary and Abernathy try to obstruct what they claim to know as the will of God. How much do they really know (understand) about the call at this point? Is the knowledge asserted here hermeneutical retrospection, existential confusion, or both? I think both; the story suggests confusion, and the narrative suggests clarity.

> That was in August. I had written a letter and received a letter in response, a very supportive letter. It was the first supportive letter I had ever gotten from a man that said, "There are a lot of men that say, 'dah dah dah dah'." I still have that letter, because that was my first written validation that God really does call women.

The narratee is told what has been suspected all along; the reason for the rejection, the resistance, and much of the confusion and tension surrounding Abernathy's call is because she is a woman. Her pastor and "a lot of men" don't believe "that God really does call women," and to some extent Abernathy's self-understanding of her call and what she should do about it is determined by this response toward her. She wrote a letter, we assume, to the college and got not only a favorable response, but a "supportive letter" upholding women's call by God.

This "validation" was important to Abernathy because it was her "first written" validation, and it confirmed for her that God does call women. So important was this validation that she has kept it all these years.

At this point Abernathy's story and narrative are different from McCreary's. As with McCreary, Abernathy's pastor resists her call (in her case the congregation resists also; rarely does a male encounter this kind of resistance, and never because of his gender), which engenders more resistance and confusion in her and deepens her liminal state, causing her to struggle over the call and go searching for understanding elsewhere. The primary reason for this in Abernathy's case, however, is that she is a woman. Her self-understanding of God's call on her life clashes with her religious community's interpretation of call, not because of lack of training, moral fitness, desire, commitment, story, or narrative, but because of one criterion — her gender. This comes up often in her story and is given prominence in her narrative as the narrative's emphasis and hermeneutics show.

> Now, what I went through trying to validate it was part of what I had said earlier about this guy from Denver coming to our church that summer. Everything fell into place. That summer a minister from Denver came to do a revival at our church. I ended up at an after-revival reception with him, and the conversation for some strange reason in this group of ministers turned to women in ministry. This pastor from Denver said, "Well, I used to be like you all, but God convicted me and converted me that he does call women." He said, "Right now I have two or three women on my staff, and they take part in the service." I was sitting there and my mouth dropped open, because this is what I asked God for. I said, "God, show me another black Baptist woman in ministry, and then I won't question you anymore. . . ." I needed to see a Black woman. . . . My pastor was invited to go there [Denver] to do something, and the church was invited to go. So, the Lord said, "You have to go." And I'm saying, "I have to go to Denver? . . ." Seems like everything fell in place for me to go. . . . Anyway, so I went to Denver and saw these women in the pulpit being a part of the service and everything. I talked to my pastor's brother. They were very open, their father is a pastor. Both of them are pastors. But they are totally different as far as what they think theologically. The brother was all for women in ministry, but my pastor was definitely, "God doesn't call women."

This part of the narrative confirms that the heart of Abernathy's problem has been her gender as suggested earlier, and that the need for validation was more crucial as a result of rejection on that basis. Her hermeneutical retrospection is that God worked her call out for her through a series of connected events. Much of Abernathy's conflict with herself and God about whether God calls women stemmed from the fact that her pastor asserted that "God doesn't call women." Abernathy needed validation from God. Therefore, she set up the fleece test: "God, show me another black Baptist woman in ministry, and then I won't question you anymore." This had to be a "black woman" because Abernathy was aware of the fact that black churches don't necessarily accept what white churches do as validation.

Abernathy's interpretation is that God takes the challenge and a series of events unfolds that fulfills her request. A revivalist who supports women in ministry and has them on his staff participating in the service comes to her church; subsequently, her pastor and church are invited to Denver for another occasion, and God tells her that she has to go. There is a slight hesitation on her part, and one wonders if it is an indication that she really didn't want God to fulfill her request since then she wouldn't have had to fulfill the call. Nonetheless, the request is fulfilled, and she observes black women "in the pulpit being a part of the service and everything." Though her pastor obviously observed it and had a father and brother who accepted women's call, his view that God doesn't call women was not altered. Thus, we see again the conflict of the inner call and outer call in the life of the church, especially as represented by some religious leaders.

> After this experience in Denver, and I call it "My Mountaintop Experience," because Denver was so high, I came home and said, "Okay God, you called, I'm doing whatever you say, you showed me what I needed to know." I no longer felt that I had to argue with people or convince people that God had called me. Prior to that, people would want to tell you why you weren't called rather than validate what God was doing. I just came home with the conviction that God had called me, and I believe that where God leads, he will provide. From then on, it was just a process of "What do you want me to do?"

As the event when the Holy Spirit tried to kill McCreary was his turning point, the "Mountaintop Experience" in Denver was Abernathy's turning point. God had validated her call by showing her what she "needed to know." Like McCreary she "no longer felt that I had to argue with people or convince people that God had called me. . . . I just came home with the conviction that God had called me, and I believe that where God leads, he will provide." Up to this point Abernathy was more concerned with convincing others that she had been called. Not only did she fail to do so, but she created doubt and tension within herself. Her interpretation of the Denver experience is that what God says and believes is what matters, not what others say. This is McCreary's conclusion also. What matters is that one follow God's lead, because where God leads "he will provide." (McCreary: "But I found out if God tells you to do, just go ahead on and do it. He will fix a way for you to do it if he tells you to do it.")

There comes a point when people who have been called by God cease trying to convince others that they have been called; they just move forward in an effort to better understand, "What do you want me to do?" This is another indication, however, that the liminality and limited knowledge about the call continue. Even at this crucial turning point in the story as well as in the narrative, Abernathy has a limited self-understanding of her call. It is indeed a process that continues.

> My whole process of school fell in place. School was a trying situation. Because, again, you are confronted with these men who don't believe God calls women. Here I am in a black Baptist school, in a religion department with all black Baptist men. Some men who were sponsors or supporters of the school resented the fact that I was a woman in a male-dominated position. It was strange, but I went with a peace. I didn't have to validate it for anybody anymore. I just had to do whatever God called me to do, which was to train and to learn.

Abernathy has just said that after the Denver experience the only thing that mattered was finding out what God wanted her to do. Part of that process was going to school. However, that she no longer feels the need to justify her call to others does not stop others from questioning her call. She finds herself in a male-dominated black Baptist school where not only her peers reject her, but the school's supporters resent her as well. Yet she "went with a peace" that she considers "strange," and has this peace because she no longer feels the obligation to "validate" her call to others. She just wants to do "whatever God called me to do." In this instance that is interpreted as "to train and to learn." Hence, the call is interpreted as the process proceeds, because she still doesn't know what ministry she has been called to. Moreover, if validation from others is a past event in the story, it is not in the narrative. Her emphasis on the struggle she had to endure as a woman trying to act on her call continues to be significant even at this point in the narrative.

During my second year, a strange thing happened. The Lord spoke to me. We had a minister's alliance which included all of the ministers on campus. It was like a fraternity or whatever. The first year I visited, but I didn't get involved, because women weren't welcomed, to put it nicely. . . . The Lord just put on my heart that I was supposed to run for office. I said to the Lord, "I don't even go; they don't want me in there. Why should I run for office?" President was what it was. The Lord said to me, "You're going to run." "No, Lord," I said, but finally, of course, being obedient I gave in. Being obedient, I won. Strange things happened. Even to the point that some of the ministers threatened to stop supporting the school, because they allowed this woman to be president of this group. They had the guys fearful at one point that they would never preach in their churches, because they let a woman do this. It was tremendous in that it was a continuation of validation by God in what he had called me to do. Some of the people were even bold enough to say, "We would rather have an unqualified man than a qualified woman, because women aren't supposed to lead the men."

The saga continues. The Lord has told her that she is to run for "president" of a male-only "minister's alliance." This is an alliance in which "women weren't welcomed." She resists the Lord's command, but ultimately is "obedient," and "being obedient," she wins. School supporters who are ministers "threatened to stop supporting the school, because they allowed this woman to be president of this group." They even threaten to withhold preaching opportunities in their churches for the male students. Abernathy's interpretation of all of this, however, is "that it was a continuation of validation by God in what he had called me to do." If, however, it was validation for her, it certainly was not for "some people" who were "bold enough to say," "We would rather have an unqualified man than a qualified woman, because women aren't supposed to lead the men." We still do not know either in the story or narrative exactly what she has been called to do. We do know, however, that at the story level gender is a major issue for others, but at the narrative level it is interpreted as a matter of God's validation by Abernathy.

But God validated it in such a way that that year we were one of the most powerful organizations that there had been. . . . We had one minister call the group on the carpet, a minister out of Houston, when we went to Houston. He said, "I'm going to be different than the rest of you, because I have heard about the way you all have treated this woman. Unless you start accepting women and everything else you are not going to preach in my church." He turned the tables on them. I saw that as God's continuing validation of what he had called me to be. Because everybody, including the adult males, as well as the campus people, had said, "God didn't call this woman and this is gonna go down the tubes." What God showed us was that through the process of whatever we did, it did prosper. To me that was part of the validation.

The matter of gender at the story level and validation at the narrative level continue to be the focal point. There continues to be resistance by the men who feel that "God didn't call this woman" and thus whatever she is involved in will fail. God uses one "Houston" minister "to turn the tables" on her peers by threatening to withhold preaching opportunities from them if they don't start "accepting women." Abernathy's interpretation of this sequence of events is that it is "God's continuing validation of what he had called me to be." We still don't know what she is called to do, and, interestingly here, it is now what she is "called to be." Undoubtedly, it carries the same meaning.

> Going back to deal with the call itself, I guess the hardest part is being alone in it — being alone in it and not having anybody else around you to say, "Yeah, this is wonderful, celebrate it." Everybody in my church, where I had been all my life (and this was always strange to me, because I had been in that church since I was three years old), was turned off by my announcement. I had worked in every department of the church, done everything that you do, but they were so programmed to believe that God did not call women, that they could not accept the fact that he called me.

Abernathy's narrative allows her to do what can't be done in the story — flash back. In order to make a connection with an earlier part of her life as well as an earlier part of the narrative, Abernathy flashes back to her life in the church during her childhood days and subsequently her public announcement of her call.

The discussion of all the rejection and resistance she faced as a woman trying to follow her call triggers a prominent thought in Abernathy's mind from her story — the loneliness of the call. "I guess the hardest part is being alone in it." This is a prominent theme in call narratives. Like Abernathy, McCreary also talked about not having anyone to help him understand the call. That, however, is as far as the similarities go. In Abernathy's case, her loneliness is due to her gender. In addition, her loneliness carries with it the pain of having no one to "celebrate" it with her. Men's loneliness comes because of the liminality of the call (women have this as well), but this dissipates as soon as they find someone to talk to who understands what they are going through.

Such is not the case with Abernathy, because as soon as she announces it, "everybody in my church . . . was turned off by my announcement." This was a church that she had been in since three years old, "had worked in every department," and "done everything that you do." Hence, the rejection was "strange" to her. There is an interesting irony in Abernathy's contention that she had "done everything that you do." This is usually the plight of women in the church; they have done everything that *they* have been allowed to do, with integrity and humility, and have done it effectively, usually without protest. However, when they assert that God has called them to do what only men are allowed to do in that church, they discover that indeed they have already done all that they will be allowed to do in that church. Both the leaders and congregation join in rejecting any other claims.

It would be rare indeed to find a man that had to endure this type of rejection in the church in which he grew up, and certainly not because of his gender; usually there is great joy in the church because one of its *sons* has been called by God, hence both men and women will embrace the *son* and celebrate the call with him. For Abernathy the reason for such rejection by the congregation is obvious — "they were so programmed to believe that God did not call women that they could not accept the fact that he called me." We observe once again the individual's self-understanding of her call clashing with the traditional understanding of her religious community.

> When I came home from seminary, there was a little lady, she was very elderly, and had been my teacher when I was three years old. She had been in this church all her life. She said to me, "When you went away to school, I thought that was the worst thing you could have ever done, but now I see what God has done." So it took all those years, but it was another confirmation that God does call women and that women could finally recognize and appreciate it. One of my prayers, because of my own struggle, was that "God always uses me to help validate somebody else's call, and maybe that's why I know about you." That was my prayer, after I became comfortable with the idea that I was called. I wanted to be able to be there for somebody else, because I didn't have anybody.

Abernathy has returned to story-time after seminary to pick up again the narrative theme of validation. She connects the two time periods (announcement of her call and return from seminary) together with her "teacher" (Sunday school, we presume), one of the programmed ones who rejected her initially ("When you went away to school I thought that was the worst thing that you could have done . . ."), but accepted her after she returned from seminary ("but now I see what God has done").

Although it "took all those years," Abernathy interprets this as "another confirmation that God does call women and that women could finally recognize and appreciate it." Validation is so important to her, because of her "struggle" as a woman rejected simply because of her gender, that one of her "prayers" is that "God always uses me to help validate somebody else's call." She wants to "be there for somebody else, because I didn't have anybody." It is striking how similar, yet dissimilar this is to McCreary's narrative ("I figure that's the reason I always try to treat everybody so kind in the ministry, because I was treated so badly. A man in the ministry needs a lot of encouragement").

Earlier in his narrative McCreary said frequently that he didn't have "anybody" to "guide" him. Hence, both Abernathy and McCreary, because of the way they were treated, feel driven to validate and encourage "anybody" who follows this path. However, there are two differences between Abernathy and McCreary: Her treatment was due to her gender, his was not; "anybody" for her includes men ("maybe that's why I know about you"); however, one gets the impression that "anybody" for McCreary includes only men ("A *man* in the ministry needs a lot of encouragement"). On Abernathy's story alone it should be self-evident that women need as much, if not more, encouragement as men.

Such encouragement occurred for Abernathy "after I became comfortable with the idea that I was called." Certainly McCreary doubted and was uncomfortable with the idea of being called also, but Abernathy's doubt and comfort level are attributable almost totally to the fact that she is a woman.[4]

> Even in my family, my in-laws more than my family, it was awful, because they don't believe that God calls women. My mother-in-law went through this thing that my husband was awful, because he was going to let me go to school and do all this other stuff. It was terrible, but the blessing was in my immediate family, meaning my husband

4. See in Myers the story of Cynthia Hale (31) and Vivian Bryant (14), as well as many of the other women in the book who raised questions with God about whether a woman could be called.

and children. . . . So that when it came time for me to deal with my call, there was my support. . . . Even when I went away to school, my kids stayed at home with my husband. That was another big incident related to my call, because these same church people who teach you and tell you that you are supposed to follow Christ were the first ones to say, "No, God didn't call you to leave your children. God made you a mother and wife first." Church people, including in-laws, were saying, "Your children are going to be juvenile delinquents, your daughters are going to be pregnant, your husband is going to leave you and have some other women. . . ." They didn't get pregnant, they are not juvenile delinquents, and they love God. When I left to go to school, my husband, who did not even go to church at that time, started going to church every Sunday, taking his kids to Sunday school. . . . This man was not that kind of person before I went to school.

Abernathy continues the discussion both of the struggle because of her gender and the confirmation by God in different ways. The resistance from her church continues and spills over into her family life. Her in-laws "don't believe that God calls women." The narrative allows her to speak about the past as present. The present tense here gives the narratee the impression that even now — many years after her ordination and the many events that Abernathy feels were confirmations from God — her in-laws still don't believe God calls women.

Her mother-in-law and the "church people" hold to a traditional view of the woman's place. The mother-in-law can't believe that Abernathy's husband (her son) would "*let* [my emphasis] me go to school and do all this other stuff." The church people say that, "God made you a mother and a wife first." Retrospectively, Abernathy is aware of the contradiction in the church's teaching since these were the same people that taught her that "you are supposed to follow Christ."

The onslaught is merciless, coming from the church people, including her in-laws. They say that her children will be "juvenile delinquents," her "daughters are going to be pregnant," and her "husband is going to leave you and have some other women." Abernathy withstood all of this because her husband and children were her support. Her interpretation of this sequence of events is that none of these predictions came true because she was following God's lead. Her children "didn't get pregnant, they are not juvenile delinquents" and her husband, ". . . started going to church every Sunday, taking his kids to Sunday school." "This man was not that kind of person before I went to school." Again, the struggle is seen as confirmation of God's will for her life.

I always say that a lot of things that are associated with my call I would have missed the enjoyment of, if I had neglected my call. I would have robbed myself and my family of a whole different kind of relationship with God. . . . Everything that happened because of my call has been positive. The negatives were the struggle of accepting it and knowing that that's what God was saying when everybody around you was saying, "God doesn't say that." And I was saying, "Well, if he doesn't do it, then why am I getting this, why am I hearing this?" I finally had to "one-on-one" say, "Lord, what are you saying? If you show me, I'll do it." He showed me, and I couldn't help but do it.

We observe Abernathy's hermeneutical retrospection: "Everything that happened because of my call has been positive." She can only say that at the narrative level, looking back on it and reinterpreting it after many years. She would have "missed the enjoyment" if she had "neglected" the call; she would have "robbed" herself and her family of a "whole different kind of relationship with God." While this is true at the narrative level, the narratee knows that at the story level everything has not been positive. Abernathy is aware of this conflict as well and immediately modifies her claim by saying that "[t]he negatives were the struggle of accepting it, and knowing that that's what God was saying when everybody around you was saying, 'God doesn't say that.'"

We are able to see again how much and how long the liminality remains and how limited knowledge and understanding are at the story level. At the narrative level a greater degree of certainty, clarity, and understanding is claimed than actually existed at the story level. At the story level there was struggle in accepting the call and confusion in knowing what God wanted her to do. In Abernathy's case it all centered around her gender, because while God was saying one thing to her, everybody around her was saying, "God doesn't say that." The conflict was even worse because these were people that she had known all her life and that she loved and respected.

As she explains at the narrative level, this conflict in communication between God and the community of faith forces her to go "one-on-one" with God. God must show her. This appears to be a flashback to the Denver experience. As in the case of McCreary, God shows her she cannot "help but do it," irrespective of what anybody else says. Abernathy abandons the story-level chronology to follow her theme of gender struggle and validation at the narrative level.

It hasn't been real easy. But now it's a whole lot better than it was, because that was ten years ago. Eleven years ago, it was totally different. Since that time, and I can honestly say, because of that time, there have been other women who have come forth and said, "I was dealing with my call, and I waited to see what was happening to you." I thank God that I really answered it. I even thank him for the struggle now that I'm out of that aspect of it. The greatest part of it was not having that human validation, but that became the greatest asset too; because then you know it's just you and God. And you know for sure, no man called you.

Abernathy jumps back to the present in order to reflect on the past. She acknowledges that "It hasn't been real easy. But now it's a whole lot better than it was" ten or eleven years ago. "Better" seems to refer to the fact that now at least women are able to come forward and make their claim. Many watched to see what would happen to her. Apparently her courage gave them courage to do the same. Therefore, Abernathy thanks God that she "answered" the call and even thanks God "for the struggle." This is truly a retrospective thanks, however, because she can do it "now that I'm out of that aspect of it." Now that she is no longer in the struggle stage and has passed through the search and sanction stage she can thank God for the struggle.

The most arresting acknowledgment of all, however, is when Abernathy emphasizes the importance of human validation. While she has argued up to this point and here that God's validation is primary, she also makes clear here what she has hinted at up to this point — the "greatest part" that she missed was the human validation. Like McCreary, Abernathy confirms that in spite of all the cataclysmic phenomena and the divine validation, callees still want to be validated by the community of faith.

Now, many years removed from the struggle, Abernathy interprets the lack of human validation as the "greatest asset." Because now "you know it's just you and God. And you know for sure, no man called you." We see here again the similarities between McCreary, Abernathy, and the apostle Paul.

You get into situations like when I first came here to my present church and said, "God, are you sure you called me? Are you sure you want me to be here? Are you sure I didn't hear you wrong?" I don't think that's any different for any man that goes through it. That is, in the fact that there are points of uncertainty once you find yourself in situations. I don't think that you are so uncertain, rather

it's that you don't want to be in that situation, and you are looking
for a way out. But all of the positive things from it I wouldn't trade
them, even to the degree that when I was in school, part of my call
was to remain Baptist, and I couldn't understand that. I said, "Lord,
why do I have to be Baptist when the Baptists won't accept me?"
When I was in seminary, people would say to me, "Well, who do you
think is going to ordain you?" . . . I said, "Well, I have to go with
whatever the Lord is saying." It kept impacting on me, "You gotta
remain Baptist. . . ." I got invited to be United Methodist, AME and
Presbyterian; I worked in the Presbyterian church and they wanted
to ordain me Presbyterian. I said, "I'm sorry, I can't. . . ." I couldn't
do it, mainly because part of my call was to remain Baptist. I did not
understand it, but I did trust God.

Abernathy makes clear here why there is so much uncertainty,
limited knowledge, liminality, and confusion about the call — the call
is a process that unfolds throughout the life of the callee and is subject
to reinterpretation the further he or she is removed from the actual
episodes and stages that make up the call. Though she knows that she
is called, when she first comes to her "present church," it engenders
doubts not only about that local calling, but her calling in general.
Abernathy doesn't think this is different for men, nor does she feel that
the "uncertainty" is really uncertainty. On the contrary, she thinks that
one is sure, but "you are looking for a way out."

For the first time we hear Abernathy acknowledge what McCreary
acknowledges early in his narrative — perhaps she didn't want the call
in first place. However, from the present vantage point she "wouldn't
trade" the "positive things" at all. She even refuses to reject the Baptists,
although they continuously reject her. She is licensed American Baptist
in Texas because that's how she understands her call — "You gotta
remain Baptist," the Lord keeps saying to her. Fellow seminarians make
her painfully aware of a problem that she has that they do not have, at
least not because of their gender — "Well, who do you think is going
to ordain you?"

She is invited into other denominations, works in the Presbyterian
church, and "they wanted to ordain" her Presbyterian. Although she
cannot find her place among the Baptists, unlike Roberts she rejects the
Presbyterians' offer. "I couldn't do it, mainly because part of my call
was to remain Baptist." The liminality continues, but so does obedience.
"I did not understand it, but I did trust God."

When I came home and went back to my church where I grew up, I
knew that I would never be ordained there and I couldn't continue

being there, because I was making them terribly uncomfortable. It was like an all-out attack to make me leave. Finally, it got to the point where I said, "Lord, I can't go there anymore, I have to resign." It hurt me to my heart, because I loved my church. I loved my church and the people in it. I wrote a letter of resignation asking for a letter of transfer. They refused to give me a letter until I found a church. I didn't have any place I wanted to go. I said, "Lord, I can't go anywhere until you send me."

Her fellow seminarians' prediction becomes a painful reality for her in her home church. It becomes evident to her that she "would never be ordained there"; therefore, she "couldn't continue being there," because she is making the people "terribly uncomfortable." She interprets what transpires thereafter as "an all-out attack to make me leave." We are not told what the all-out attack consisted of, but it was sufficient to make her write a letter of resignation asking for a letter of transfer which they say they will reject until she finds a church. It hurts her to do so, because she loves the church and the people in it. She doesn't have anywhere to go and awaits the Lord's direction. Like McCreary who has to leave his local church and Roberts who has to leave his denomination because they cannot find their place within, Abernathy has to leave her local church because there is no place for her. Their self-understanding of call clashes with the traditions of their religious communities, at least as seen from the perspective of the leaders and in most instances as supported by the congregation. Unlike McCreary and Roberts, however, Abernathy has to leave because she is a woman. This is the unfortunate plight of many women who receive a call from God; many times they have to leave their local churches in order to be accepted, and sometimes they have to leave their denomination entirely. Like that of Abernathy, women's options are often limited; either they don't have any place they want to go, or they have no place that will accept them for who they are.

Somebody from CBA [Cleveland Baptist Association] knew what I was going through. This white guy called me up and said, "We can ordain you, and you can be part of our church, but it's not the black church." I said, "Well, I don't think that is where God is leading. I don't think it's ordination as much as it is that I needed a place where I can do ministry where God wants me to be. Then finally they told me to go visit this church on Lee Road, Lee Road Baptist. I went and really didn't like it and really wasn't quite ready to join a church; but I went because they had asked me to go visit. The next Sunday, the Lord led me to go back, but I said, "I don't want to go, Lord." I went, and I think about the second or third time I went, they opened the

doors of the church. I was going up there and I didn't know why. . . .
I guess I joined the church there, and it was one of the best things
that could have ever happened to me. I was there a little less than a
year before they voted to ordain me. They were the most wonderful
people and accepted all of my gifts. I taught Bible class for adults.
They just went all out and did for me what I would have expected
my home church to do. But it was like God kept giving me that
Scripture, *"A prophet is without honor in his own country,"* to let me
know that I was not to be at my home church, I was to be right where
he had placed me. Since then he's done nothing but bless me.

The struggle and validation theme continues. Though rejected at
home, Abernathy finds another avenue opened by God. Initially it is not
an avenue that she wants. It even causes her to reinterpret what she has
claimed all along was her calling — the ordained ministry. However,
when God answers her prayer by sending her to a place that is willing
to ordain her, her response is, "I don't think it's ordination as much as it
is that I needed a place where I can do ministry where God wants me to
be." This sounds very much like Roberts, who was looking for a place
to do ministry acccording to his self-understanding of his call — a
broader ministry than his denomination was willing to allow.

Throughout the narrative, however, Abernathy has always been
obedient, if not initially at least ultimately. She goes to the church that
she is directed to and joins. Because she doesn't know exactly why,
when, or how she joined, the liminality continues. However, her retrospective interpretation of the move is that it was "one of the best things
that could have ever happened to me." In less than a year she is
ordained, teaches Bible class, and is fully accepted by the people. These
are all of the things that she "would have expected" from her "home
church." She recalls biblical rhetoric to interpret this sequence of events.
Though one door closes, another opens. God continues to validate her
call by letting her know that she is ". . . not to be at my home church,
I was to be right where he had placed me." Her interpretation of
everything since then is that God has "done nothing but bless me." By
now the narratee recognizes that though this may be the case at the
narrative level, it is not necessarily what obtains at the story level.

It was kind of strange, because there were a few people in my home
church that came forward and said different things; they may have
come to the ordination or the installation here. But the most different
part was letting go of people and things you held dear. It was just
letting you and God be, and just letting everybody else go by the

wayside. Because when you love and respect people they can have too much of an influence on you the wrong way. That's what God did for me. He moved the people. At first it was real strange. It's always real lonely, always really lonely. But then God will do something to make you satisfied.

Human validation emerges again at the end. Though she cannot be ordained in her home church, "a few people" from that church "came forward and said different things." The narrative allows Abernathy to bring together two events separated by years at the story level (ordination and installation at her present church). Abernathy says this "was kind of strange." Perhaps what is strange is that so few came and so few positive things were said by her "home church" members.

Abernathy again raises what may be one of the most difficult aspects of the call — the clash between the individual's self-understanding of the call and the understanding of the church's tradition. She says, "the most difficult part was letting go of people and things you held dear. It was just letting you and God be, and just letting everybody else go by the wayside. Because when you love and respect people they can have too much of an influence on you the wrong way." This indeed is a difficult balancing act, not only because the callee loves and respects these people who are wedded to certain traditions, but because he or she is one of these people who, up to the time of the call, may have embraced the same beliefs they do now. They have not had Abernathy's mountaintop experience and thus don't find it easy to embrace. Moreover, the callee is fighting them and himself or herself, and it is easier to let go of the people and things one holds dear at the narrative level than at the story level. At the story level people the callee's love and respect can indeed have "too much of an influence on you the wrong way."

Just how difficult it is to make this break is seen when Abernathy observes that it was not she that initiated the break, but God that "moved the people." It is better stated that God moved Abernathy away from the people. Moreover, although Abernathy earlier interpreted all of this as blessings, it is clear that the narrative closes on a bittersweet note. It is still "strange" and "It's always real lonely, always really lonely. But then God will do something to make you satisfied." Although God continues to validate Abernathy's call and ministry, the lack of human validation is a constant reminder of how much more lonely the call can be when Christians, male and female, reject a callee because she is a woman. Thus the theme of struggle and validation dominant throughout the narrative brings the narrative to a close.

Vashti M. McKenzie:
"From a Broadcasting Career to Preaching"

Vashti McKenzie was born in Baltimore, Maryland, in 1947 to parents who were born in Maryland and Illinois. She was called in 1981 and ordained an African American Episcopal elder in 1986. She earned a master of divinity degree from Howard University's Divinity School and now pastors Payne Memorial Baptist Church in Baltimore. McKenzie's story is an example of a type B (noncataclysmic/reluctant). As with Abernathy's story, McKenzie's story demonstrates that this type is unique neither to males nor to one generation. Yet her call is slightly different from Abernathy's, at least at the narrative level, since she interprets it very specifically as a call to preach and pastor.

> Well, if you had asked me about the call to preach maybe about seven years ago, I would have said it began eight years ago or nine years ago. But having been in the ministry now eight years, eight or nine years — well, almost a decade — I can tell you now that the call to the ministry began as a girl growing up in church. I can't remember a time when I was not in church. I remember wanting to sing [in] the junior choir and I couldn't read, I was not old enough to read. . . . At that particular time only men, only boys, were allowed to serve the altar. I thought it was unfair that only the boys could carry the cross, carry the Bible, be a part of the procession. I wanted to serve on the altar too. But, of course, that wasn't a part of our tradition at the time.

McKenzie makes the narratee aware of the impact of hermeneutical retrospection from the very opening of the narrative. She is aware of how time changes perspective and interpretation of the call. If asked about the call "seven years ago," she would have said it began eight or nine years ago. We must be careful with time here because story time and narrative time are converging. McKenzie is telling us something very important about the distinction between story time and narrative time. In story time, if asked seven years ago about her call, she would have said she was called a year or two earlier, which would date it in story time in the year 1981, not fifteen or sixteen years before the narrative was recorded (1973-74). In narrative time, however, McKenzie is able to reinterpret her call and date it much earlier — "I can tell you now that the call to the ministry began as a girl growing up in church."

This is a distinction of the utmost importance for our understanding of call. At a period closer to her call, one or two years after the call, McKenzie would have dated her call at the story level in the year 1981.

However, given the opportunity of hermeneutical retrospection eight years later she dates it during her childhood years growing up in church. Not only does the date change in the reinterpretation of the call, but so does the perspective of how it occurred — from a specific date to a gradual process beginning in childhood.

Like all four callees examined earlier, McKenzie was a child of the church. "I can't remember a time when I was not in church." As with Abernathy she participates in all of the areas she is allowed to, which means that because of her gender there are limitations on that participation. "At that particular time only men, only boys, were allowed to serve the altar." She feels this deeply, because she "wanted to serve on the altar too." However, her desire clashes with her religious community's "tradition" at that time.

In contrast to Abernathy, who resists interpreting her call as a call to preach, McKenzie's interpretation from the very beginning of the narrative is that of a "call to preach."

> And, going through college years, the regular adolescence, [I was] still not recognizing that pull, that closeness to Christ, that presence of God and serving him other than doing. As an adult at Bethel Church, which is my home church — John and Cecelia Bryant are my parents — walking into the door of that church for the first time, I felt such an extraordinary pull that I had never experienced in my religious life up until that point.

What McKenzie recognizes now, many years later, at the narrative level, she was not able to recognize at the story level — "such an extraordinary pull" of God on her life. All of this is now seen as part of the call process, though clearly it was not understood as such when it was happening. Contrary to Abernathy who meets with immediate rejection by her pastor and congregation in the church she has attended from age three, it appears that a supportive pastor and his wife create a more positive atmosphere for McKenzie — "walking into the door of that church for the first time, I felt such an extraordinary pull that I had never experienced in my religious life up until that point." John Bryant's reputation for supporting women in the ministry is almost legendary in the AME church.

> I couldn't find anybody who could explain what was happening to me at that time. I really couldn't until later, of course, when all of it became clear. But God just made it so in my life that in order for me to live out my faith would be to preach the gospel and then later to

serve as a pastor. He cuts off all your options, makes it very clear, very plain that the only thing that he wants you to do and that you can do is to preach the gospel; there is no peace in any other line.

Liminality emerges for McKenzie at the story level. She understood neither the call nor "what was happening to me at that time." Only later did things become "clear." Again, we see that clarity prevails retrospectively, not when things are happening. Everything appears to be very clear to McKenzie in the narrative. She knows that her call is "to preach the gospel and then later to serve as a pastor"; she knows that God "cuts off all your options," and "makes it very clear, very plain" that you are to "preach the gospel"; and that you will find "no peace" in any other vocation. But when does she know this? This is her interpretation of events long after they have occurred. If she understood them at the story level, when they were happening, then we wouldn't hear the retrospective assertion that, "I couldn't find anybody who could explain what was happening to me at that time." Like all callees who find themselves in the liminal state of the call, she needed help in understanding her experiences. However, this help always comes "later."

This seeking and searching, knowing and not knowing, clarity and confusion unfolds as a process as God "cuts off all of your options," and makes it "very clear" and "very plain" that you will find "no peace in any other line" of work. As with all the other callees, the call for McKenzie is a process that unfolds over time and is understood gradually.

Now, when God is pressing you in this manner, of course, all of us think, "Who? Why me at this time?" I had been married for ten, twelve years, settled, [with] a house, a husband, a career in broadcasting — program director of a radio station. Now why the call to the ministry? If God wanted me in the ministry, why didn't he call me when I was in college and go straight through seminary? Why now? Why now? And it was just very clear that God called me as a woman, as a mother, and as a wife; that all of these gifts and all the experiences that I had up to that point would be beneficial for whatever use in his ministry. And it's true. All of those things — wife, mother, all of the other vocational experiences — have become quite significant in my pastoral ministry and in my preaching ministry. God has used all of those aspects. I knew God wanted me to do something other than where I was. Where I was at the time is — you're talking about 1978 — I was program director of a gospel radio station in Washington, D.C., and it seemed to me that, as God begins to pull — that what I was doing was not enough for him as far as the ministry is concerned.

The liminality, limited understanding, and limited clarity emerge in this part of the narrative. McKenzie has just asserted in the previous paragraph that God made things clear and plain, cutting off her options. However, that clarity is at the narrative level. At the story level, there are numerous questions like "Who?" "Why me at this time?" "Why now?" She has a husband and a career in broadcasting. Since this is gospel broadcasting, a form of ministry, it should be sufficient. Perhaps this is one of the options and other lines of work that McKenzie refers to God cutting off. Ultimately she got the impression that it was "not enough for him as far as the ministry is concerned."

That she is "a woman," "a mother," and "a wife" are not seen as stumbling blocks for McKenzie. On the contrary, these aspects of her life as well as her "other vocational experiences" would be "beneficial" in her ministry. Her assertion that they "have become quite significant in my pastoral ministry and in my preaching ministry" makes it abundantly clear that this is a retrospective viewpoint. McKenzie does not place the same emphasis on gender as does Abernathy, nor do we hear up to this point anything like the negative and hostile response that Abernathy was subjected to. Obviously a supportive pastor and congregation make a significant difference.

> One night in studying the Bible, God brought me right on through to Acts, the sixth chapter, verses one through six, and those were, I guess you would call, my "call scriptures" — the call-to-action scriptures. Then the other particular point is in the scriptures where God tells us to wait on our ministry and that we are to minister out of the power . . . as far as those who are called to prophesy, go ahead and prophesy in faith, and so forth and so on. And that, I guess, you would call my "call scripture."

As with Abernathy biblical rhetoric has a place in McKenzie's interpretation of her call. The six chapter of Acts and what appears to be an allusion to Paul's thirteenth chapter of 1 Corinthians serve as "call scriptures" for McKenzie. Though they are not the typical biblical call narratives cited by many who feel called to preach, her citation of them demonstrates the importance of both the Bible and retrospective interpretation.

> Going to church and being uncomfortable, uncomfortable in that present state. I mean, it's a decided consciousness of disobedience if you did not. Knowing that every time when people asked you to say something, it was as if you were preaching, and finding that you are

not able to say anything else but. In my capacity at the radio station, there were many times when I was asked to emcee a gospel concert. But all of a sudden somewhere in the middle of the gospel concert . . . all of a sudden you are proclaiming the gospel, and it's nothing you intended, it's nothing you planned. . . . Then others, of course, coming and they are affirming what God is already doing on the inside of you, making it clear. So, finally, one time I said, "Lord, this is it. I mean, there's no halfways. We're not going to 'Maybe, maybe not/is He, is He not.' We're just not going to go through that anymore. I mean, just make it clear to me exactly what your calling needs to do." It's like laying out the fleece.

McKenzie speaks about "being uncomfortable in that present state." That present state is at the story level and it is a liminal state. She is caught between what she is doing and what she thinks she should be doing. It's a "decided consciousness of disobedience." In her "capacity at the radio station," she is involved in gospel concerts, but she finds herself suddenly "proclaiming the gospel," though she does not plan to do it. It is evident that McKenzie sees this as confirmation of God's call on her life to preach. In addition, others are "coming and they are affirming what God is already doing on the inside of you, making it clear." This is the kind of human validation that Abernathy and many other women desired and missed so much.

How we are to understand the assertion that things are made clear arises again. McKenzie reaches the point where the liminal state is no longer acceptable to her; it will no longer be "Maybe, maybe not/is He, is He not," obviously referring to whether God has really called her. If, however, we are to accept her assertion that things were clear, the narratee wants to know how to interpret McKenzie's request to "just make it clear." We observe once again that at the story level clarity and understanding of the call are limited, while at the narrative level hermeneutical retrospection clears away most ambiguity.

Two things seem evident: McKenzie wants more clarity about the specific ministry or function of her call, what she is called to do; and she wants some kind of supernatural sign to confirm it — "It's like laying out the fleece." Here McKenzie is obviously using biblical rhetoric in referring to Gideon. This is clearly story level because the narratee knows that at the narrative level she has been called to preach and pastor and that God has confirmed it through people and events.

So, of course, I'm on my way to church . . . sitting as far away as I could, and the word is being preached, and at the end of the sermon then Reverend Bryant says, "Turn to the person who is next to you and ask them if they're in Christ, and if they're not in Christ then you witness to them." Of course, I turned to this sister and I began to witness to her and to share with her. . . . And I helped walk her down and led her down and off she went. She went in, but when she came out it wasn't a she, it was a he. . . . And, you know, I was through. . . . I was just totally undone . . . but it was just that thorough; it was just that clear. So I went home and I said, "No, God. You really can't mean this."

McKenzie continues the confirmation theme. She interprets an event when she witnessed a man dressed as a woman in church and the person confessed and repented as another confirmation of God calling her to preach. "I was just totally undone." This must refer to more than the shock of seeing someone in church dressed this way; in the context of wrestling with her call, that individual's transformation as a result of her witnessing is paramount.

She starts shouting and praising God for it because "it was just that clear." "So I went home and I said, 'No, God. You really can't mean this.'" Again liminality, clarity, and knowledge emerge. Although she claims that it's clear — obviously a reference to this event as another confirmation that God is calling her to preach — she goes home to question God about its clarity. There is not only resistance here — "No, God" — there is the matter of knowing and understanding — "You really can't mean this." Irrespective of the whole sequence of confirming events and affirming people, at the story level McKenzie is still uncertain.

Through a process of fasting and praying and fasting and praying and God just pressing in on you, then he just tells you, "You were called to preach. You were called to pastor," and that's it. Period. Of course, at that time, you're talking about in a very turbulent time in the church when men and women are grappling, "Are women called to preach? Are women called to pastor?" And I sat in a convocation in 1978, it was a Baptist woman conducting a workshop on black women in the ministry, and she wrote a sentence across the blackboard that just really pierced through my confusion. She wrote, "God does call women to preach. I know because God called me." That just, boom, reverberated right in my heart, and then finally I said, "Yes, Lord. Yes, Lord. Yes, Lord." I'll just never forget that. It was in November that I walked down the aisle and finally told my pastor that I'm accepting my call to preach and I've got to be about my Master's business, my Father's business, and that is to preach the gospel.

McKenzie continues her quest for a crowning confirmation sign from God since it is not yet clear to her that she must take this path. We do not yet know why McKenzie continues to resist the call, if it is resistance; it may be just ambiguity and uncertainty. Through a "process of fasting and praying" God tells her she is "called to preach" and "called to pastor." It is not clear to the narratee whether this is to be taken as a literal voice or merely a consciousness. Also, one wonders whether McKenzie has once again compressed story time in the narrative, or whether in fact the call to preach and the call to pastor came at the same time.

For the first time the narratee becomes aware of what may have been at the root of McKenzie's resistance all along. The period of McKenzie's liminality is a "turbulent time in the church where men and women are grappling, 'Are women called to preach? Are women called to pastor?'" There is no emphasis in the narrative to this point on McKenzie's gender; thus the narratee to this point has the impression that, unlike Abernathy, it was not an issue for her even though her call occurred during exactly the same time period (Abernathy was called in 1978).

Gender is an issue; McKenzie just has not focused on it in her narrative up to now. It was at a "convocation in 1978" when a "Baptist woman conducting a workshop on black women in the ministry . . . pierced through my confusion. She wrote, 'God does call women to preach. I know because God called me.'"

For the first time McKenzie acknowledges directly that gender was an issue for her just as it was for Abernathy and that she was confused. Her liminality, like Abernathy's, is dual; it is not just confusion over whether God is in fact *calling* her, but whether God is in fact calling *her*, a woman. Undoubtedly, what made McKenzie's struggle less traumatic was her supportive, affirming pastor and congregation. As a result, she does not emphasize her gender struggle as much as Abernathy does in her narrative.

This experience is the turning point for McKenzie. Finally she says, "Yes, Lord. Yes, Lord." As with Abernathy this is her mountaintop experience; an experience she will "never forget." In Abernathy's case, the turning point is seeing black women in the pulpit participating in the service; in McKenzie's case it is hearing another black woman affirm that God had called her to the ministry. Given the fact that McKenzie had an affirming church and pastor and Abernathy did not, the observation of other women in ministry is the turning point and culminating moment for both. After this experience McKenzie finally tells her pastor that "I'm accepting my call to preach."

Then after that, I experienced such a peace I had never experienced. It seems like for the whole year and a half it was like a fighting and struggling, waking up every morning and saying, "Who's going to win today? Who's going to win out?" After that I never had such a peace. I mean, it was just like, whew! I was just at peace with the world, at peace with God, at peace with myself. I mean, just the whole future became clear. Then the turbulence of the past was just the bridge that you came over. That was it. I mean, lightning didn't strike, a voice didn't come out and say, "You are called to preach my gospel." I mean, it didn't happen. God didn't write across my house, "You are called to preach." But he just makes it clear on the inside of your heart that you will not be happy, you will not be satisfied, you won't do anything unless you preach my gospel. And that's it.

The liminal state is broken, the "fighting and struggling" is over, and "peace" prevails. She is at peace with herself, God, and the world. As with Abernathy she can now look back on the "turbulence of the past" as a necessary part of her call. As the narrative closes, McKenzie clears up some questions that the narratee has wanted answered. God's communication to her was not in a literal voice. Her call was not a cataclysmic-type call. No supernatural phenomena occurred in her call experience as with Abernathy's. "God didn't write across my house, 'You are called to preach,'" and "lightning didn't strike."

"But he just makes it clear on the inside of your heart that you will not be happy, you will not be satisfied, you won't do anything unless you preach my gospel." The narratee now understands that this is narrative clarity and not story clarity; this is hermeneutical retrospection at its best. A limited kind of clarity emerges in the story, but a slower, deeper kind of clarity unfolds for the callee retrospectively.

Manuel Scott, Sr.: "An Irresistible Compulsion"

Manuel Scott, Sr., was born in Waco, Texas, in 1926 to parents born in Texas. He was called in 1944 and ordained a Baptist minister in 1948. He earned a B.A. from Bishop College and now pastors the St. John Missionary Baptist Church in Dallas. Scott's story is an example of a type C (noncataclysmic/nonreluctant) call. Scott's call story was selected because of its denominational significance. He is a Baptist from the same generation as Newman, the Methodist, who also has a type C call. And yet many Baptists would think that type C calls don't occur in their denomination.

My call to the ministry was a consciousness that I felt at the earliest stages of my life. I've never dreamed or proceeded to desire any other type of life pursuit other than preaching. At the very elementary school level, I felt deeply persuaded that it was my business. The call didn't come at any ecstatic moment. It came with a growing and gradual awareness that the lesson, as far as a church's mission and to be a messenger of the master, broke on me. It was irresistible. The fulfillment of expression of my inner awareness, with respect to preaching, became an irresistible focus.

Scott describes his call as a "call to the ministry" and a "consciousness" that he has "felt" from an early age, as early as "elementary school." He interprets that call as a call to preach. By a "consciousness" it seems apparent that Scott simply means an awareness. His call isn't sudden or cataclysmic; it "didn't come at any ecstatic moment. It came with a growing and gradual awareness. . ." and is "irresistible." It is an "inner awareness" that "preaching" is to be his "business" and that "became an irresistible focus" for him. Scott does not refer to any family tradition of preachers as does Newman, but it is evident that religious exposure at an early age has had an impact on him. Like Newman, he "never dreamed or proceeded to desire any other type of life pursuit other than preaching."

The consciousness of the call and the confirmation came with gradual and increasing impact. I could no longer be satisfied with participation outside of the pulpit ranks. There wasn't no lightning flashes from heaven or no emotional tears or exceptional joy. As the intensity of awareness grew, it became a compulsion at the age of seventeen, when I acknowledged my call. The call to preach for me never came as a burden. I wasn't no reluctant prophet. It was no burden for me. Yes, there are the Jeremiah type — a reluctant prophet — and the Isaiah type, who see the world situation and see themselves in relationship to that, to the nature of things. And they just say, "Here am I, send me." I was the Isaiah type.

Scott picks up the emphasis that the call was a gradual consciousness again, and adds that the "confirmation" also "came with gradual and increasing impact." We are not given any details about confirming events or people. It is the "intensity" of the awareness that increases for Scott and that he wishes to emphasize. This intensity makes him dissatisfied with doing anything "outside of the pulpit ranks."

The dual theme that the call is not cataclysmic but yet irresistible repeats. It is such a "compulsion" that he finally acknowledges it at the age of seventeen. There are "no lightning flashes from heaven or no emotional tears or exceptional joy." The lack of tears and joy is connected to the fact that the "call to preach . . . never came as a burden." This is in obvious contrast to McKenzie and McCreary and the many others who emphasize what peace and joy they receive and how much of a burden is lifted after acknowledging the call.

Whereas these others are hesitant, resist, and struggle with accepting the call, Scott is "no reluctant prophet." Since he has always wanted to be a preacher and has never dreamed of doing anything else, "it was no burden" to him. He is aware of the fact that there are callees of the reluctant type, like Jeremiah, but he is an "Isaiah type," one of those "who see the world situation and see themselves in relationship to that, to the nature of things."[5] We take this to mean that Scott understood his call and saw his role as a change agent; one who could do something about "the nature of things" as a "messenger of the Master."

In retrospect Scott uses the biblical rhetoric of two Old Testament call narratives to interpret his own. Although Isaiah's call is the very type that he says his is not — a cataclysmic, phenomena-laden type, one aspect of Isaiah's call is enough to make the entire call serve as a model for Scott. Isaiah is not a reluctant prophet. Scott is suggesting that their responses were the same — "Here am I, send me" — although obviously the type of their calls is not the same.

In point of fact, all interpreters do not understand Isaiah as a nonreluctant prophet. There may be some hesitation in the response: "Woe to me! . . . For I am a man of unclean lips, and I live among a people of unclean lips . . ." (Isa. 6:5). Perhaps Isaiah felt the unworthiness to the call that many callees express in their narratives. Such may have been the case also at the story level for Scott, but the narratee is not told. This is the advantage of hermeneutical retrospection — the callee gets the opportunity to reinterpret the story at the narrative level.

Some Observations and Hermeneutical Implications

Whereas there are obvious similarities among these six narratives, enough distinctions exist when story and narrative are juxtaposed to support the thesis of at least three different call types in this collection.

5. See, among others in Myers, the Hoyt (37) and Waller (76) stories.

The first observation is that all six callees were exposed to religious environments at an early age. This had an important influence on their ultimate acceptance of ministry as a life vocation. There are some obvious differences for PK's, due perhaps to the intensity of their religious setting, and the influence is not always interpreted as positively as in Newman's case. Roberts's interpretation of his early environment is decidedly negative, yet the ultimate positive impact of his decision is as strong as that of the others.

A second observation is that only the nonreluctant call type (type C) has no clear elements of a liminal state at the story level. Liminality prevails in both reluctant types (types A and B). Liminality is observed best at the story level. It consists of limited knowledge and clarity, confusion, doubt, and ambiguity, and engenders reluctance, resistance, and struggle in the life of the callee. However, at the narrative level the callee will often interpret the call in a nonliminal way. The narratives assert more knowledge and clarity, and less ambiguity and doubt, than is usually the case in the story.

The third observation is an outgrowth of the second. Often both an internal and external struggle arise for the callee; as a result, reluctance and sometimes outright resistance occurs (obviously, this is not the case for type C). The struggle occurs for a variety of reasons: lack of freedom, feeling of unworthiness, ambiguity, and rejection by others (significantly on the basis of gender for women). Rejection by others, especially one's own local congregation, sometimes forces the callee to go to a different congregation, perhaps even a different denomination, to find acceptance.

Rejection on the basis of gender (the particular plight of women) is a fourth observation. Women in both reluctant types experience such rejection, and this contributes to their liminality and reluctance to accept the call. The pain is greatly exacerbated when the resistance comes from loved ones, especially male callees and the community of faith. It is mitigated, though not totally erased, when other callees, in particular the pastor, and a woman's own local congregation support her. As important as pastoral and congregational support are, for those struggling with call nothing seems to surpass the experience of being exposed to other women who are full participants in ministry at this level. Sometimes, however, it is necessary for a woman to leave her congregation or denomination to get validation.

The importance of validation is the fifth observation. Divine validation is important for both men and women in overcoming the liminality and struggle. For the cataclysmic calls such validation may come from voices and visions and other supernatural phenomena, whereas for the noncataclysmic type it may come as a series of confirming events such as the cutting off of all other options in life that are fulfilling. Divine validation is in some sense more important for women because they don't receive the same quantity or quality of human validation as men do.

As important as divine validation is, human validation is equally important. Irrespective of how immediate the divine validation is, both men and women continue to seek human validation. Most often some event correlated with human validation is the turning point of a call. Although women may emphasize divine validation more often because of the dearth of human validation they receive, when women receive human validation it is highly emphasized, and its absence may often inflict lasting wounds.

The clash over narrow traditional interpretations of the call is the sixth observation. Sometimes there is a clash between the personal interpretation of the call and the religious community's traditional interpretation of the call, especially as seen through the eyes of the pastor (the first portal in the callee's rites of passage). Among women callees gender is almost always the source of their clash with the community of faith. Some callees draw upon biblical rhetoric to help interpret their own call experiences. In some instances biblical call narratives are appealed to, whereas in others Scriptures completely unrelated to a call are utilized.

A seventh observation is thematic emphasis. The greatest difference between narrative and story is observed in how callees reshape their stories, both chronologically and linguistically, to emphasize a theme unique to their call. McCreary emphasizes the cataclysmic nature of his call; Roberts emphasizes the noncataclysmic, gradual nature that includes a desire for a freer, broader ministry; Newman emphasizes the family tradition and committed life; Abernathy emphasizes the gender struggle, yet constant validation by God; McKenzie emphasizes the search for validation discovered in a unique event in church and culminating in the encounter with another woman who publicly and forcefully asserts her call; and Scott emphasizes the noncataclysmic, nonreluctant, gradual but irresistible aspects of his call.

A final observation is that the call types are not bound by gender, generation, or denomination.

The hermeneutical implications of these narratives are numerous. This closer analysis of selected narratives by type supports the general analysis of parts I, II, and III. We must appreciate the hermeneutical differences between call as story and call as narrative, since at the narrative level every callee puts his or her own twist on their story. Part of this twist is cultural conditioning engendered by the traditions of their respective communities of faith and part of it is their own hermeneutical retrospection of their story. How much their interpretation changes depends to a great degree on how long it has been since they had the call experience, how much theological reflection they have been exposed to academically, and what other traditional understandings of call they have been exposed to.

The fact that callees' retrospective narratives can be interpreted differently when viewed at the story level is not cause for alarm. It does, however, have hermeneutical implications for how we should rethink call to ministry. It should be self-evident that one individual's hermeneutical retrospection of call to ministry cannot be the paradigm for all others, because this is an individual subjective attempt to make sense out of the call experience; often it is an interpretation that changes as time passes. This is not deception; it is hermeneutical retrospection.

The best example of this is the prevalence of liminality at the story level that is deemphasized, reforged, or reinterpreted by the callee at the narrative level. The fact that callees manifest a limited knowledge, lack of clarity, and confusion about more things in their stories than their narrative interpretations suggest should caution all of us not to restrict call to ministry to any one type and especially not to any one individual's experience.

However, an analysis of call to ministry as story may serve as a better heuristic device for broadening our understanding as well as appreciation for similarities and differences among calls. When call to ministry as story is juxtaposed to its narrative transformation, we learn even more about the hermeneutics of call to ministry and can appreciate the differences in call types both at the story and narrative levels.

We observed that at the narrative level some individuals might interpret their call as sudden; however, upon closer examination at the story level most calls appear to be a gradual series of events, in some instances beginning as early as childhood. Some events might be crucial turning or culmination points at the story or narrative level or both. However, it does not appear possible to disentangle the call, at least at the story level, from the earlier life of the individual in a manner that allows the call to be discontinuous with the callee's earlier life. If such discontinuity is possible at all, it is most likely at the narrative level.

Moreover, an examination of call to ministry from this dual perspective should force religious communities to reexamine their traditional views of call to ministry. We may discover that they are too restrictive and are in need of updating to keep up with who, how, and to what God is calling lately. In this regard, we must wrestle anew with the trio of the inner call, the outer call, and the education necessary to fulfill the call.

We should not cast aside two thousand years of church history, right, and responsibility to validate and certify inner calls, if for nothing more than to protect the church from charlatans. Yet at the same time we must be open to what God may be doing differently in our time through the inner call that is in conflict with the church's traditional views.

The issue of women's call to ministry is an example of the latter. The fact that female call stories and narratives are of every type and contain the same constituent parts and structure as those of males has serious hermeneutical implications for some religious traditions. If the call as narrative can be used as a valuable piece of data to legitimate a man's call to ministry, but not a woman's — especially when they are similar — then the church must wrestle anew with whether this phenomenon has outlived its usefulness for anyone. It is striking to note, however, that these stories are no less frequently required in our time by the church than previously as significant testimony by claimants of a call. In addition, these stories are offered and accepted by people from a variety of traditions at crucial times as legitimization or authorization to speak on behalf of God. As long as that continues to be the case, it will be hard to argue that they have outlived their usefulness.

PART V

THE CALL AS THEOLOGICAL AND CULTURAL PERSPECTIVES

CHAPTER 11

The Call as Theological and Cultural Perspectives

The theological discussion of call did not begin in America, neither with European Americans nor African Americans. This dialogue has been going on for some time. Moreover, no theological discussion about call is without some cultural worldview undergirding it; any view of call is culturally determined. This chapter will discuss briefly the theological-cultural continuities and discontinuities that African Americans share with other cultural perspectives of the concept of call.

Biblical Perspectives

The concept of call is prominent throughout the Bible. Its significance in Scripture provides the central backdrop for understanding African-American call narratives. Indeed, throughout the history of the larger church, hermeneutical and theological discussions in various parts of the church have wrestled with restricting the doctrine of calling. Ironically, the lexical meaning of the biblical terms for "calling" as well as the narratives of "callings" are much broader than many of these twentieth-century discussions allow.

The most dominant term in the Old Testament signifying "to call" is the Hebrew *qarâ*.[1] The term is not restricted to one event or person, but is used in many different ways. It is used for naming,

1. L. J. Coppes, *"qarâ,"* in *Theological Wordbook of the Old Testament*, vol. 2, eds. R. Laird Harris, Gleason L. Archer, Jr., and Bruce K. Waltke (Chicago: Moody Press, 1980), 810-11.

calling a nation into relationship with God, an invitation, as well as a divine call to mission. It is the last use of the term that concerns us in this study.

Numerous call narratives recorded in the Old Testament emphasize a divine encounter and a commission as key aspects of the narrative. The calls of Abraham, Moses, Samuel, Amos, Hosea, Isaiah, Jeremiah, Ezekiel, and Gideon are but a few. Although not all of the call stories use *qarâ* explicitly in the narrative, as the content and structure of the narrative reflect the sense of the term, they have been the basis for acceptance of these experiences as divine calls of God.

While these biblical narratives have been investigated from a number of different perspectives, the conclusions of form-critical discussions have proven the most useful for this study. These studies have given us an appreciation for the content and structure of these narratives as a corpus. Habel asserts six basic parts to the structure of these call narratives: the divine confrontation, the introductory word, the commission, the objection, the reassurance, and the sign.[2]

(1) The divine confrontation. Basically, the callee explicitly (e.g., Moses, Jeremiah) or implicitly (e.g., Amos) asserts that he has had a direct one-to-one encounter with God or an angel (e.g., Gideon) or that the call occurred in a vision (e.g., Isaiah). The encounter creates a sense of *mysterium tremendum et fascinans* in the recipient. "The call, therefore, appears as a disruptive experience for which there has been no obvious preparation. The call marks the initial interruption of God in the life of the individual."[3] Moreover, it is a consecrating, purifying event.

(2) The introductory word. An introductory word is given before the direct commission. It functions in an explanatory manner and thus will differ according to the historical situation. It may suggest the special personal relationship between God and the individual. In addition, it may serve as a confessional word in which the callee professes his faith (e.g., Gideon, Jeremiah).

(3) The commission. It is conferred at the same time as the encounter (e.g., Amos 7:15; Hos. 1:2; Ezek. 2:2-3; Isa. 6:9; Jer. 1:5). It is always specific — perhaps to a nation or all nations — and insists on the prophet realizing that he is a spokesman for God. It is the commission that drives the prophet. While the diversity of the commission depends upon the times, situations, and no doubt the personality of

2. N. Habel, "The Form and Significance of the Call Narratives," *Zeitschrift für die alttestamentliche Wissenschaft* 77 (1965): 297-323.
3. Ibid., 298.

the prophet, the commission always invokes a sense of awesome responsibility and inability to accomplish such a task.

(4) The objection. This sense of awesome responsibility causes the prophet to recoil, at least initially, and respond as he does. In addition to the responsibility, the potential response of the people to the prophet also causes consternation. The primary objection is one of inability. Moses objects because of poor speech, Jeremiah because of his youth (*na'ar*), and Amos because he feels unworthy of the title.[4]

(5) The reassurance. In order to calm the callees' fears, God gives them a word of assurance. It takes on many forms, but it is all centered in legitimating the commission, granting power to fulfill the mission, and providing the knowledge that God will be present to the end. More than any other aspect of the experience, it is this element that will steady the prophet in difficult times. On the basis of this assurance the prophet will distinguish himself from false prophets and meet all challenges to his authority. The assurance and the ability to appeal to God during difficult times give the prophet the necessary ingredient for the success of his mission.

(6) The sign. The purpose of the sign is to bolster the words of assurance given to the callee. Basically, it is a sign requested by the callee to insure him that it is God who has spoken to him.

For the black church the Old Testament remains primary. The dominance of the narrative genre in the Old Testament, the ease with which narratives can be committed to memory, as well as the liberation motif in most of them made this portion of the Holy Scriptures very appealing to the preliterate black church. It has not lost this appeal during literate times. Consequently, these call narratives hold a place of prominence equal with those of the New Testament in wrestling with divine call in the black church. African-American callees identify with the call stories of Old Testament prophets like Jeremiah, Isaiah, Amos, and Ezekiel in the self-understanding of their calls as much as with any New Testament call story.

The term (and its cognates) which most often signifies call in the New Testament is the Greek *kaleo*. As with the Old Testament term, this term is used in many different ways. For example, it may be used to name, designate, or give title to someone (e.g., Luke 1:13; John 1:42), or to invite or to call into relationship with God (e.g., Rom. 8:28-30; 9:11;

---

4. Obviously it could be argued that Ezekiel (2:1–3:15), who is described as not conversing with God, and Isaiah (6), who shows no resistance at all, are exceptions to Habel's pattern at this point.

1 Cor. 1:9; 7:17-24; Gal. 1:6).[5] The last usage takes on many more theological connotations than the others. It may refer to the call to salvation in Christ, the body of Christ, Christian living, or to specific ministry within the body of Christ. This latter usage of the term leads us to the call narratives that are background for this study.

New Testament call narratives have not received nearly the amount of attention that those in the Old Testament have received. This is probably because of the prominence given to the call of Paul in the New Testament. However, in addition to Paul there is the call of John the Baptist, Jesus, the Twelve, Timothy, Titus, and a host of others. The difficulty presented the interpreter with these figures is that their narratives are not nearly as clear-cut as those concerning the Old Testament prophets or Paul. Hence, emphasis in the black church on New Testament call stories has been primarily limited to Paul's.[6] This study will focus primarily on the call of Paul.

Paul's call, both as recorded by Luke and at various points in Paul's own letters, has been the object of great scrutiny. Much recent attention has focused on the structure of the Pauline narrative material, as well as on Paul's retrospective interpretation of the experience.[7] Such

5. K. L. Schmidt, *"Kaleo,"* in *Theological Dictionary of the New Testament*, vol. 3, eds. Gerhard Friedrich and Gerhard Kittel (Grand Rapids: Eerdmans, 1972), 487-96. Hereafter referred to as *TDNT*. See also L. Coenen, "Call," in *The New International Dictionary of New Testament Theology*, vol. 1, ed. Colin Brown (Grand Rapids: Zondervan, 1975), 273-76. Hereafter referred to as *NIDNTT*.

6. In a study of over 600 black preachers Glass concludes, "Paul's conversion is emphasized much in the Negro's call to preach." Victor T. Glass, "An Analysis of the Sociological and Psychological Factors Related to the Call to Christian Service of the Negro Baptist Minister," 164.

7. As a result of this recent debate these works are now legion. I list here only some of the most important ones. E. P. Sanders, *Paul and Palestinian Judaism* (Philadelphia: Fortress, 1977); Krister Stendahl, "The Apostle Paul and the Introspective Conscience of the West," in *Paul among Jews and Gentiles* (Philadelphia: Fortress, 1976), 78-96, also in *Harvard Theological Review* 56 (1963): 199-215; James D. G. Dunn, "The New Perspective on Paul," *BJRL* 65 (1982-83): 96-122; Charles W. Hedrick, "Paul's Conversion/Call: A Comparative Analysis of the Three Reports in Acts," *Journal of Biblical Literature* 100 (1981) 415-32; John Knox, "On the Meaning of Galatians 1:15," *JBL* 106 (1987): 301-4; J. Peter Bercovitz, "*Kalein* in Gal. 1:15," *Proceedings of the Eastern Great Lakes and Midwest Biblical Societies* 5 (1985): 28-37; William W. Klein, "Paul's Use of Kalein: A Proposal," *Journal of the Evangelical Theological Society* 27 (1984): 53-64; William Baird, "Visions, Revelation, and Ministry: Reflections on 2 Cor. 12:1-5 and Gal. 1:11-17," *JBL* 104 (Dec. 1985): 651-62; Paula Fredriksen, "Paul and Augustine: Conversion Narratives, Orthodox Traditions, and the Retrospective Self," *JTS*, n.s. 37 (Apr. 1986): 3-34. See also two classic earlier works which have great bearing on this subject: Johannes Munck, "La vocation de l'Apôtre Paul,"

attention to this material has broken new ground both in our appreciation of Paul's theology and his self-understanding of his call. It is these recent conclusions about his self-understanding of call that prove most useful for this study.

The first major conclusion is the argument that no discontinuity exists between Paul's preconversion Judaism and his conversion Christianity. In fact it is the very concept of conversion around which much of the controversy centers. None of the call-narrative passages in Luke or Paul refers to his Damascus road experience as conversion. Krister Stendahl argues that it is our reading — better, misreading — of this material through a Western introspective mind-set that causes us to refer to it as a conversion.[8] Nowhere does Paul refer to it in this manner. In fact, when Paul does speak about his call, and he doesn't speak about it much,[9] his narration of it is similar to the Old Testament prophets' call narratives.[10] This leads us to our next point.

The second major conclusion is that Paul's call narration reflects the features of the call genre. William Baird argues persuasively when he says, "Although Gal. 1:11-17 does not constitute a formal call narrative, it reflects features of the call genre."[11] Baird's comparison utilizing Habel's paradigm is so significant that it bears repeating in its entirety.

> 1. Divine confrontation. Jeremiah says, "The word of the Lord came to me" (1:4). Paul says that his gospel (word) was received by a revelation from God (Gal. 1:12, 16).
>
> 2. Introductory word. Yahweh says to Jeremiah, "Before I formed you in the womb, I knew you" (1:5). Paul says that he was called by "the one who set me apart from my mother's womb" (Gal. 1:15).
>
> 3. Commission. To Jeremiah God says, "I appointed you a prophet to the nations" (1:5). Paul says that the purpose of his call was that, "I might preach him (the son) to the Gentiles *(ethnesin)*" (Gal. 1:16).
>
> 4. Objection. Jeremiah complains, "I do not know how to speak, for I am only a youth" (1:6). Paul confesses that he persecuted the church (Gal 1:13) — behavior which he says (elsewhere) made him "unfit to be called an apostle" (1 Cor. 15:9).
>
> 5. Reassurance. God comforts Jeremiah, "Be not afraid . . . for I am

---

Studia Theologia 1 (1947): 131-45; John Knox, *Chapters in a Life of Paul,* rev. edition with an intro. by Douglas R. A. Hare (Macon: Mercer Univ. Press, 1987). Knox's original work appeared first in 1950.

8. Stendahl, 78-96.

9. Knox, *Chapters* . . . , 93-106.

10. Stendahl, 7-23.

11. Baird, 656.

with you" (1:8). Paul says that God "called me through grace" (Gal. 1:15) — a grace that works in Paul's ministry despite his unworthiness (1 Cor. 15:10).

6. Sign. According to Jeremiah, "Then the Lord put forth his hand and touched my mouth; and the Lord said to me, Behold, I have put my words in your mouth" (1:9). For Paul, the sign is the revelation of the son (Gal. 1:16) — the revelation through which he receives the gospel (the word; Gal 1:11-12).

On the basis of these data, it can be concluded that Gal. 1:11-17 echoes the main themes of the prophetic call narrative.[12]

Paul and his call to ministry have held a place of great importance in the black church throughout its history. The recent emphasis on the nature and narrative of Paul's call unveils two points that prove instructive for this study. First, Paul's narration of his own call retains remnants of his ethnic background. And second, his narrative is a continuation of an earlier paradigm that has biblical grounding.

The theological concept of calling that focuses on a call to ministry has undergone some significant changes in the history of biblical interpretation. The New Testament knows of no distinctions in the use of the terms for call (kaleo, kalein, klesis, kletos) into ministry (diakonia). All of those called into relationship with God are called into ministry. In fact, even the distinction between clergy and laity as we know it today is articulated neither in the lexical meaning of these terms nor in the New Testament itself. The people of God (laos) are the ministers (diakonos) called (kletos, ekkletos) into ministry (diakonia). Even the term clergy is derived from a Koine term (kleros) that is basically equivalent to another Greek term (laos) that refers in the New Testament to all of the people of God.[13] Thus, the calling (klesis) of God in the New Testament refers to God's calling people out (ekkletos) of the world to be his people (laos); it does not have the official clerical meaning that it is often restricted to today.[14] How did the broader doctrinal understanding of call to ministry for all become relegated to call to the preaching ministry in a very large part of the church today?

I think part of the answer lies in Scripture itself. We observe that different people are called in different ways to different ministries. Some

12. Ibid., 656-57.

13. This connection is echoed in 1 Peter 2:4-10, esp. vv. 9-10.

14. Schmidt says, "The fact that God is the kalon and that Christians are the keklemenoi, with no qualifying addition, makes it clear that in the NT kalein is a technical term for the process of salvation." TDNT, 489.

call stories (e.g., those of Isaiah, Jeremiah, Paul) are given a prominence and emphasis different from those of others who are also called into ministry (e.g., Timothy, Titus, Junia). Furthermore, Paul adds to the difficulty when he argues that there are gifted people whom God gives to the church to function in certain capacities and that the Holy Spirit distributes gifts to people in order that they might fill different specialized ministries.[15] Finally, Scripture contributes to this situation even more when it spotlights certain people that have been called out for ministry going through a ritual — laying on of hands — that is very similar to what we call ordination: a ritual set aside for certain restricted ministries.[16]

Thus, in the history of biblical interpretation the church has wrestled and continues to wrestle with the concept of call in the broad sense found in the New Testament as well as call in the narrow sense observed in the numerous call narratives found throughout the Bible. Frank Stagg, a Southern Baptist New Testament scholar, says, "Beyond the calling common to all of God's people is his special calling of some as attested throughout the Bible, from people like Moses and Huldah to people like Peter and Philip's four daughters."[17] Several observations about Stagg's statement merit highlighting. First, his restrictive sense of calling is quite broad. It is inclusive enough to contain a prophet, prophetess, men, apostles, and prophetesses. Second, the actual Hebrew or Greek term for call is not used in reference to most of these people. Third, all of them are spotlighted because of the prominence of their narratives in the biblical text.

As various parts of the church have wrestled with the biblical understanding of call, this dichotomy between a broad sense of calling and a restrictive sense has remained with us. Indeed, it seems that the very Scripture from which we have derived this dual meaning of call to ministry has complicated the matter. Some of these biblical narratives

15. See particularly Rom. 12, 1 Cor. 12, and Eph. 4.

16. The relevant passages are Acts 6:1-6; 13:1-3; 14:23; 1 Tim. 4:14; 5:22; and 2 Tim. 1:6. See a most penetrating analysis of the biblical basis for this ritual in R. Alan Culpepper, "The Biblical Basis for Ordination," *Review and Expositor* 78 (Fall 1981): 471-84. Cf. Eduard Schweizer, "The Nature of Ministry in Reformed Understanding: New Testament Dimensions," *Horizons in Biblical Theology* 9 (June 1987): 41-63, who argues against the necessity of ordination today. Schweizer also says that there are two biblical models for ministry: the rabbinic and the prophetic; the former required training for legitimization, the latter did not. Schweizer, however, does not deny the importance of education today for those going into ministry.

17. Frank Stagg, "Understanding Call to Ministry," in *Formation for Christian Ministry*, eds. Anne Davis and Wade Rowatt, Jr. (Louisville: Review and Expositor, 1988), 31.

have been emphasized greatly by particular authors of Scripture, often betraying their theological interest and bias. Furthermore, these accounts often include extraordinary events. While these are descriptive accounts, the mysterious nature of their supernatural phenomena has often prompted interpreters in the church's history to take these accounts as prescriptive. Whether the term call is used in the narrative is moot because the reader is left with the impression that there is something unique about this call narrative when compared to others. Mysterious may be the best way of describing it.

> How do we really distinguish between the general calling common to us all and the special calling which comes to only some? The mystery cannot be completely dispelled. For reasons known only to God, he seems to call some to be "ministers" in a sense not common to all his people. Both Bible and continuing experience attest to this. God called Moses in a sense in which he did not call the thousands in Israel, even though all were his people by calling.[18]

Theological Perspectives

The black church is not the only church that has shown an interest in the call to ministry. The importance of the call to the ordained ministry as different from other ministries and vocations has a significant place in the church's history.

John Fostor examines ninety cases of calls to the ministry in what he names the first five Christian centuries.[19] While admitting the difficulty of this endeavor, Foster places the cases into ten categories based on his judgment of the greatest influence on the callee's decision to go into ministry. Some of these categories and cases are of particular interest for this study.

1. *Manifestation or Vision:* Fabian, Bishop of Rome from 236 to 250, and Jerome, the author of the Vulgate, were influenced particularly by a dramatic vision. Fostor's conclusion about this category is as follows: "The most surprising thing about this first category is that it contains only two cases. Both are related to the Bible; indeed the type of experience might be called biblical."[20]

---

18. Stagg, 32.

19. John Foster, "The Call to the Ministry in the First Five Centuries," *London Quarterly and Holborn Review* 179 (1954): 169-80.

20. Ibid., 171.

2. *Boyhood inclinations:* Felix of Nola, Athanasius, Ephraim Syrus, and Martin, Bishop of Tours, showed inclinations for ministry from early childhood. Ephraim's inclination is accompanied by a dream as he lay in his mother's arms.

3. *Simultaneous conversion and call:* Pachomius, Eudoius, Florentinus, Heliodorus, Peter, Tertullian, Arnobius, Cyprian, and Possidius were "converted to the faith and called to the Ministry in one and the same experience."

4. *Influence of a great man.* Some went into the ministry because of the influence of a great person. Irenaeus was influenced by Polycarp; Dionysius of Alexandria and Gregory Thaumatourgos by Origen; Festus by Basil of Caesarea; Paulinus of Nola by the combination of great figures like Martin of Tours, Ambrose of Milan; and Felix of Nola; and Hilarion of Gaza by Antony.

5. *Appeal of the ascetic ideal:* Pamphilus of Ceasarea, Innocent of Jerusalem, Theodore of Tabenna, Epiphanius of Cyprus, and Isidore of Pelusium are but a few of those that went into ministry via the monastic route.

6. *Influence of family and home:* Another category of significance involves those who were influenced by family and home. In most instances they followed a long line of family members who went into ministry. Polycrates, Bishop of Ephesus, was the eighth bishop in his family. Domnus, Bishop of Antioch, was the son of a bishop, as was Aristages, son of Gregory the Illuminator, his father's successor. Isaac, great-great-grandson of Gregory, continued his family's tradition as ruler over the Armenian church. Macedonius, Bishop of Constantinople, followed his uncle into the ministry. A number of these figures, John Chrysostom, Rabbulas, Bishop of Edessa, Peter of Sebaste, and Gregory, Bishop of Nazianzus, were influenced by female figures in their family.

Those that I have highlighted from Foster's study are listed in ascending order of importance. What is interesting about his study is how some factors that influence these callees' decisions for ministry are products of their time (e.g., the monastic life), whereas others cross time barriers (e.g., simultaneous conversion and call, influence of a great person, childhood inclination, and influence of a religious home environment). It will be interesting to observe the extent to which similar factors appear in our contemporary study.

The Protestant church has debated how the call to ministry should be understood and constituted. Various parts of the Protestant church have emphasized different aspects of the call in their denominational history. For example, Luther clearly believed that God with the church calls ministers. In Luther's concept of the "priesthood of all believers" he emphasized the importance of spiritual gifts as the basis of ministry for the entire congregation, not just pastors.[21] Calvin added to the debate by distinguishing between the inner (personal) and outer (congregational) call of ministers. It is beyond doubt that Calvin argued for a decisive role of the congregation in the call of a minister.[22] However, though Calvin was never officially ordained, he had no difficulty accepting the authority of ministry in certain situations on the basis of the certainty of his inner call.

Since that time interdenominational and intradenominational distinctions have emerged regarding the relative importance of the inner and outer call in validating ministry. Certain groups have added their own insights to this debate. For example, the Puritans emphasized the experiential aspect of the call. The Pietists also emphasized the experiential aspect of the call, especially the role of the Holy Spirit in the call.[23]

The emphasis that the Pietists placed on the Holy Spirit can also be observed in the Methodists' emphasis on the Holy Spirit in holiness. As a result they emphasize the importance of "fruits" as the major

21. See particularly Helmut T. Lehmann, gen. ed., *Luther's Works*, 55 vols. (Philadelphia: Muhlenberg Press, 1958), vol. 40: *Church and Ministry*, edited and translated by Conrad Bergendoff, 383-94; and Henry E. Jacobs, *The Book of Concord* (Philadelphia: The Board of Publication of the General Council of the Evangelical Lutheran Church in North America, 1883).

Later interpreters of Luther have differed over how Luther's concept of the call should be understood. Cf., e.g., Martin Chemnitz quoted in David J. Peter, "A Lutheran Perspective on the Inward Call to the Ministry," *Concordia Journal* 12 (July 1986): 121-29; Morris Ashcraft, "Called by God: Affirmed by the Church," in *God-Called Ministry* (Cary, N.C.: The Baptist State Convention of N.C., 1983), 13; Richard Jungkuntz, "Theses Toward a Lutheran Theology of the Call," *Currents in Theology and Mission* 8 (June 1981): 141-45; William F. Arndt, "The Doctrine of the Call into the Holy Ministry," *Concordia Theological Monthly* 25 (May 1954): 337-52; and Waldemar W. Wehmeier, "Calling a Pastor: How it Evolved in the Missouri Synod," *Currents in Theology and Mission* 4 (Oct. 1977): 269-75.

22. See John Calvin, *Institutes of the Christian Religion*, 2 vols., ed. John T. McNeill and trans. by Ford Lewis Battles (London: SCM, 1960): 1055-1166. (Book IV.3.10, 11, 15, 31).

23. See particularly Peter C. Erb, ed., *Pietists: Selected Writings* (New York: Paulist Press, 1983); Philip Jacob Spener, *Pia Desideria*, trans. and edited with an intro. by Theodore G. Tappert (Philadelphia: Fortress, 1964). Williston Walker et al., *A History of the Christian Church*, 4th ed. (New York: Charles Scribner's Sons, 1985), 587 argue that it was the Pietists' turning from scholasticism as a group while emphasizing "the primacy of feeling in Christian experience" and holiness as reflected in the outward life that impacted the shape of American Protestantism.

proof of whether an individual has been called.[24] Baptists also have emphasized the importance of the experiential dimension of the call.[25] Although the Methodists and Baptists clearly have emphasized the importance of the inner call, it is also true that they recognize the importance of the outer call.[26] Thus, in their acknowledgment of the role that both play they are similar to Calvin. The Congregationalists and Presbyterians have also leaned toward Calvin in their acknowledgment of the importance of the inner and outer call. More than the Baptists and Methodists, however, they have emphasized a third element of the call, the role of formal education (training or preparation).[27]

24. Benjamin Lakin (1794-1820), one of the pioneer Methodist circuit riders, records these words in his journal: "I believe that God hath called me to travel and preach the Gospel. . . . My belief is founded on . . . (2) seeing some *fruit* of my labours" (my italics). William W. Sweet, *Religion on the American Frontier, 1783-1840: The Methodists*, vol. IV (Chicago: The Univ. of Chicago Press), 247. See particularly Leslie F. Church, "The Call to Preach in Early Methodism," *London Quarterly & Holborn Review* 179 (1954). Church, 155, records that "fruits" was part of the Methodist's pattern of confirmation because, "The 'fruits' justified the sower in continuing to sow and reap." In addition, Church, 185, records Wesley's reply to a man that doubted Wesley's call to the ministry. "Perhaps you do not [believe that I have a call]. But I do. To me His blessing my work is an abundant proof."

25. See Winthrop S. Hudson, "The Protestant Concept of Motivation for the Ministry," in *Conference on Motivation for the Ministry*, ed. Samuel Southard (Louisville: Southern Baptist Seminary, 1959). Bill J. Leonard, ed., *Early American Christianity* (Nashville: Broadman, 1983), 75 says, that "conversion and call under divine inspiration were the basic criteria for all ordinations among Baptists. Education was less important and sometimes feared as a detriment to 'heart religion.'" Hudson and Leonard state that this reversal to the primacy of the inward call was a reversal from earlier Baptists who held a similar view to Calvin about the call, without specifying when this so-called "reversal" occurred. Thomas R. McKibens, Jr., "The Role of Preaching in Southern Baptist History," *Baptist History and Heritage* 15 (Jan. 1980): 32 says "The suspicion of academia goes back to the uneducated frontier preachers who resented the intellectual preachers from the East."

26. See particularly Sidney E. Mead, "The Rise of the Evangelical Conception of the Ministry in America: 1607-1850," in *The Ministry in Historical Perspectives*, eds. H. Richard Niebuhr and Daniel D. Williams (New York: Harper & Brothers, 1956); H. Richard Niebuhr, *The Purpose of the Church and Its Ministry* (New York: Harper & Row, 1956), 58; Walter B. Shurden, "Documents on the Ministry in Southern Baptist History," *Baptist History and Heritage* 15 (Jan. 1980): 45-54. Shurden examines some rare documents from the period 1808-48 which demonstrate that this view existed up to this period of time at least for some Baptists.

27. Documentation that supports this perspective can be observed in Elwyn Allen Smith, *The Presbyterian Ministry in American Culture: A Study in Changing Concepts, 1700-1900* (Philadelphia: Westminster, 1962); L. E. Cooke, "The Call to the Ministry in the Congregational Church," *London Quarterly & Holborn Review* 179

Therefore, it might be argued that three elements have arisen in Protestant attempts to articulate their understanding of the call to ministry: the inner or personal call, the outer or congregational call, and the role of training in the call.[28] Suffice it to say that the debate continues in the church today, with various emphases upon these three elements among the church's various parts.

Black Religious Experience Perspectives

The black church is part of American Protestantism. Therefore we should expect similar understandings about the concept of call in the black church and other Protestant traditions. The black church in America, at least as a visible institution, came into existence subsequent to other Protestant traditions. Therefore, one might conclude that the origin of the black church's concept of call is located solely in American Protestantism. It might appear that influence has been in one direction — American Christianity's influence on the black church

This idea was given great impetus by Frazier's thesis that African Americans have no continuity with their African heritage and that their

---

(1954): 200-202; and William T. Youngs, Jr., *God's Messengers: Religious Leadership in Colonial New England, 1700-1750* (Baltimore: John Hopkins Univ. Press, 1976).

In contrast to the perspective found in the above sources it should also be observed that in these two groups some have experienced dramatic personal calls like those among the Baptists and Methodists. See, e.g., the following biographies: Garth M. Rosell and Richard A. G. Dupuis, eds., *The Memoirs of Charles G. Finney: The Complete Restored Text* (Grand Rapids: Zondervan, 1989); John Rogers, *The Biography of Elder Barton Warren Stone, Written by Himself* (Cincinnati: J. A. & U. P. James, 1847); and Dwight L. Moody's biography.

28. I use the term "training" because it is broad enough to incorporate formal education as in seminary as well as nonseminary training that might take place, for example, within the denomination. In this sense education was important to all of these groups. See Sidney E. Mead, "The Rise of the Evangelical Conception of the Ministry in America: 1607-1850," in *The Ministry in Historical Perspectives* for documentation that "training" was a part of at least some Baptists' conception of ministry in the latter part of the nineteenth century.

In addition, I use the term "training" as a third element, because it is not clear to me that all groups use it merely as an element to qualify one for the outer call. This makes it merely a subset of the outer call, thereby relegating the discussion to two elements — inner and outer call — with various parts. It may be that for some within Protestantism it is a third element that is used as confirmation of the inner or outer call or both. This then would create three distinct elements in the consideration of the call. Any definitive answer on this matter is beyond the scope of this study.

religious practices are due to influence by American Christianity. "From the available evidence, including what we know of the manner in which the slaves were Christianized and the character of their churches, it is impossible to establish any continuity between African religious practices and the Negro church in the United States. . . . It is our position that it was not what remained of African culture or African religious experience but the Christian religion that provided the new basis of social cohesion."[29]

Examples of continuity between American Protestantism's concept of call and that of the black church abound, but two categories among the Baptists will suffice to make my point.[30] As we discovered in other Protestant traditions, the black church also has emphasized the importance of the "inner call" and religious experience. Frazier explains, "The 'call' was supposed to have come through some religious experience which indicated that God had chosen him as a spiritual leader."[31] Booker T. Washington supports this insight by an observation from his time. Obviously, his description is meant as a negative caricature; it nevertheless demonstrates the primacy of the "inner call" experience among African Americans.

> In the earlier days of freedom almost every coloured man who learned to read would receive "a call to preach" within a few days after he began reading. At my home in West Virginia the process of being called to the ministry was a very interesting one. Usually the call came when the individual was sitting in church. Without warning the one called would fall upon the floor as if struck by a bullet, and would lie there for hours, speechless and motionless. Then the news would spread all through the neighbourhood that this individual had received a "call." If he were inclined to resist the summons, he would fall or be made to fall a second or third time. In the end he always yielded to the call. While I wanted an education badly, I confess that in my youth I had a fear that when I had learned to read and write well I would receive one of these "calls"; but, for some reason, my call never came.[32]

29. E. Franklin Frazier, *The Negro Church in America* (New York: Schocken Books, 1974), 24.

30. For example, in those traditions in which whites (e.g., Methodists and Presbyterians) emphasized education, so did blacks (e.g., AME).

31. Frazier, 24.

32. Booker T. Washington, *Up From Slavery: An Autobiography* (New York: The Sun Dial Press), 82.

The second category observed in the black church is also found among other Protestant traditions — the role of training in the call to ministry. Again, observations from Washington's time are helpful. "The ministry was the profession that suffered most — and still suffers, though there has been great improvement — on account of not only ignorant but in many cases immoral men who claimed that they were 'called to preach. . . .' When we add the number of wholly ignorant men who preached or exhorted to that of those who possessed something of an education, it can be seen at a glance that the supply of ministers was large. In fact, some time ago I knew a certain church that had a total membership of about two hundred, and eighteen of that number were ministers."[33]

Frazier adds: "One qualification which the Negro preacher among the slaves needed to possess was some knowledge of the Bible. However imperfect or distorted his knowledge of the Bible might be, the fact that he was acquainted with the source . . . gave him prestige."[34] Victor Glass, in his 1952 study of more than six hundred Negro Baptist ministers, describes a condition similar to that painted by Washington and Frazier.

> The Negro minister has the title "reverend," which usually carries with it the equal of physician or lawyer. . . . This is an important element in status because there are no long hours of study or large outlay of money paid for this title. He literally jumps full-grown into it. . . . The average Negro minister does not believe that education has anything to do with the call to the ministry. . . . A survey made for this study showed that for 856 churches located in ten Southern states, there were 1,796 ordained ministers. These men are not educated men. Of the 1,796, only forty-four of them have the Bachelor of Divinity degree. Nine hundred seventy-eight of these men have no degree at all.[35]

It may be a bit too quick to suggest, as does Frazier, that the African-American religious experience is wholly dependent upon Amer-

---

33. Ibid.

34. Frazier, 24.

35. Glass, 112, 159-60. Three important studies that offer important statistical data on this matter are as follows: Benjamin E. Mays and Joseph W. Nicholson, *The Negro's Church* (New York: Negro Universities Press, 1933), ch. 3; Harry V. Richardson, *Dark Glory: A Picture of the Church among Negroes in the Rural South* (New York: Friendship Press, 1947), ch. 8; C. Eric Lincoln, "In the Receding Shadow of the Plantation: A Profile of Rural Clergy and Churches in the Black Belt," *Review of Religious Research* 29/4 (June 1988): 349-68.

ican Christianity simply because Frazier was unable to trace it to African religious practices. Frazier is reacting against Herskovits's theory of African religious continuity in America. Though Herskovits claimed too much, he[36] did succeed in demonstrating continuity between African-American religious practices and African religious practices.[37]

Others have argued for an even broader continuity between African-American phenomena and their African heritage. Sterling Stuckey argues the point for folklore;[38] Talley for historical myths;[39] Stepto for slave narratives;[40] Jules-Rosette for conversion experiences;[41] Pitts for Afro-Baptist rituals found in the worship service like hymnody, prayers, trances;[42] and Raboteau in all forms of spirit possessions like shouting, conversion, and call experiences.[43]

I am unaware of any published work which addresses directly either the possibility of a call tradition in African religions or possible continuity between some African precursor or exemplar and the African-American call tradition. However, this does not mean that such a case cannot be made.[44] Although it is beyond the scope of this study to make such a case, certain obvious connections can be observed.

John Mbiti argues persuasively that the cultural traditions of Africans linger on — especially things like emotions, beliefs, and thinking patterns — even under the most rapid change.[45] We observed above

36. Melville J. Herskovits, *The Myth of the Negro Past* (Boston: Beacon Press, 1958).

37. See Albert J. Raboteau, *Slave Religion: The "Invisible Institution" in the Antebellum South* (New York: Oxford Univ. Press, 1978), 48ff., for an excellent critique of Herskovits's thesis.

38. Sterling Stuckey, "Through the Prism of Folklore: The Black Ethos in Slavery," *Massachusetts Review* 9 (1968): 417-37.

39. Thomas W. Talley, "The Origin of Negro Traditions." *Phylon* 4 (1943): 30-38.

40. Robert B. Stepto, "I Rose and Found My Voice: Narration, Authentication, and Authorial Control in Four Slave Narratives."

41. Bennetta Jules-Rosette, "The Conversion Experience: The Apostles of John Maranke," *Journal of Religion in Africa* 7 (1976): 132-64.

42. Walter Pitts, " 'If you caint get the boat, take a log': cultural reinterpretation in the Afro-Baptist ritual." *American Ethnologist* 16/2 (1989): 279-93.

43. Raboteau. See also Henry H. Mitchell, *Black Belief: Folk Beliefs of Blacks in America and West Africa* (New York: Harper & Row, 1975), who argues this point for the entire black religious experience.

44. In addition to my own research on this matter, I have spoken to no scholar familiar with this area of research that is aware of any work that has been done from this perspective. However, they all express the belief that such a connection can be made.

45. John S. Mbiti, *African Religions and Philosophies* (New York: Doubleday, 1970).

some phenomena in which continuity is established.[46] If we shift our conceptual language to a different set of terms, then the connections are not difficult. The anthropological concept of a shaman (diviner, medium) who is a religious specialist that receives a divine call from a deity, often accompanied by spirit possession, is as common in African life[47] as in Jewish life. This connection is made extremely well by Martin Buss.

> For instance (as is well known in anthropological circles), many parallels obtain between Israelite and African life. . . . Most African-Israelite parallels, however, quite likely reflect the operation of both historical connection and sociological conditioning. . . . A call summons a person to a specialized role. . . . As a society grows, normally the first emerging specialty (the practitioner of which can be called a shaman) is one that combines the performance of curing and other rituals with the giving of advice on the basis of a special relationship with normally unseen realities. . . .[48] Frequently, the role of a comprehensive religious specialist is believed to be assigned by one or more spirits through dreams, protracted illness, or special experiences of some kind. At the same time family connections are important, in that a new shaman is quite commonly chosen from among the relatives of an older one. . . . In practice, a personal call received by a shaman or a medium often also needs to be recognized as such by an established diviner, and a period of apprenticeship commonly follows. . . . A call by a deity or spirit commonly summons the recipient to a lifetime of special service; that is true especially if selection occurs already at, or before, birth.[49]

46. See also "The National Office for Black Catholics and The Liturgical Conference," *This Far by Faith: American Black Worship and Its African Roots* (Washington: The Liturgical Conference, 1977), especially Henry H. Mitchell, "The Continuity of African Culture," and Clarence Jos. Rivers, "The Oral African Tradition Versus the Ocular Western Tradition."

47. See detailed examples of this concept in Audrey Butt, *The Nilotes of the Sudan and Uganda* (London: International African Institute, 1952); and Karl Eric Knutsson, *Authority and Change: A Study of the Kallu Institution among the Macha Galla of Ethiopia* (Göteborg, Sweden: Elanders Boktryckera Aktiebolag, 1967).

48. Martin J. Buss, "An Anthropological Perspective Upon Prophetic Call Narratives," *Semeia* 21 (1981): 18 n. 4, says that the role of shaman is the oldest specialization. "For instance, the shaman is the only prominent specialist of any kind among Eskimos . . . and the only one among many South-American tribes. . . . Since no other useful term is available, the word 'shaman' will here be used to designate a religious specialist with a quite comprehensive task. . . ."

49. Ibid., 10-13.

We have seen that a possible exemplar to an African-American minister that receives a call is an African shaman who receives a call, and that spirit possession may accompany these call experiences. In addition, we have observed that Raboteau argues persuasively that spirit possession is a specific phenomena that demonstrates continuity between the African-American religious experience and its African heritage.

One last connection needs to be made; the connection between conversion experiences and call experiences. Of particular note is the research of Bennetta Jules-Rosette on an indigenous African church, "independent of mission aegis." She says:

> Conversion was presented to me as a struggle rather than a gift or act of grace. . . . This simultaneous clarity and incommunicability of experience is considered by Apostles to characterize a "true" conversion of the heart. . . . conversion appears to be a powerful clash resulting from the shift from one realm of thought and action to another, a moment of specific shock. . . . Apostles stress that acceptance must be witnessed as an individual experience. New members give accounts of personal visions and prophecies that signaled a change of life for them. . . . Acceptance includes rejection of "the ways of the world" through strict tabus, fasting, prayer and song. Every aspect of the convert's behaviour is scrutinized with respect to the requirements of holiness.[50]

Jules-Rosette describes conversion experiences that are without question similar to the conversion experiences described among African-Americans in Charles Johnson's work. Referring to his collection of pre–Civil War and post–Civil War narratives, Johnson says:

> A conversion experience — whether it be in religious or other form — is marked by a sudden and a striking 'change of heart,' with an abrupt change in the orientation of attitudes and beliefs. It is accompanied by what can be described as an 'emotional regeneration, typically sudden in its advent and consummation.' Conversion thus affects radically one's outlook toward life and one's conception of oneself.[51]

50. Jules-Rosette, 134-35.

51. Charles S. Johnson, ed., *God Struck Me Dead*, xvii. Glass, 117-18, 124-25, draws this conclusion from his study of "call" narratives: "One or more of the following factors should accompany a valid call. It should be cataclysmic, supernatural, emotional. . . . These phenomena usually follow a definite pattern of 'vi-

There is another interesting feature about Johnson's work that has not been emphasized. What is striking about Johnson's collection of "conversion" narratives is that many of the people assert in the narrative that their call experience occurred simultaneously with their "conversion" experience. Glass misses this important connection in his study when he concludes that many an informant "frequently confuses the call with a conversion experience. . . . Those who wrote articles on the call seemed to equate a conversion experience with the call."[52]

The narrators in the studies by Johnson and Glass are not confused. They are merely relating their retrospective experiences as requested. It is the analysts that have missed the potential significance of the association. This is no small matter. If African-American conversion narratives can be definitively linked with call narratives, then another possible trajectory through which to trace the African-American call narrative back to Africa emerges.

Mechal Sobel addresses the subject of religious influence between African Americans and American Protestantism from an Afro-Baptist perspective. Sobel looks at similar religious experiences found among black and white Baptists and writes as follows: "Critics who maintain that all of the black Christian's practices can be traced to white Christianity are in error. They overlook the fact that blacks influenced white culture in significant ways.[53] They err further in that a great deal of the content of black Christianity is not shared by whites."[54]

---

sions and dreams, seasons of unrest, and giving up to God. . . .' Every one is expected to validate his call by some such experience. . . . Young men are advised by some pastors to wait until they see or hear something." Of course, this has precedence from the time of slavery and perhaps is traceable back to the slaves' African heritage. Lawrence W. Levine, *Black Culture and Black Consciousness: Afro-American Folk Thought from Slavery to Freedom* (Oxford: Oxford Univ. Press, 1977), 36, quotes an ex-slave who is speaking about her conversion experience: "We must see, feel and hear something . . . for our God talks to his children."

52. Glass, 118-19.

53. Mechal Sobel, *Trabelin' On: The Slave Journey to an Afro-Baptist Faith,* 98. Regarding an 1819 work describing a revival, Raboteau, 67, writes, "Besides shedding some light on 'the original religious songs of blacks — as distinguished from the standard Protestant hymns that they sang — ' the account above is significant because it tends to support the argument that black patterns of behavior influenced white revivalists at the camp meetings."

Additionally Sobel, 98, writes, "Blacks began to participate in revivals in the South at a very early date and no doubt influenced the emerging so-called white patterns."

54. Sobel, 98. Examples of these differences according to Sobel are visions and dreams in religious conversion experiences, 98-122.

Glass, 165, argues similarly. He writes, "The hearing of voices does not rank

Little doubt should remain today that continuity exists between the African-American religious experience and African religions. What is much more complex and difficult to assess is the degree and direction of influence between the African-American religious experience and American Protestantism.[55] A detailed focus on this matter is beyond the scope of this study and perhaps beyond our ability to uncover. It is necessary, however, to place this study in that overall historical context. Some scholars have argued for the thesis of mutual influence.[56] In particular we may not improve greatly upon the balanced syncretism thesis of Raboteau.

> Perhaps the religious heritage of American Protestants and the African religious background were not completely antithetical. . . . Elements of African behavior and belief could have been modified by contact with European culture and could have merged with it in a new syncretistic form. Conversely, European traits could have been shaped and reinterpreted by the slaves in the light of their African past. On the other hand, the similarity of some traits may make it very difficult or even impossible to separate what is African from what is European in origin; on the other hand, this very commonality might have served to reinforce certain African elements while others withered under severe prohibition and attack. That some elements of African religion survived in the United States not as separate enclaves free of white influence but as aspects hidden under or blended with similar European forms is a thesis worth considering in more detail, especially since there are strong arguments for its validity in the areas of music, folklore, and language.[57]

In the introduction we raised a question about the extent to which the callee's use of the narrative to legitimate his or her claim to be an instrument of God has prior theological and cultural traditions to which

---

as high as dreams and visions, but it is a significant factor in the call of Negro Baptist ministers. . . . Negro ministers are markedly different from white ministers with respect to voices, dreams, and visions. In three separate studies of white ministers, these phenomena had very little place; in fact, in a study of 1,704 white ministerial students, these subjects were not mentioned at all as factors contributing to the call."

55. Witness, however, Glass's completely different interpretation of similar phenomena in white and black call experiences in American Protestantism. He traces the phenomena in the black experiences not to white American Protestantism, but to the sociological and psychological circumstances of African Americans in America. See parts II, III, and IV.

56. For example, Mitchell and Sobel.

57. Raboteau, 58-59.

it can be associated. This chapter answers that question in the affirmative. First, this use of narrative is deeply rooted in the Judeo-Christian biblical tradition — to which all of these denominations appeal theologically — traceable to Old Testament prophets such as Moses, Jeremiah, Isaiah, and Ezekiel and the New Testament apostles, especially as seen in the call narratives of Paul. Second, we observed that this narrative approach continued in American Protestantism as a result of the theological positions held about the call. Although denominations differ in the amount of emphasis they place on the "inner call" (personal), how it should be validated vis-a-vis the "outer call" (congregational), and the role of training in the call, it is noteworthy that all Protestant denominations accept the inner call as a key component. This is crucial because the callee rests his or her claim to be an instrument of God primarily on the "inner call." Finally, we observed a cultural link between African traditional religions and the black church's easy acceptance of call narratives for purposes of legitimation. This is traceable to two events in African traditional religions: the shaman stories of divine call to leadership roles and conversion stories of divine change, both of which are usually accompanied by spirit possession and subsequently articulated, orally, to legitimate the callee's new status.

PART VI

THE CALL AS HERMENEUTICS
AND MINISTRY

CHAPTER 12

Betwixt and Between: Rethinking Call to Ministry — Call, Called, and Calling

However, as the years have passed on, I have learned and as I pursued the New Testament in a far deeper sense, I articulate my calling in a little different fashion since that particular event. First of all, I think the whole issue of the call has been misunderstood not only by blacks, but it's been misunderstood by white people also. In a broad sense, in the New Testament there is no such thing as "the call to preach" as we have articulated. Everybody is called to preach in a New Testament sense, and the call to preach is inseparable and cannot be extricated from the call to salvation. When I'm called to salvation, I'm also called to preach in the sense of spreading the word. What we have confused with a call to preach is the cultural phenomenon of sermonizing. Sermonizing is not biblical, sermonizing is cultural. . . . Therefore, usually we would say that in my case, prior to really coming to grips with this, I was saved in 1953 and I was called to preach in 1966. I personally articulate it in this fashion now. I was saved in 1953 and I was called to preach in the New Testament sense in 1953; but I received a special anointing in 1966 to be a pastor-teacher, upon which I later would go on and receive training for the gift that God had given me in this particular area.[1]

Mack King Carter
Mt. Olive Baptist Church
Ft. Lauderdale, Fla.

1. Myers, 72-73.

217

But, see, one of the things about asking about your calling, you still haven't asked is "Called to what?" You know, you are assuming that it's preaching. And I think that one of the things that especially women bring to this new movement of the ministry is that we are reinterpreting what it means to be in the ministry. We are reinterpreting ministry. . . . I think that our presence in the ministry forces the church, forces us, forces our colleagues to have to rethink ministry, rethink gifts, rethink the notion that in the black church only the preaching ministry is the ordained ministry in our churches. That needs to be seriously rethought, because many of us come with all kinds of other gifts, whether it's gifts in administration, and some of the men do too. I would hope that our presence even opens doors for them to be able to exercise other kinds of gifts and really give thought to developing other kind of gifts. . . . I know that I was called to the ministry ten years ago but I think now, ten years later, I would say that it wasn't just the preaching ministry. . . . Ten years ago I might have articulated it as the preaching ministry, because I didn't know anything else.[2]

Renita Weems
Vanderbilt Divinity School
Nashville, Tenn.

Black churches are betwixt and between, caught in a liminal state, on the hermeneutical issue of questioning the call. For some it is blasphemous to even consider testing or challenging a claimant's call. The caricature drawn by Booker T. Washington about those called to preach in his day, though obviously an exaggeration, should not be scoffed at so easily.[3] We are still plagued in many of our churches with the notion that all one needs to do is wake up one morning and say, "God called me to preach," and it should be accepted without having to undergo any rigorous testing of that claim. The complexities of our world in this technological computer age, and especially the plight of the masses of African Americans, the poor, and the disenfranchised, demand that we take more seriously the testing of any claim to be called by God.

2. Myers, 342.
3. See 205 n. 32.

The key questions that emerge in this debate are: Who does the calling? How is the call to be certified? What is the claimant called to do? These questions turn the spotlight on this very difficult matter that needs to be addressed anew in black churches in light of the problems that African Americans face in this country today. The black church finds itself trapped betwixt and between the desire to hold onto long-standing hermeneutical traditions in this debate on the one hand, and the reality, on the other hand, that if the church doesn't make some important ministerial adjustments it will no longer be relevant to the very people that the church has been called to serve; this is especially the case with our younger generations today. They do not see the institutional church as relevant to the pressures and problems that they face daily.

The difficulty can be best understood by looking at how these churches have responded to the three questions raised earlier: Who does the calling? How is the call to be certified? What is the claimant called to do?

Call and Called — Who Does the Calling?

Either in their written disciplines or oral traditions black churches, as with other Protestant traditions, place great emphasis on the inner call (personal) issued by God, not humankind. It is not unusual to hear black clergy, either as an apology or description of their call, appeal to biblical rhetoric similar to that of Paul to the Galatians, "For I did not receive it from a human source, nor was I taught it, but I received it through a revelation of Jesus Christ" (1:12). Indeed, this may be one of the important differences in how black churches view the call as a vocation when compared to other secular vocations. Whereas one may choose — for economic or other reasons — other secular vocations, one is chosen for the ministry. Moreover, the call of God is ultimately an irresistible call.

Although this inner call is a prevalent part of the retrospective interpretation of the call observed in oral call stories of black clergy, it is but one aspect of the understanding of call. Whereas all will acknowledge in one sense that only God calls, they will also acknowledge that one is called by a congregation (outer call) of believers. We observed this in the sanctioning stage of the call while analyzing the content of these stories. All callees went to the church for confirmation and validation of their call. Not only does the church perform the ritual of ordination and have the power to move one through the rites-of-passage portals, but unless one is called by a congregation of believers as well, it is often very difficult to get anyone to believe that one has indeed received a call from God.

Although many callees' interpretations suggest that theirs is a call only from God, the juxtaposition of story to narrative in this study gives a different view. Irrespective of the type of call, how cataclysmic and phenomenologically laden some stories are, or how convinced these callees are that they have heard the voice of God, all of them seek confirmation and validation from the church.

Therefore, we can argue that the outer call (congregational) is as important as the inner call (personal). Furthermore, our juxtaposition suggests that the church has the right, indeed the responsibility to test any purported call from God. We observed earlier that the black church as well as other Protestant churches have wrestled for centuries with the relative importance of each of these calls. However, the very fact that these callees could not reach ultimate fulfillment in their call until they moved into the orbit of the congregation's call accentuates the importance of this aspect of the call.

This tension is reminiscent of that which we see in the life and writings of Paul to selected congregations of believers, but perhaps also in his self-understanding of call. He makes what at first glance appear to be two irreconcilable arguments in his rhetoric to the Galatians. Initially, he seems to argue that he neither sought nor needed the church's sanctioning of his call (1:11-24) and just as quickly acknowledges that he both sought it, needed it, and received it (2:1-2). Interestingly both assertions are attributed to revelations from God. Scholars through the ages have wrestled with the many apparent conflicts of Paul's statements within these first two chapters of the Galatian epistle as well as their conflicts with Luke's assertions in Acts. They have resolved the conflicts in a variety of ways.

Perhaps an additional way to resolve this conflict of statements is to suggest that like the callees we have observed, Paul had to wrestle with his own self-understanding of call. What we have are interpretations and reinterpretations of that event. Whereas at one given moment he articulates that the call is only of God, at other times he is made painfully aware of the fact that congregations of believers are a part of the process. He may grudgingly yield to the latter, but yield he does. In so doing he both gives and acknowledges the church's right to test not only the content of his message, but the call of God itself. The answer to the question, "Who does the calling?" is both God and the church.

Calling — Called to Do What and Who Certifies It?

The black church needs to address these questions anew along with the two concerns they highlight: the interpretation of what one is called to do and the education necessary to do it. We observed earlier how the personal call and congregational call have been a part of black churches' understanding of the call. However, in far too many of our churches the concept of a "call" has been restricted solely to "the call to preach."

There is a need for us to rethink the interpretation of call and the education necessary to carry it out in our churches, as the Carter and Weems quotations that open this chapter suggest. Carter draws attention to the issue of training when he makes a distinction between his "call to preach," which he believes everyone is called to do and his call ("special anointing") to pastor. He connects his specific calling to the need for specific training to perform his ministry: "I was saved in 1953 and I was called to preach in the New Testament sense in 1953; but I received a special anointing in 1966 to be a pastor-teacher, upon which I later would go on and receive training for the gift that God had given me in this particular area."

When someone says that they have been called, the church should ask, "Called to do what and what is the training necessary to perform that particular ministry?" The more specific our understanding of the call, the more specific should be our demands for its training. Certainly one whom God calls and gifts to be a pastor-teacher, and whom the church calls to be pastor, needs a different kind of training than that of a minister of music or counseling.

Black churches approach this matter in a variety of ways. Some of our churches, especially those who are minorities in predominantly white denominations, require the seminary degree (e.g., master of divinity) as the specific training necessary for ordination and performance of the pastoral ministry. Others combine some seminary training or degree with denominational training. Still others require no seminary or academic training at all. Thus, the idea that all people acknowledging a call to ministry need training suited for a specific call requires more attention in our churches.

The mixed feelings about training in many of our black churches is exacerbated by a confusion over the call itself, especially what one is called to do. Weems's question and assertion, "Called to what? You know, you are assuming that it's preaching" puts the spotlight on this problem. Indeed, the assumption — this confusion, as Carter calls it — from the time that the call is uttered is that a call from God is a call to preach. This not only creates a problem of testing and training, but it creates an even greater problem of ministry. What ministry will these people be certified to perform? For example, Weems and others, though gifted preachers, have acknowledged as well as demonstrated gifts and training necessary for a teaching and writing ministry.[4] In some instances callees even acknowledge dual ministerial interest with a preference for ministry other than the preaching ministry. Weems is very direct about this matter:

> And there are days when I wonder, do I enjoy preaching more than I enjoy writing? It's a toss-up. It's a toss-up for me. I know that that may be rather scandalous language in the black church, in the black tradition; and that's probably because for us preaching is only an oral event. I don't just think it is just an oral event, not if you are a good writer, it doesn't have to be. . . . although the carnal woman in me enjoys the preaching moment as much as anyone else, the other woman in me — and I pray it's the spirit woman in me — prefers the written sermon or written word or written essay, article, whatever.[5]

Scandalous? Blasphemous is better. Unfortunately, there are corners in the black church where, had Weems or any of those similar in mind articulated this retrospective reinterpretation of their call during their initial articulation, they would not have been ordained or certified.

The impact of this confusion on ministers is enormous. Ministers find themselves in an identity crisis. Do I deny my call or deny my ministry? If God has called and gifted me to work with youth, both in desire and results, but my church only understands and accepts a call to ministry in terms of a call to preach, how should I articulate my call to the church? What about those with similar gifts and callings in the area of teaching or counseling? Are a professor in the guild and a pastor in the church the only acceptable options for the former, called to teach, and para-church groups for the latter, called to counsel? Must all of these callings be reduced to, interpreted, and articulated as calls to preach in order for these people to preach, be certified, and ordained? What if preaching is not high on their list of preferences, especially in view of how they interpret their call?

4. See in Myers, e.g., the following stories: McMickle (Baptist), Felder (UM), Carpenter (Disciples), and Hoyt (CME). Hoyt, Carpenter, and Felder are examples of preachers whose primary area of ministry is the academy, whereas McMickle's primary area of ministry is pastoral, though he also teaches preaching as well as other courses in the academy.

5. Ibid., 343-44. Cf. also the McMickle, Hoyt, and Felder narratives.

The impact of this identity crisis on ministry is just as enormous. While black children are dying in the streets, a gifted youth minister may be sitting in the pulpit waiting for his turn to preach; or perhaps he or she is sitting in the pew trying to determine how best to articulate a call to work with youth without naming it a call to preach. In addition, there are those gifted and skilled legal, financial, medical, and administrative people who feel called to a new and different kind of ministry, but either have been forced to articulate it as a call to preach or haven't articulated it at all because they don't understand it in that way.

How do we get out of this confused labyrinth that we have created for ourselves through centuries of tradition about what it means to be called to preach? The stories in this collection are not just accounts of past experiences, they are retrospective accounts. They are part story, narrative, and hermeneutics. Like the Gospels they are a combination of historical events wrapped in theological and hermeneutical rhetoric.

Sometimes, because of our interest in the story (what happened), we forget that it is also narrative (how it is told) and hermeneutics (how the narrator interprets the story). The fact that it is a historical event, retrospectively interpreted, should alert us to the need to continue our hermeneutical exploration for a better way to both understand and articulate this phenomenon known as call in our time.

Therefore, we should be open to rethinking the idea of call. A good starting place would be to wrestle anew with our hermeneutical understanding of call to ministry over against call to preach. The reductionism that takes place with these two very different concepts is a large part of the problem. The Carter and Weems stories are especially helpful in this regard.

The first matter we must address is what we mean by a "call to preach." If Carter is correct — and I believe he offers an angle on the truth that should be explored — in his assertion that we confuse preaching with sermonizing and that everyone in a New Testament sense is called to preach, then we certainly need to rethink our use of this very reductionistic phrase.

A couple of New Testament examples will broaden the dialogue. Deacons in certain black denominations are not allowed to preach because they haven't been "called to preach." It is ironic, then, that the communities holding this position usually hold the view that the seven in chapter 6 of Acts are the first deacons. It is irrefutable that at least two of the seven, Philip and Stephen, are described as preaching in chapters 7 and 8. Furthermore, when the scattering of the church takes place (Acts 8:1-4), Luke records that all went about proclaiming the word, except the apostles. Even if one could argue successfully some type of apostolic succession to the modern preacher, based on these texts alone — to say nothing about numerous others — it is difficult to argue from a New Testament perspective that those who preached in the first-century church are restricted to the types of those who are allowed to preach today.

Carter is also insightful when he distinguishes between sermonizing and preaching. Gerald Davis, as suggested in the introduction, has demonstrated persuasively that the African-American sermon is performed art that can be seen as a genre in its own right.[6] He does so primarily by describing its form and structure. This does not necessarily say anything about the content of the sermonizing. Hence, to say someone preached may refer to content; as with the various people referred to in the New Testament who proclaimed the word of God. And yet it may refer only to form — as with the genre of the African-American performed sermon.

A third point to consider further is Carter's distinction between his call to preach and his call to be a pastor-teacher. Although like most people who initially articulate a call to preach he reduces both ideas to one, his later retrospective reinterpretation makes a clear distinction between the call to preach, which everyone receives, and the call to be a pastor-teacher, which further distinguishes between the functions of those called to preach.

It is precisely at this point that Weems's perspective broadens to fit neatly with that of Carter's. Weems wants us to rethink and reinterpret not just our understanding of the call to preach, but our understanding of the call to ministry. She argues that the variety of gifts present among those entering the ministry in our time, especially the gifts of women, should be cause enough for us to rethink our understanding of call to ministry. She refers specifically to second-career people like teachers, nurses, and others. Furthermore, she asserts that strong abilities in preaching and/or pastoring are not enough reason to relegate these callees to roles that satisfy the way we have understood call. This is a very important insight because Carter's shift from call to preach as the defining term to pastor-teacher is a concrete shift also in ministry. Preaching is but one possible ministerial activity; it certainly is but one possible function and responsibility of a pastor-teacher. For some it is the defining activity for the role of pastor-teacher; others would argue with that point. Nonetheless, few who fill

6. See 1 n. 1.

this job would deny that many other responsibilities claim their time, even if they try to argue theologically that only preaching should do so. Moreover, the pastor-teacher is not the only person functioning ministerially in the church that preaches in addition to performing other duties.

Weems further broadens Carter's insight when she argues that we need to "rethink the notion that in the black church only the preaching ministry is the ordained ministry in our churches."[7] This certainly would be revolutionary for the black church, focusing the discussion where it needs to be, on the call to ministry, not just an elusive call to preach. Gifts, skills, desire, commitment, and fitness for specific ministry can be tested, and individuals can be academically and ministerially prepared.

What, then, constitutes a ministry deserving of ordination? It is beyond the scope of this book to deal with all of the complexities of this hotly debated question in the church's history. However, we need to ask whether a person who hears the call of God to minister to youth, is uniquely gifted by God to do so, goes to seminary without ecclesiastical help to get adequate training, spends all of his or her time in the street with youth learning how to minister to them, and neither wants to preach in the traditional sense of the term nor wants to articulate his or her call as a call to preach should be ordained as one called to ministry.

Why not? In light of the problems African Americans face, shouldn't we focus more on calls to ministry that are relevant to the needs of our people? Shouldn't the times, cultural conditions and circumstances, and the new faces that are making themselves available and the different kind of gifts they bring to the table cause us to think about what God may be doing in our time? Shouldn't this make us rethink our understanding of call?

Never in the history of our churches have so many women attended seminary and directly or indirectly articulated a call to ministry in our churches. Weems argues that "one of the things that especially women bring to this new movement of the ministry is that we are reinterpreting what it means to be in the ministry. We are reinterpreting ministry. . . . I think that our presence in the ministry forces the church, forces us, forces our colleagues to have to rethink ministry. . . ."[8]

7. Ibid., 342.
8. Ibid.

Without question the entrance of women into the discussion of call to ministry, especially in untraditional roles such as pastor, has forced many to rethink their understanding of call to ministry. We turn now to a broader discussion of that issue.

CHAPTER 13

Betwixt and Between: Women, the Black Church, and the Call to Ministry

Now please allow me to share a personal experience of related existential estrangement and ontological assault. Philadelphia is my home town. Every spring there is a great revival in town and the nationally prominent revivalist comes to preach. The church is at least half full of preachers. For a few years, I attended that revival desiring to find medicine for my own needy soul. It was the practice of an assistant pastor to very specifically welcome what he called the ministerium strimium reverends. He asked all those to stand. Then, the revivalist came out and thanked God for . . . the presence of all the brother preachers; and, then invited all the brother preachers to stand. Sitting in the pew, I was immediately confronted with a crisis of identity. Which do I own, my call or my gender? Do I sit and deny this call, this claim of God on my life decreed by God before I was formed in the womb? Do I sit and now again, another time add to my own history of shame, for the years I tried to do everything else but answer this call? Or do I stand and deny my gender? A preacher I am, a brother I am not. I finally resolved the violent conflict by standing. Because, when I stood I stood as I am. I stood in the total authenticity of my being — black, preacher, Baptist, woman. For the same God who made me a preacher is the same God who made me a woman. And, I am convinced that God was not confused on either count.[1]

Prathia Hall Wynn
United Theological Seminary
Dayton, Ohio

Wynn's dilemma is an excellent example of the black church's liminality over the role of women in certain ministerial positions in the church. Like other communities of faith, both Catholic and Protestant, black churches are betwixt and between on this issue. They are divided; this is the case if one compares local congregations, ministerial councils or associations, state or national conventions. Few theological issues in our time engender more acrimony and discord than this issue in the black church. Some pastors have been put out of ministerial councils; other pastors and congregations have broken or strained fellowship with churches that ordain women and especially if these women seek a seat in the pulpit. Some pastors deny a woman access to their pulpits irrespective of her credentials, ordination, or fellow sponsor. And yet I'm not aware of any ministerial council that has put a brother out of the council or voted to close its membership to any brother because of his *theological position* on abortion or inerrancy, though numerous ecclesiastical bodies in the black religious community have taken different positions on doctrinal issues like these, as well as others.

The difficulty with this issue of women's roles is that, like many others (e.g., slavery, war, abortion, inerrancy), it is adversely determined in the name of God and Scripture, and who wants to be against God and Scripture? There are some who launch this debate from other points of departure, but for the most part the few published pieces and the numerous oral debates at religious gatherings that have addressed it take Scripture as their starting point.[2]

The obvious conclusion is that this is an exegetical matter irrespective of anyone who tries to make it a sociological, economic, or theological one. It is an issue that must start with and be settled in Scripture. The articles and books from other, nonblack communities of

---

1. Prathia Hall Wynn, "Becoming Sisters and Brothers in Struggle," lecture at Kelly Miller Smith Institute, Vanderbilt University Divinity School Conference, "What Does It Mean To Be Black and Christian?" October 1991.

2. See, e.g., Ella Mitchell's edited works, *Those Preachin' Women*, vols. 1 and 2 (Valley Forge: Judson Press, 1985) and *Women: To Preach or Not to Preach* (Valley Forge: Judson Press, 1991), all three collections of sermons that support in different ways women as preachers. As sermons, however, their point of departure is Scripture also.

faith that have made exegesis of critical passages the battleground for settling this issue are vast indeed.

In this chapter, however, I want to offer another perspective by reversing the hermeneutical point of departure for the discussion. Many have believed that issues like these can be resolved strictly on the basis of exegesis. However, a quick glance at the amount of published material, the number and credentials of scholars, as well as the piety of many on both sides of the issue should cause us to conclude that on exegetical grounds alone we are at an impasse at best. This is not to say that the exegetical debate and dialogue should cease; rather, it is to acknowledge that fewer people than we wish to admit have changed their positions on the issue because of an opponent's exegesis.

From a hermeneutical perspective the stories in this corpus raise questions about whether Scripture is the appropriate starting point for this debate. If it is, then based on the exegesis of their day our ancestors during slavery and shortly thereafter may have never accepted calls to ministry. Many couldn't read these Scriptures and the power of exegesis lay in the hands of others.

What is self-evident in the stories on which this study is based is that all of the narrators, male and female, ultimately accepted a call to ministry not because of someone's polished exegetical apologia on their behalf; on the contrary, they became convinced of its authenticity because of a process that focused primarily on a personal (inner call) divine-human encounter as well as a corporate (congregational call) human-human encounter among a community of believers.

In fact, this is the way all calls occur, those in Scripture as well as those outside of Scripture. Paul, to use but one of the many examples in Scripture, accepts his call because of a process that includes a personal encounter with the divine — in his case the resurrected Jesus — on the Damascus road and a corporate encounter with divinely designated individuals in a specific community of believers in Damascus. Later, other communities of faith, namely the Antiochene and Jerusalem church, become a part of the confirmation process. Only much, much later does the place of Scripture in all of this emerge.

Such is the case with the calls of this collection. The process involves an encounter with the divine; this may be internal, external, or both, cataclysmic or noncataclysmic, and may be to a willing or unwilling callee. Ultimately the callee goes to people in the community of faith to tell the story and gain clarity, advice, support, confirmation, and legitimation. A specific congregation and pastor are crucial at this point. A period of preparation and apprenticeship will begin, leading to the final rites of passage when a group of already ordained believers gather for the ritual of ordination.

What is intriguing about this process — a process that we observe both in these stories and in actual black churches today — is that Scripture is not usually invoked until the process is nearly complete — that is, ordination. More basically, Scripture is not the point of departure for assessing the authenticity of the call. What the individual has to say about self-authenticating aspects of the existential encounter with the divine, what the corporate body has to say about its experiential encounter with the callee, as well as how it assesses the callee's story — these together make up the point of departure. Indeed, each of these components is central to confirmation and ordination, and without them the process is truncated.

In every aspect of the story similarities occur between the stories of women and men. Like the men, women were influenced in the ministerial direction because of early religious exposure. One interesting aspect of this early exposure is how pervasive women are in influencing male callees toward ministry. Rarely is there a man in this corpus that does not attribute his religious interest either partially or wholly to some female figure. Some of these women are viewed as resident theologians and religious leaders, sometimes challenging the restraints of their time.

As this study has demonstrated, there are female call stories of all three types. Though some obvious differences emerge in the struggle of women, there are numerous similarities with men as well. Women struggle with whether they are worthy to be called, whether they want to give up certain freedoms or more preferable careers, and with families that think they can do better. They also resist the call for some of the same reasons as do men. Like some men, for example, women resist because they do not see adequate role models in ministry.

The search of the woman is essentially the same as that of the man. She wants someone to insure her sanity, someone to help her interpret the events and feelings, someone to help move her through the liminal state. In addition, women and men go to the same kinds of people for support: family, friends, pastor, and the community of believers.

Women receive sanctions in ways similar to men: people and events. Family members, pastors, and believers in the community are key.

The surrender to the call by women brings about the same kind of feelings as felt by men: a heavy burden lifted, peace, fulfillment. It occurs in similar ways and places: at the point of saying yes or after preaching the trial sermon.

There can be no doubt that the structure of women's stories as narratives are designed to do the same thing as those of men — to persuade the hearer of the authenticity of their call.

The major difference in the stories of women centers around the matter of gender. Although some men state that they did not have adequate role models, this refers to type of ministry. In the case of women this usually refers to gender or forbidden roles (e.g., pastor). Some men state that they encountered resistance from family, friends, pastors, and others. However, this usually deals with economics, ex- pectations, age, or some other factor, never gender. In addition to these same kinds of resistances, women encountered resistance from family, friends, parishioners, peers, and pastors strictly because of their gender. Moreover, included in the sanctioning of women was, on occasion, an acceptance of their gender as well.

The one structural difference in the women's narratives when compared with men's is the amount of space devoted to gender dis- cussion.

In light of these similarities and differences as well as the past and present value placed on the personal and corporate call story in black churches, we must rethink call to ministry and the place of call stories in this process. For example, if call stories are the starting point and key data for confirmation of men, why not for women? If one factor (i.e., gender) can negate the value of call stories, why not other factors (e.g., lack of seminary training)? Does not the negation of call stories on the basis of gender undermine the value of call stories in the black church for all? If the form and content of male call stories are to be treated as essential in the call process, what does this mean for female call stories that are essentially the same as those of males?

Since Scripture ultimately does enter the picture, though far later than we have conceded heretofore, two passages not usually invoked should be considered. One argument that circulates among male preachers for accepting men in the ministry even when there is some doubt about their call is that if God did call a man, they don't want to put anything in his way. I've often wondered why the same reasoning is not applied to women.

We need not tarry over the obvious dangers and potential abuse inherent in accepting any call, whether male or female, based on this kind of reasoning. However, two passages from Scripture that follow this line of reasoning might be appropriately extended to apply to the call. Paul argues this way about certain callees: "Some proclaim Christ from envy and rivalry, but others from goodwill. These proclaim Christ out of love, knowing that I have been put here for the defense of the gospel; the others proclaim Christ out of selfish ambition, not sincerely but intending to increase my suffering in my imprisonment. What does it matter? Just this, that Christ is proclaimed in every way, whether out of false motives or true; and in that I rejoice. Yes, and I will continue to rejoice" (Phil. 1:15-18).

What an incredible thought. Paul knows that some of those who are preaching the gospel are doing it for the wrong reasons; they have ulterior motives. However, his focus is on the content of the proclamation. As long as the content of the gospel is pure, it doesn't seem to matter to Paul who the vessel is or what the motives for preaching are. He will rejoice regardless. Perhaps men who have trouble with women in the ministerial role should think about the depth and implications of this Scripture.

Another passage that follows this line of reasoning comes from Luke. When the apostles are brought before the council during the church's infancy for preaching in the name of Jesus after being ordered to stop, Gamaliel, a Pharisee, teacher of the law and highly regarded by all the people, speaks indirectly on their behalf: "So in the present case I tell you, keep away from these men and let them alone; for if this plan or this undertaking is of men, it will fail; but if it is of God, you will not be able to overthrow them. You might even be found opposing God! So they took his advice . . ." (Acts 5:38-40a). I know of no better counsel from the New Testament to help break the present impasse.

Perhaps men who have problems with God calling women should ponder this thought anew. Why would women go through all the tribulation that these stories make clear if God had not called them? For some of the same wrong motives as some men? Then let Paul's reasoning to the Philippians prevail. However, if women pursue their call for the right motive — they have been called by God, but you are trapped by your communities traditional beliefs, then let Gamaliel's reasoning prevail.

CHAPTER 14

Betwixt and Between: Where Have We Come From and Where Do We Go?

A divine messenger posed this dual question to the African slave girl Hagar who was attempting to free herself from bondage: "Where have you come from and where are you going?" We might ask a similar question about the call as seen through the lens of this study. We have emerged from this study with the understanding that the call comes in a variety of types and crosses gender, denominational, geographical, and generational boundaries. As a result it should not be reduced to a narrow understanding of merely the call to preach. Rather, the call unfolds in a variety of different ministries and possibly changes throughout the life of the callee. The following observations are among the most important in this study.

The Call Is Both Story and Narrative

As story the call consists of at least six, sometimes overlapping, stages: stage one — early religious exposure; stage two — call experience; stage three — struggle; stage four — search; stage five — sanction; stage six — surrender. The story is the narrator's attempt to tell what happened and the interpreter's attempt to reconstruct the preverbal sequence of events. The content of the story is determined to a large extent by the type of call. As narrative the call consists of three types: cataclysmic/reluctant, noncataclysmic/reluctant, and noncataclysmic/nonreluctant. The narrative is the narrator's way of telling his or her story through a retrospective interpretation of its events. Thematic emphasis is para-

233

mount at the narrative level in order that the narrator might persuade the narratee to believe the story. Chronology and historical precision, though important, are not as important as plot in the narrative.

The Liminality of the Call

The call is a rites-of-passage ritual whereby a layperson moves through a threshold to become a member of clergy. One of the more significant observations of this study, discovered in the juxtaposition of story and narrative, is how prevalent liminality is in the call. At the narrative level the callee's knowledge is broader, clearer, and more certain; however, at the story level liminality prevails in terms of limited knowledge, ambiguity, and confusion. The pastor is the primary portal through which a callee must pass. The call stages should probably be seen as more circular and overlapping than Van Gennep's theory allows. However, a general description of call as rites of passage would categorize the stages as follows: preliminal (stage one); liminal (stages two through four); postliminal (stages five and six).

The Cultural and Transcultural Nature of the Call

In American Protestantism the transcultural nature of the call is observed in the threefold discussion of the inner call (personal), outer call (congregation), and training (education) necessary to fulfill the call. The emphasis placed on each of these aspects of call highlights the cultural differences. While divine elements of call that are transcultural (e.g., visions and voices) exist at the story level, at the narrative level cultural conditioning is evident. In some instances, a clash might even occur between the cultural traditions of the religious community and the self-understanding of a call that breaks with cultural traditions.

The Hermeneutics of the Call

The hermeneutical implications of this study for the understanding of call to ministry in black churches are vast. The call as narrative is an individual's interpretation of his or her story. As the years pass, sometimes there is a reinterpretation in light of new data. Narrative is an individual's attempt to explain his or her present in light of the past.

In this regard the narrative is indispensable for understanding how different people interpret call. However, it cannot stand alone as the basis for defining or describing the variety of calls. The call as story is necessary as well and may, in fact, be a better starting point for broadening our recognition of a variety of call types. The prevalence of liminality in call as story, though deemphasized at the narrative level, should make us cautious about reducing all calls to one type and speaking too absolutely about what all calls look like. The clash between religious communities' traditional understandings of call and individuals' self-understandings of call should make us rethink some outdated and some simply wrongheaded traditions. We need to reconsider what is meant by a call and how we are to recognize one.

Where do we go from here? If we do not rethink how we have approached call to ministry heretofore, the answer to that question might be: Nowhere! We are where we are going. In rethinking the call this study offers the following broad recommendations.

Rethinking the Call to Ministry

The first step that we must take is to broaden our language and our perspective. We need to begin to think in terms of "call to ministry" as opposed to the overly reductionistic phrase "call to preach." When the New Testament addresses gifts, gifted people, and offices, a variety of ministries is always listed and none of them is reduced simply to the call to preach.

In light of the problems the masses of African Americans face today, a host of different ministerial gifts are needed. Our people are hungry, homeless, unemployed, without health care, inadequately educated in substandard inner city schools and generally powerless as individuals. However, an enormous amount of resources, economic and human, lies untapped in black churches.

Perhaps we need to consider more ministries of economic and educational empowerment, as well as ministries that address social and physical needs. These ministries go beyond the traditional preaching hour on Sunday at 11:00 a.m., and go beyond building sanctuaries of limited uses. A gymnasium, for example, can serve as a place for youth to gather at certain times and for the hungry and homeless to sleep in and be fed at other times. A multipurpose family center can be utilized to offer social services, physical services, and educational services at the same time or different times.

Why couldn't black health-care professionals (doctors, dentists, nurses, et al.) and other professionals (lawyers, bankers, accountants, educators, and administrators) that belong to our churches be supported by our churches to establish low-cost services in centers built to minister to the whole person? For this we would have to view ministry much more broadly than preaching. Ministry needs to be concretized more specifically and tied more directly to gifts that people have been given. Moreover, such a proposal recognizes that none of these gifts is distributed on the basis of gender.

We must begin to recognize ministries and ministers on a basis other than that of someone's cultural preaching ability. Ministry is not limited to or defined primarily by preaching. In fact, not even the pastoral ministry is defined by preaching. Rather, this ministry is filled by what the New Testament calls the pastor-teacher. Hence, a teaching (training) dimension is emphasized along with a shepherding (nurturing, caring) dimension. Youth ministers could fulfill this type of ministry with youth; a counseling minister could fulfill this type of ministry with a variety of age groups; the minister of administration could fulfill aspects of this ministry. Yet none of these ministers should be forced to think of their ministry in terms of preaching anymore than the senior pastor should think of his or her ministry only in terms of preaching.

If we think of ministry in this manner, then our concern is with who has the demonstrated gifts, commitment, and preparation to fulfill these ministries, not whose vocal chords and inflections get the best response, nor whether one is male or female.

Recognizing a Call to Ministry

As this study has demonstrated, recognizing a call to ministry is a divine-human and human-human encounter; an individual as well as a community of believers are involved. Historically three key elements have entered the discussion: the personal call (inner call), the congregational call (outer call), and the education necessary to fulfill the call. Whereas this study has brought additional insights to this discussion, these three elements are still valuable as broad categories for recognition of the call. Toward that end, the following observations are offered for recognizing a call.

An irresistible urge that ministry is one's life work. No other vocation in life fulfills the individual like ministry.

This inclination may be acknowledged early or later in life. However, it should be so overwhelming that the individual is unfulfilled doing anything else. For some the desire is accompanied with a variety of cataclysmic events, but for just as many others no such events are ever encountered. For some it will appear to come suddenly, while others will experience it as a much more gradual series of events. Some will be reluctant, but others will not. For a rare few the call will be clear, but for the vast majority it will be confusing, bewildering, and just plain unsettling. Once it has been accepted, however, peace and fulfillment tend to take over, and more clarity and certainty start to reign. Do not look for the call to remain static throughout the callee's life; it can change and unfold in different ways as the process continues.

A recognition among the community of believers that a calling is evident in the life of the individual.

Because the call to ministry is for the common good, it is a call that is perfected within the community of faith. Therefore, the best place for recognition, confirmation, and support should be the church. Unfortunately, this doesn't always mean the callee's local church. It may be (and it should be) because these are the people that should know about the life of the claimant. Sometimes, however, our traditional beliefs get in the way of acknowledging that God is doing something contrary to what we think God could do. If the call is genuine, God will open up places and send people to confirm it. A sensitive, open-minded pastor is an excellent starting place. Hopefully, that will be the claimant's pastor; if not, there are others. One should seek the advice of those in the community of faith; tell them one's story, and listen to their response.

In order to help people further define their calling, our churches must redesign their structure along areas of specific ministry as opposed to other traditional structures (e.g., auxiliaries, many of which have nothing to do with ministry, but the perpetuation of the institutional church). This should be done according to the needs of the community they serve and the gifts that are resident in the church. When done this way, ministries are created on the basis of need and gifts, and a host of new ministries may emerge that no one considered in the past. God's gifted people and God's needy people are the mothers and fathers of creativity.

A commitment to preparation in fulfilling a specific ministry.

Education is paramount. Anyone not willing to make this sacrifice is unworthy of the calling. In plain and simple terms the callee must go to school. This may be the best place to determine just how committed the claimant is to the call. If claimants are unwilling to go to

school, then the church should be unwilling to allow them apprentice-
ships in the church. If, however, they are willing to make the necessary
sacrifice to go to school, then the church should be prepared to aid them
financially and any other way possible as well.

No other vocation, career, or job accepts people without some kind
of academic standard. Why should the church sanction anyone not
willing to accept the rigors of preparation to fulfill a calling that he or
she claims comes from God? The call must be tested, and testing should
not only take place in the field but in the classroom that helps prepare
one for the field. The individual, the church, and the community need
to know, "To what specific ministry has this person been called?" Preparation in the academy and practice in the field can help the claimant
find that specificity. Our world is too complex and our people's problems too vast and complicated for the church to be willing to turn loose
an army of untrained callees to help remedy these ills.

Loose Ends

A few research matters emerged as a result of this study, but were
beyond the study's scope. For example, a larger study of call to ministry
representing all black churches, especially those in the deep rural South
and other rural areas, is needed. Because of financial reasons many
black churches in a variety of denominations were not included (e.g.,
COGIC, Apostolic, Nondenominational, Episcopalian, Presbyterian)
that I sorely wish could have been. What additional insights and understanding of call to ministry would these additions offer?

Furthermore, are there more than three types? Is there anyone out
there who would say, "I don't fit in Type A, B or C?" Would enough
similarities among others exist to justify other types? Is there, for example, a cataclysmic/nonreluctant type? Or is that a contradiction?
Does a nonreluctant type need a cataclysmic experience? Perhaps the
larger study mentioned above could help answer questions like these.

A final matter that will need attention in black churches is ordination. To my knowledge, this subject has not been addressed at all
from a black perspective. Basically, most black churches follow traditional positions on this matter. We need to be raising new questions,
however, about who should be ordained on the basis of functions,
needs, and gifts.

On the one hand we do not want to make ordination inefficacious
by ordaining everybody; however, on the other hand the time has come

for us to rethink the notion that only those who claim a "call to preach" should be ordained. Ordination is a hermeneutical matter, something that has been reinterpreted time and again in the church's history. There is no clear position on this in Scripture. In fact, Scripture only speaks to it by inference in situations about laying on of hands. It is not an easy connection, however, to get from laying on of hands to the modern concept of ordination, especially when it comes to the question of who should be ordained.

We must address this matter, however, from our own cultural perspective, in light of our needs and the gifts that God has given our churches.

APPENDIX A: DEMOGRAPHICS

Name	Gender	Denomination	Age	Age called	Marital status	First told	Birth place	Parents birthpl.	Ed.	Parents religious	Rel. in ministry	Voc. status	Ministry residence	Church size
1. Abernathy, L.	F	UCC	46	34	M	husband	MS	MS	M.Div.	both	Uncle	Pastor	OH	120
2. Adams, C. G.	M	Baptist	55	0	M	mother	MI	GA/NC	M.Div.	both	grand rel.	Pastor	MI	7500
3. Adams, H. J.	M	AME	61	17	M	father	SC	SC	S.T.M.	both	PK	Bishop	GA	0
4. Anderson, H.	M	AMEZ	67	33	M	wife	NC	SC	B.D.	both	PK	Bishop	NC	0
5. Alston, A.	F	Comm. Ch.	69	17	S	pastor	VA	VA	B.Th.	both	Cousin	Ass. Min	MD	3200
6. Austin, S.	F	Baptist	35	20	M	friend	NY	FL	M.Div.	both	PK	Ass. Min.	GA	1500
7. Bailey, E. K.	M	Baptist	45	19	M	father	TX	TX	M.Div.	both	PK	Pastor	TX	5000
8. Blake, J.	M	Baptist	63		M	pastor	AL	AL	B.Th.	both	PK	Pastor	OH	300
9. Booth, C.	M	Baptist	43	14	M	mother	MD	VA	D.Min.	both	grandf.	Pastor	OH	1200
10. Booth, L. V.	M	Baptist	71	17	M	mother	MS	MS	B.D.	both	PK	Pastor	OH	150
11. Brogdon, J.	F	Disciples	52	8	D	mother	OH	AL/SC	D.Min.	mother	nephew	Pastor	OH	140
12. Bryant, C.	F	AME	44	9	M	mother	NY	NC	M.A.	both	aunt/uncle	Elder	MD	0
13. Bryant, J.	M	AME	47	10	M	father	MD	IN/SC	D.Min.	both	PK	Bishop	MD	0
14. Bryant, V.	F	AME	52	46	M	husband	MI	AL	M.A.	both	none	minister	MI	1200
15. Carpenter, D.	F	Disciples	46	14	M	mother	MD	MD	Ed.D.	mother	none	Pastor	DC	500
16. Carter, M.	M	Baptist	43	9	M	pastor	FL	AL/FL	D.Min.	both	Yes	Pastor	FL	5300
17. Caviness, E. T.	M	Baptist	62	17	M	pastor	TX	TX	B.D.	both	none	Pastor	OH	2500
18. Chapelle, T. O.	M	Baptist	74	16	M	mother	OK	TN/VA	B.Th.	both	Yes	Pastor	OK	800
19. Churn, A.	F	Baptist	60	5	D	grandm.	PA	PA	D.Hum.	grandma	none	Pastor	NJ	300
20. Clark, C.	M	Baptist	76	9	M	mother	LA	LA	Gram.	mother	none	Pastor	TX	6002
21. Cotton, E.	M	Baptist	68	0	W	pastor	TX	TX	D.Min.	both	none	Pastor	CA	500
22. Delk, Y.	F	UCC	51	5	S	mother	VA	VA	D.Min.	both	grand rel.	admin.	NY	0
23. English, R.	M	Baptist	47	23	M	father	GA	GA	M.Div.	both	gr. grandf.	Pastor	W.Va.	387
24. Essek, B.	F	UCC	39	30	S	friend	AL	AL	M.Div.	both	none	admin.	NY	0
25. Felder, C.	M	UM	47		D		SC	SC	Ph.D.	mother	none	Prof.	DC	0
26. Forbes, J.	M	UCC	55	9	M	bishop	NC	NC	D.Min.	both	PK	Pastor	NY	2000
27. Ford, J.	M	Baptist	48	33	M	father	AL	AL	M.P.A.	both	none	Ass. Min.	AL	600
28. Fowler, R.	M	Ch. of God	55	27	M	father	OH	GA	M.Div.	both	PK	Pastor	OH	850
29. Gilkes, C.	F	Baptist	43	34	D	friend	MA	PA/IN	Ph.D.	both	grandf.	Ass. Min.	ME	300

APPENDIX A: DEMOGRAPHICS (Continued)

Name	Gender	Denom-ination	Age	Age called	Marital status	First told	Birth place	Parents birthpl.	Ed.	Parents religious	Rel. in ministry	Voc. status	Ministry residence	Church size
30. Glover, S.	M	Baptist	65	0	M	father	NJ	NC/GA	Th.M.	both	PK	Pastor	OH	1100
31. Hale, C.	F	DC	38	23	S	mother	VA	VA	M.Div.	mother	grandf.	Pastor	GA	280
32. Henderson. C.	M	UM	56	19	M	pastor	GA	GA	B.D.	both	none	D.Supt.	GA	0
33. Hill, E. V.	M	Baptist	57	11	W	pastor	TX	TX	B.S.	both	grandf.	Pastor	CA	2000
34. Hines, S.	M	Ch. of God	61	17	M	pastor	W.Ind.	W.Ind.	B.Th.	both	PK	Pastor	DC	540
35. Holly, J.	M	Baptist	47		W	pastor	PA	WV	Ph.D.	no	grandf.	Pastor	MI	3086
36. Hopkins, S.	F	UCC	33	19	M	friend	DC	VA/SC	M.Div.	both	grandf.	Admin.	NY	0
37. Hoyt, T.	M	CME	49	17	M	bishop	AL	AL	Ph.D.	both	PK	Prof.	CT	0
38. Jackson, A.	M	DC	40	21	M	professor	MS	MS	M.Div.	both	grandf.	Pastor	TN	3300
39. Jackson, J.	M	Baptist	90+	8	M	father	MS	AL	M.A.	both	PK	Pastor	IL	2000
40. Johnson, S.	F	Baptist	33	13	S	pastor	NY	NC/VA	D.Min.	both	cousin	Pastor	NY	600
41. Johnson, W.	M	Baptist	48	37	M	mother	OH	TN/VA	B.A.	both	none	Ass.Min.	OH	250
42. Jones, H.	M	Baptist	49	24	M	father	KY	KY/IN	M.Div.	both	PK	Pastor	OH	1300
43. Jones, O.	M	Baptist	58	9	M	professor	AR	AR	D.Min.	both	uncle	Pastor	MI	1386
44. Jones, W. A.	M	Baptist	56	22	D	father	KY	KY/IN	B.D.	both	PK	Pastor	NY	5000
45. Kemp, A.	M	Baptist	61	23	M	pastor	NC	SC	D.Min.	both	none	Pastor	OH	1000
46. Kimbrough, W.	M	UM	50	22	M	pastor	GA	AL/GA	M.Div.	mother	uncles	Pastor	GA	6200
47. King, B.	F	Baptist	27	17	S	mother	GA	AL/GA	M.Div.	both	PK	Minister	GA	0
48. Knight, C.	F	Baptist	34	0	S	pastor	CO	TX	M.Div.	both	cousin	Pastor	NY	150
49. Lightner, A.	F	AME	45	36	D	pastor	NC	NC	M.Th.	no	cousin	Pastor	MD	250
50. Mackenzie, V.	F	AME	43	34	M	pastor	MD	MD/IL	M.Div.	both	cousin	Pastor	MD	217
51. Massey, J.	M	Ch. of God	60	16	M	mother	MI	AL	M.A.	both	PK	Dean	AL	0
52. McCreary, C.	M	Baptist	73	5	M	cousin	AL	AL	D.D.	both	none	Pastor	OH	1000
53. McCreary, L.	M	Baptist	44	23	M	aunt	AL	AL	M.A.	mother	cousin	Pastor	OH	120
54. McKinney, S.	M	Baptist	64	23	M	father	MI	AL/GA	D.Min.	both	PK	Pastor	WA	2800
55. McMickle, M.	M	Baptist	42	16	M	pastor	IL	IL/NC	D.Min.	mother	uncle	Pastor	OH	1200
56. Mitchell, E. P.	F	Baptist	73	21	M	church	SC	SC	D.Min.	both	PK	Prof.	GA	0
57. Mitchell, H. H.	M	Baptist	71	20	M	mother	OH	OH/VA	Th.D.	both	grandf.	Prof.	GA	0
58. Morgan, E.	M	AMEZ	72	27	M	pastor	AL	AL	B.D.	both	PK	Pastor	OH	800

APPENDIX A: DEMOGRAPHICS (Continued)

Name	Gender	Denomination	Age	Age called	Marital status	First told	Birth place	Parents birthpl.	Ed.	Parents religious	Rel. in ministry	Voc. status	Ministry residence	Church size
59. Moss, Otis	M	Baptist	55	17	M	pastor	GA	GA	D.Min.	both	none	Pastor	OH	3800
60. Newberry, A.	M	AME	34	11	M	father	OH	OH/GA	M.Div.	both	PK	Pastor	OH	354
61. Newman, E.	M	UM	62	16	M	father	SC	SC	B.D.	both	PK	Bishop	TN	0
62. Payden, H.	M	Baptist	67	23	M	wife	OH	AL/SC	M.A.	both	PK	Pastor	OH	1400
63. Pounds, R.	M	Baptist	32	21	M	mother	OH	OH	B.A.	both	grandf.	Pastor	OH	1250
64. Proctor, S.	M	Baptist	69	18	M		VA	VA	Th.D.	both	uncles	Pastor	NY	6000
65. Reid, F.	M	AME	39	20	M	father	IL	LA/KY	M.A.R.	both	PK	Pastor	MD	6000
66. Richardson, W.	M	Baptist	41	18	M	mother	PA	VA/SC	M.A.R.	both	grandf.	Pastor	NY	2000
67. Roberts, J.	M	Baptist	55	??	M	father	IL	IL/GA	Th.M.	both	PK	Pastor	GA	3000
68. Sampson, F.	M	Baptist	62	18	M		TX	LA	B.D.	both	none	Pastor	MI	5000
69. Scott, M.	M	Baptist	64	18	W	pastor	TX	TX	B.A.	mother	sons	Pastor	TX	1800
70. Shaw, William	M	Baptist	58	11	M	pastor	TX	TX	D.Min.	both	none	Pastor	PA	2000
71. Shuttlesworth, F.	M	Baptist	68	18	W	mother	AL	AL	B.S.	mother	PK	Pastor	OH	350
72. Smith, J. Alfred	M	Baptist	60	17	M	pastor	MO	MS/LA	D.Min.	mother	son	Pastor	CA	3100
73. Taylor, G.	M	Baptist	72	19	M	sch.pre.	LA	LA	B.D.	both	PK	Pastor	NY	9000
74. Tunstall, C.	M	Baptist	78	20	W	cousin	AL	AL	M.A.	both	PK	Pastor	AL	2000
75. Walker, Wyatt T.	M	Baptist	62	21	M	prof.	MA	VA	D.Min.	both	PK	Pastor	NY	2300
76. Waller, A.	M	Baptist	70	23	M	pastor	VA	VA	B.D.	both	uncles	Pastor	OH	1000
77. Weems, R.	F	AME	36	25	S	pastor	GA	GA	Ph.D.	no	none	Prof.	TN	0
78. Wheeler, E.	F	Baptist	44	15	M	mother	NY	GA/NY	Ph.D.	both	uncles	Pastor	OH	850
79. Wiggins, A.	F	UM	49	23	S	minister	MD	MD/VA	M.Div.	no	grand rel.	Pastor	MD	257
80. Williams, R.	M	Brethren	38	17	M	father	SC	SC/Jam	M.Div.	both	PK	Pastor	OH	900
81. Wright, J.	M	UCC	49	18	M	father	IL	VA	D.Min.	both	PK	Pastor	IL	4500
82. Wynn, P.	F	Baptist	50	0	D	a pastor	PA	VA	M.Th.	both	PK	Pastor	NJ	50
83. Young, J. S.	M	Baptist	70	32	M	minister	FL	AL	B.Th.	both	PK	Pastor	FL	1500
84. Young, M.	M	AME	46	19	M	grandm.	GA	SC/GA	M.Div.	both	PK	Pastor	GA	2433
85. Youngblood, J.	M	Baptist	42	22	M	mother	LA	LA/MS	M.Div.	both	great uncle	Pastor	NY	2500
86. Zak, F.	M	CME	32	20	M	mother	AL	AL/S.A.	D.Min.	both	brother	Pastor	OH	500

APPENDIX B: CALL STAGES

Name	Gender	Denomination	Call Type exposure	Early religious experience	Call	Struggle	Search	Sanction	Surrender
1. Abernathy, Lucille	F	Baptist/UCC	A	X	X	X	X	X	X
2. Adams, Charles	M	Baptist	C	X		X	X	X	X
3. Adams, John H.	M	AME	C	X			X	X	X
4. Anderson, H.	M	AMEZ	C	X		X	X		X
5. Alston, Agnes	F	Baptist/CC	A	X	X	X	X	X	X
6. Austin, Sharon	F	Baptist	B	X	X	X	X	X	X
7. Bailey, E. K.	M	Baptist	A	X	X	X	X	X	X
8. Blake, Joseph	M	Baptist	A	X	X	X	X	X	X
9. Booth, Charles	M	Baptist	C	X				X	X
10. Booth, L. V.	M	Baptist	C	X		X		X	X
11. Brogdon, Julia	F	Baptist/DC	A	X	X	X	X	X	X
12. Bryant, Cecelia	F	AME	A	X	X		X	X	X
13. Bryant, John	M	AME	A	X	X	X	X	X	X
14. Bryant, Vivian	F	Baptist/AME	A	X	X	X	X	X	X
15. Carpenter, D.	F	Baptist/DC	A	X	X	X	X	X	X
16. Carter, Mack K.	M	Baptist	A	X	X			X	X
17. Caviness, E. T.	M	Baptist	B	X		X		X	X
18. Chapelle, T. O.	M	Baptist	C	X		X		X	X
19. Churn, Arlene	F	Baptist	A	X	X	X	X	X	X
20. Clark, C. A. W.	M	Baptist	C	X		X	X		X
21. Cotton, Earl C.	M	Baptist	C	X		X			X
22. Delk, Yvonne	F	UCC	B	X			X	X	X
23. English, Ronald	M	Baptist	B	X		X	X	X	X
24. Essek, Barbara	F	UCC	A	X	X		X	X	X
25. Felder, Cain	M	UM	B	X		X	X	X	X
26. Forbes, James	M	Pentecost./UCC	A	X	X	X	X	X	X
27. Ford, Johnny	M	Baptist	B	X	X	X	X	X	X
28. Fowler, Ronald	M	Church of God	B	X	X	X	X	X	X
29. Gilkes, Cheryl	F	Baptist	A	X	X	X	X	X	X

APPENDIX B: CALL STAGES (Continued)

Name	Gender	Denomination	Call Type	Early religious exposure	Call experience	Struggle	Search	Sanction	Surrender
30. Glover, Sterling	M	Baptist	A	X	X	X	X	X	X
31. Hale, Cynthia	F	DC	B	X	X	X	X	X	X
32. Henderson, C.	M	UM	B	X		X	X	X	X
33. Hill, E. V.	M	Baptist	A	X	X	X	X	X	X
34. Hines, Samuel	M	Church of God	B	X	X	X	X	X	X
35. Holly, Jim	M	Baptist	B	X		X	X	X	X
36. Hopkins, Susan	F	Baptist/UCC	A	X	X	X	X	X	X
37. Hoyt, Tom, Jr.	M	CME	C	X				X	X
38. Jackson, Alvin	M	DC	B	X		X	X	X	X
39. Jackson, Joseph	M	Baptist	C	X					X
40. Johnson, Suzan	F	Baptist	B	X	X	X	X	X	X
41. Johnson, Wm.	M	Baptist	A	X	X	X	X	X	X
42. Jones, Henry W.	M	Baptist	B	X	X	X	X	X	X
43. Jones, Odell	M	Baptist	B	X	X	X	X	X	X
44. Jones, William	M	Baptist	B	X	X	X	X	X	X
45. Kemp, Arthur	M	Baptist	A	X	X	X	X	X	X
46. Kimbrough, W.	M	UM	A	X	X	X	X	X	X
47. King, Bernice	F	Baptist	B	X	X	X	X	X	X
48. Knight, Carolyn	F	Baptist	C	X				X	X
49. Lightner, C.	F	AME	A	X	X	X	X	X	X
50. Mackenzie, V.	F	AME	B	X	X	X	X	X	X
51. Massey, James	M	Church of God	B	X	X	X	X	X	X
52. McCreary, C.	M	Baptist	A	X	X	X	X	X	X
53. McCreary, L.	M	Baptist	A	X	X	X	X	X	X
54. McKinney, S.	M	Baptist	B	X		X	X	X	X
55. McMickle, M.	M	Baptist	A	X	X	X	X	X	X
56. Mitchell, E. P.	F	Baptist	B	X		X	X		X
57. Mitchell, Henry	M	Baptist	B	X	X	X	X	X	X
58. Morgan, Eugene	M	AMEZ	B	X	X	X	X	X	X

APPENDIX B: CALL STAGES (Continued)

Name	Gender	Denomination	Call Type	Early religious exposure	Call experience	Struggle	Search	Sanction	Surrender
59. Moss, Otis, Jr.	M	Baptist	C	X			X	X	X
60. Newberry, A.	M	AME	B	X		X	X	X	X
61. Newman, Ernest	M	UM	C	X				X	X
62. Payden, Henry	M	Baptist	B	X	X	X	X	X	X
63. Pounds, R.	M	Baptist	B	X	X	X	X		X
64. Proctor, Samuel	M	Baptist	C	X	X	X	X	X	X
65. Reid, Frank, III	M	AME	B	X		X	X	X	X
66. Richardson, W.	M	Baptist	A	X	X	X	X	X	X
67. Roberts, Joe	M	AME/Baptist	B	X		X	X	X	X
68. Sampson, F.	M	Baptist	B	X	X	X	X	X	X
69. Scott, Manuel	M	Baptist	C	X					X
70. Shaw, William	M	Baptist	C	X					X
71. Shuttlesworth, F.	M	Baptist	B	X			X	X	X
72. Smith, J. Alfred	M	Baptist	B	X	X	X	X	X	X
73. Taylor, Gardner	M	Baptist	B	X	X	X		X	X
74. Tunstall, C.	M	Baptist	A	X	X	X	X	X	X
75. Walker, Wyatt Tee	M	Baptist	B	X	X	X	X	X	
76. Waller, Alfred	M	Baptist	C	X					X
77. Weems, Renita	F	AME	B	X			X		X
78. Wheeler, E.	M	Baptist	A	X	X	X	X	X	X
79. Wiggins, Alfreda	F	UM	B	X	X	X	X	X	X
80. Williams, Ron	M	AMEZ/Brethren	A	X	X	X	X	X	X
81. Wright, J.	M	Baptist/UCC	A	X	X	X	X	X	X
82. Wynn, Prathia	F	Baptist	B	X	X	X	X	X	X
83. Young, James S.	M	Baptist	A	X	X	X		X	X
84. Young, McKinley	M	AME	B	X		X	X	X	X
85. Youngblood, J.	M	Baptist	B	X	X	X	X	X	X
86. Zak, Frederick	M	CME	B	X	X	X	X	X	X

APPENDIX C

Narrative Sequences

Kemp's narrative sequence is as follows:

Par. 1[1]

1. About eight years old I accepted Christ as my Saviour in response to the superintendent's call for a decision.

Par. 2

2. My family predicted that I was going to be a preacher.
3. I had spent a lot of time reading the Sunday school books.
4. We were living in Washington, D.C.
5. But I had moved back to North Carolina with my family when I accepted Christ as my Saviour.
6. We moved back to Washington, D.C.
7. I went through that public school system until I graduated from high school.
8. As one of seven children ours was a sheltered life in a religious home where my mother and father were very active in church.
9. I turned eighteen and graduated from high school.
10. I was forced by economics to get out in the world and make my own living.

1. See the narrative in Myers. This number refers to the paragraph (par.) in the narrative where these data are located.

11. I had turned down a four-year scholarship to Howard University because I didn't want to go to a black school.
12. In order to go to a white school, I would have to work and save money. I took a job in the federal government in Washington, D.C. to save money to go to Ohio State University. I was torn between sociology and the medical profession.
13. My youngest sister graduated from Dunbar High School in Washington, and I took the money I had been saving to send her to Ohio State.
14. This meant that I didn't start my college until twelve years after I graduated in 1948. I started Ohio State in 1960 in the summer session.
15. I moved to Columbus.
16. It had still never crossed my mind to take seriously the predictions people had made about my becoming a preacher.

Par. 3

17. An odd thing happened in 1952, eight years earlier. I was in a special signal corp unit of twenty-six men in the United States Army in Fort Monmouth, New Jersey.

Par. 4

18. Then my mother had a heart attack.
19. The Red Cross arranged for me to come home to be with her while she was recovering.
20. Meanwhile this special outfit that I was in shipped out to Canada on a field trip and they would be gone for six months.
21. I went back to the Army after looking after my mother.
22. My slot had been filled by my backup man and I couldn't join the team.
23. They put me in the supply room handing out fatigues.
24. I became really really embittered with the Army.
25. I started to rebel against them.

Par. 5

26. I had just reenlisted for a six-year period.
27. I was really bent out of shape by being pulled off that team and not allowed to join it in Canada.
28. I started to take my revenge out against the Army. I refused to suit up in military clothes. I wouldn't do anything. I wouldn't take orders.
29. That brought me into disfavor with my commanding officers.
30. They put me on company punishments.
31. I broke that.
32. They court martialled me.
33. I disregarded that.
34. The company commander said, "This was one of the best soldiers I had and all of a sudden he's gone off the deep end. Maybe something has happened to him. Maybe he's cracked up." So he remanded me to the custody of the military hospital there at Fort Monmouth.

Par. 6

35. But before I got to the hospital the commanding general had me to come in for a personal consultation with him because I was trying to get out of the Army.
36. I had written a letter to the Communist Youth Party seeking admission.
37. That raised quite a stir among the intelligence officers on the post.
38. So the general had called me up and wanted to interrogate me to see whether or not I was communist.
39. When the determination was made that I wasn't communist, then he concluded that I must be crazy.
40. So he called a doctor, a psychiatrist from the military hospital, to give me a personal examination.

Par. 7

41. He determined that there was nothing wrong with me psychologically, but like him who had been forced to give up a lucrative practice I was bitter with the army.

42. He made the commitment that he was going to work toward my discharge.

Par. 8

43. I was there in the hospital in a private room and on one occasion where I had been reading I heard a voice, a voice of a male.
44. I heard a voice saying to me, "Go feed my sheep."
45. I looked around and I was really kind of befuddled and wondering who had said it.
46. The first thing I did was got up and went to the door to look out the window to see if there was anybody out there that was talking to me.
47. I left the door to go back to sit down on the bed where I had been lying down.
48. In an interval of about five minutes, exactly the same statement, "Go feed my sheep."
49. And by now I'm really having some apprehension.
50. I know I keep hearing somebody talking to me, and when I check back at the door a second time I don't hear any movement out there and I don't see anybody.
51. It was nearly half an hour later that I heard the third, the same voice the third time. It said, "Go feed my sheep." I was restless all of that night.

Par. 9

52. I was scheduled to see the psychiatrist that next morning.
53. I was quick to share with him what had happened.
54. He then wanted to go back and go back over some of the files to see whether [there was] any history of hallucination in my own psychological profile.

Par. 10

55. At the same time of the call an impacting, heavy weight came over me that I could not get out of my mind the sense that I had to respond, that I had to obey this voice saying, "Go feed my sheep."

56. Those words made a lot of sense to me because I had read that that was the words that Jesus had said to Simon Peter after Christ had been crucified and raised from the dead and preparing to ascend into heaven again. That's precisely what he told Peter.

Par. 11

57. It sometime later on dawned on me that that would have been a call for me to go into a preaching ministry.
58. Then I determined that I was not going to do that because preaching was the furthest thing from my mind.
59. I had been taught that if you are going to be a vessel for God you've got to be a fit vessel and you got to have good behavior, good morals, good ethics.

Par. 12

60. So I determined that I was going to be the worst possible human being that you could be, to make myself unfit to be a minister of the gospel.
61. I wasn't drinking then, but I started drinking. I had been gambling occasionally, but I became an avid gambler. And subsequently drove getaway cars for thieves. I participated in criminal money-raising ventures related to narcotics and aided users of narcotics, but I did not ever use narcotics.

Par. 13

62. Well, in short, I had prostitutes working for me.
63. I had just become a dyed-in-the-wool rascal through and through with the avowed intention and purpose that I was never ever going to respond to that call in that hospital room, "Go feed my sheep."
64. And oddly enough, virtually everything I touched was successful, even though it was criminal.
65. I made a lot of money. I spent it as fast as I made it and had a good time.

Par. 14

66. In 1959 I left Washington, D.C., and moved to Columbus, Ohio.
67. I intended to go to Los Angeles, because in Washington, I had what the old folks use to call, "I had run out."
68. I was going to visit my mother and father for ten days, who were living at the time in Columbus, Ohio, and then go out to make a new life for myself out in Los Angeles.
69. I had really hit the pits. I had lost self-respect. I was really in the gutter, a street person, sleeping in fourth-rate hotels.

Par. 15

70. I left Washington, D.C., January 11, 1959. I sobered up enough to come to Columbus, Ohio.
71. I had my final drunk in Washington on January 10.
72. While spending some time there with my parents.
73. When they came home from church that day they didn't recognize me until she got close enough to see me and were shocked to see "this little old man" as my mother described it sitting on her front porch all bearded and bedraggled.

Par. 16

74. After a good shave and a bath I was recognizable and it was a good family reunion.
75. As I stayed there for a while my mother and dad began to ask me to stay longer than the ten days.
76. They were getting older and they kind of needed somebody to look after them.
77. I didn't know anybody in Los Angeles.
78. So they put that kind of parental beg on me and I stayed there.
79. And my mother asked me if I would go to church with her sometime.
80. And I did a couple of times.
81. Then after that, I guess after the first month, maybe into the second month I was going to church on Sunday.
82. She asked me one Wednesday night if I would go to prayer meeting with her.

83. And I did.

Par. 17

84. This was the third month that I was there, in March of 1959.
85. I was sitting in prayer meeting and prayer meeting was almost broke up.
86. It was just about time that the pastor would usually make his closing commentary and pronounce the benediction and we would all go home.
87. There would have been twenty to twenty-five persons in that prayer meeting.
88. And, just before he got up to make his remarks, I had a sudden flush of heaviness to impact on my heart, just as though I was carrying the weight of the world around me.
89. I broke out in uncontrollable sobbing.
90. And nobody could understand what was going on.
91. And the pastor, who is now deceased, said, "I know what's wrong with him. I know what's wrong with him. He hasn't told me but I know what's wrong with him."
92. I got to the point that I could stop crying well enough to make audible words.
93. The first words that came out of my mouth were, "I've got to preach, I've got to preach, I've got to preach."
94. And he said, "I know it, and you're not going to have any peace until you do."
95. It was at that point that I made the determination that I would not ever again spend a moment of my life outside of the call of Christ to be a preacher of the gospel. It had taken me eight years to make that determination.

Par. 18

96. I learned under Pastor Johnson's tutelage in church.
97. And I subsequently, in 1960, went to Ohio State, again in sociology.
98. I really didn't like Ohio State because it was too big, so I transferred to Capital University.
99. I took the bachelor in religion in nearly fourteen years of on and off,

100. because I had married and had a son and was not able to go to school full-time.
101. And I was working at Westinghouse with very little seniority. I'd get bumped a lot from job to job. So this was kind of tough trying to hang on to a job and go to school.
102. So it took me twelve years to get the bachelor's degree on a part-time status.

Par. 19

103. After that, I took a pastorate in a country church down in Renville, Ohio, for three years.
104. And commuting sixty-five miles one way that became too much and I stopped.
105. And I went back to school.
106. I did all the course work on a master in criminology and got to the point of writing the thesis.

Par. 20

107. It was at that point that I had received the call to come to pastor the Mt. Olive Baptist Church in Akron, Ohio, in 1978.
108. I responded to that call by the church to come and pastor Mt. Olive.
109. I have been happily engaged here ever since.
110. In the meanwhile, once coming to Akron I started attending Ashland Seminary.
111. I took the master in religion there.
112. Ultimately [I earned] the doctor of ministry at Ashland Seminary.
113. So, there you have the call experience of Arthur Kemp.

Par. 21

114. There is no question in my mind as to what I heard. It was male, it was a voice, it was audible.
115. Now, the question that I have always raised for myself, since there was nobody else in the room with me and there was nobody to witness what I had heard; did I in fact experience the auditory

phenomenon of hearing the voice or was it something that was subconsciously or psychologically placed on my mind, within my mind?

Roberts's narrative sequence is as follows:

Par. 1

1. I grew up in an AME minister's and his wife's home,
2. coming out of three generations of AME folk.
3. So there was a certain extent in which I feel that I was almost always in part a child of the church. I knew nothing other than that.
4. I went through the natural rebellion that a person will go through in my teenage years, feeling that if I wanted to do anything it would not be in the ministry.

Par. 2

5. I was bothered by the poverty of ministry, the lack of material acquisitions, as was evident in my father's life.
6. I was bothered by the solicitous nature and stance which I felt was demeaning as he had to deal with trustees. They would often feel that it was quite appropriate for them to pass on third-hand things to us.
7. I lived in Chicago, Illinois.

Par. 3

8. The third thing I found offensive was the demeaning nature of the black AME bishopric assistant, which was definitely a plantation sort of pecking order.
9. So I just didn't like the lack of freedom that one had in all of that.
10. And really I thought that I would have very little to do with the ministry.
11. I was talking about law and dentistry and all the rest.
12. But I found that after I was really honest, there was a love for the

people shown of all of these entrapments that I have already talked about that made me feel that I wanted to do my ministerial role.

13. But I was not sure just where.

14. So I think the call was not a traumatic thing that came to me but something that I yearned to do.

15. But I fought it because I thought the political trappings and the infrastructure of my denomination mitigated against fulfilling the kind of ministry I wanted to fulfill.

Par. 4

16. The next thing that I really knew was that I wanted to have a ministry that was broad enough to let me address some political, social, and economic problems and would not be so narrow that I would be wedded to a particular parochial situation.

17. So I went looking for some sort of quasi-political bridge that would allow me to be comfortable in both camps. I went to college.

18. While in college I had the opportunity to meet some Presbyterian folk.

19. They encouraged me to consider going into the Presbyterian church.

20. And it was for political reasons that I went into the Presbyterian church because I saw that it gave me more freedom to be unencumbered by a number of folk, to be independent, and to be able to do the kind of ministry that I wanted to do.

21. When that opportunity for education really came on to me, then I think that the call was really sort of authenticated.

22. At heart I was an AME. I enjoyed everything that the church was about. I admired all of that but the present manifestations got in my way.

23. The Presbyterian church made me feel like I could take that tradition and blend it into whatever I wanted it to be.

24. So my call was not a catastrophic, vertical thing that suddenly came upon me.

25. It was rather the accumulation of a number of experiences that nudged me on toward ministry that were encumbered by some political problems of infrastructure.

Par. 5

26. So it is not something that I can date in terms of a Tuesday at one o'clock when anything happened, but rather something that I think was rather gradual.
27. And not to sound defensive, but I believe when people stop lying most of them will admit that it was a gradual thing that they were nudged to and not a catastrophic, one-day piece that suddenly came and hit them like a bolt of lightning out of the air.
28. I think all of those stories if we looked up are but the pinnacle of a long series of God's prodding and nudging us toward decision. Then we talk about one that was critical and that was it.
29. I can remember the day when Frank Gordon, who was pastor of Shiloh Presbyterian Church, talked to me.
30. And I could say it was on that day after we had that talk and that prayer that my call was confirmed, I came out of the darkness, but that would be a lie. So I'm not going to do that. So that is my answer.

Par. 6

31. But if you ask specifically about how that call came into being that's another story. I went to Knoxville College.
32. Then I went to Union Seminary.
33. Then to Princeton.
34. These perfected the ministry.
35. But this is how I actually was drawn to it. I was finally able to reconcile myself with a system of governance in a denomination that would not impede my view of a broad ministry and my view of a free ministry.

Par. 7

36. I think there is a certain extent as to which a connectional church that has bishops who are not sensitive that can be demeaning to the sacredness of human personality. It can almost be another form of slavery.

Newman's narrative sequence is as follows:

Par. 1

1. I am from a large family of preachers.
2. It is seemingly a kind of family tradition.
3. My father was a Methodist preacher. My grandfather was a Methodist preacher. I am one of seven boys and six of us went into the ministry.

Par. 2

4. Now going back my father was a Methodist preacher.
5. At the age of sixteen I completed high school.
6. I had a sense of call.
7. Of course, it's been pretty much understood as far as my entire life up until that time that I was going into the ministry.
8. I did not see any other profession or calling as to what would be my life's commitment.
9. At the age of sixteen I received a local preacher's license by the charge conference that my father was pastor of at that time.
10. Then after completing high school, at the age of sixteen, I entered Clafflin College, which is one of our eleven black colleges supported by the United Methodist church.

Par. 3

11. Upon my completion of my college work I did some preaching across the state of South Carolina.
12. Even during the time I was in college I preached.
13. Then upon completion of my college work my father was desperately ill.
14. I did not find it possible to continue my education on to seminary.

Par. 4

15. Shortly after I got out of college he died.

16. Then I was asked by the district superintendent to carry on my father's work.
17. I completed one year of the tenure that was his.
18. Then, at the end of that year I asked to be moved and assumed a pastorate of two other congregations in South Carolina.
19. After two years' pastoring these two churches, I felt that it was necessary for me to ask for another move, because I wanted to have rural pastoral experience.
20. I was in a county seat town and I wanted something that would give me a different exposure.

Par. 5

21. I became pastor of two little churches in South Carolina.
22. I stayed at these churches for approximately a year and a half, and then transferred to the Florida Conference.
23. I still lacked my theological education.
24. After about eight months, I guess, I went back to school in Atlanta at Gammon where I did my theological work — which I completed.
25. I went back to Florida and pastored in Florida the remainder of my Florida ministry.

Par. 6

26. While in Florida I pastored what was at that time one of our most historic black churches, Ebenezer Church in Jacksonville, Florida.
27. After seven years I became a district superintendent of a merged Florida conference in 1971 and became the first black district superintendent in Florida.
28. After six years, which is a tenure, [I] became pastor of a church in Ft. Lauderdale with 2200 members.
29. [I] pastored there for five years.
30. Then from there [I went] to the Conference Council on Ministers, where I served as associate director for a year.
31. Then [I] went back to the position of district superintendent of Florida for one and one-half years.
32. Then [I] was elected to the bishopric out of the Florida Conference.

Par. 7

33. Upon my election to this position I was assigned then to the Nashville area comprising two annual conferences, the Tennessee Conference and the Memphis Conference.
34. And that's where I am now after five years in the Nashville area.

Par. 8

35. My call to the ministry was almost a kind of thing that I considered I had no choice.
36. I had been born and brought up in the Methodist church and the family of preachers.
37. I just assumed that on the day of my own knowledge of ministry that this would be my calling.
38. So my call to some extent comes out, I guess, of a family tradition.
39. There was never a time that I considered I would do anything else.
40. It was a life commitment.
41. So my call I don't think is anything unique, it's not unique to any extent of any other person's call.
42. I feel that there is the call and you make the commitment to it and dedicate your life to it.
43. I did not see any spectacular vision of some kind or some unknown mysterious voice that came to me. I did not see that.
44. I saw mine as a family tradition, heritage.
45. It was a desire to be a participant in working with people, looking at their concerns, developing a ministry that would respond to their concerns. Let's say it was social and at the same time it was a commitment, and out of this commitment a dedication.
46. I tie the call and history together. And this has been my response to the call to the ministry.

Index of Names

Names of interview subjects appear in SMALL CAPITALS.

ABERNATHY, LUCILLE, 28, 34, 42, 45, 56, 127, 158-77, 181, 184-85, 189
Abrams, M. H., 93n
ADAMS, CHARLES, 127
ADAMS, BISHOP JOHN HURST, 18, 35, 38, 55
Allen, William Lloyd, 4n
ALSTON, AGNES, 29, 57
ANDERSON, BISHOP HERMAN, 26
Aristotle, 94, 95n
Arndt, William F., 202n
Ashcraft, Morris, 202n
AUSTIN, SHARON, 25, 56

BAILEY, E. K., 20n, 25, 62
Baird, William, 196n, 197
BARTHES, ROLAND, 69
Bennett, Lerone Jr., 3n
Bercovitz, Peter, 196n
BLAKE, JOSEPH L., JR., 20, 30n, 58, 61
Blanchard, Jean-Marc, 70n
Blenkinsopp, Joseph, 65n
BOOTH, CHARLES, 49, 129
BOOTH, L. VENCHAEL, 25, 41, 42n
Booth, Wayne C., 76
BROGDON, JULIA, 22, 30, 34, 45
Brooks, Cleanth, 75, 93, 94, 95
BRYANT, CECILIA, 34
BRYANT, BISHOP JOHN, 21, 27n, 33, 179
BRYANT, VIVIAN, 30n, 34, 38, 53, 56, 58, 59n, 62, 170n

Buss, Martin J., 29n, 32n, 208n
Butt, Audrey, 208n

Calvin, John, 59n, 202
CARPENTER, DELORES, 19, 21, 22, 33, 42, 59, 62, 127, 220n
CARTER, MACK KING, 22, 30, 215, 219-23
CAVINESS, E. THEOPHILUS, 26
CHAPPELLE, T. OSCAR, 26n
Chatman, Seymour, 69, 74n, 76, 81n, 93-95
Chemnitz, Martin, 202n
Church, Leslie F., 203n
CHURN, ARLENE, 19n, 20n, 22, 29n, 30n
CLARK, CAESAR, 27, 64n
CLEVELAND, BISHOP ELMER E., 1, 2
Coenen, L., 196n
Cone, James H., 3n
Cooke, L. E., 203n
Coppes, L. J., 193n
COTTON, EARL, 19, 20n
Crane, R. S., 93n, 95n
Crites, Stephen, 65n
Culpepper, R. Alan, 70n, 199n

Davis, Gerald, 1, 222
DELK, YVONNE, 19, 35, 56
Driver, Tom F., 119n, 120, 121
Dunn, James D. G., 196n

Erb, Pater C., 202n

260

Essek, Barbara, 34, 39n, 55, 63

Felder, Cain, 19n, 35, 220n
Finney, Charles G., 204n
Forbes, James, 57
Ford, Johnny, 25, 63
Forster, E. M., 93
Foster, Steven, 119n
Fostor, John, 200
Fowler, Ronald, 35
Frazier, E. Franklin, 204-7
Fredriksen, Paula, 80, 196n

Geertz, Clifford, 6n
Genette, Gérard, 69, 70, 74-78, 81, 89, 92
Gilkes, Cheryl, 22, 31, 41, 48
Glass, Victor T., 4n, 18n, 22n, 24n, 28n, 33n, 36n, 37n, 40n, 43n, 44n, 52n, 71n, 196n, 206, 209n, 210, 211n
Glover, Sterling, 30n, 39, 59
Grimes, Ronald, 120

Habel, N., 194, 195n, 197-98
Hale, Cynthia, 25, 38, 41, 64, 127, 170n
Harris, Marvin, 6n
Hedrick, Charles W., 70n, 196n
Henderson, Cornelius, 21, 26
Herskovits, Melville J., 207
Hill, E. V., 39n, 62
Hines, Samuel, 28n
Holly, Jim, 20n
Hopkins, Susan Newman, 34n, 59n
Hoyt, Thomas, 35-36, 187n, 220n
Hudson, Winthrop S., 203n

Isaiah, 74, 121, 187, 194, 199

Jackson, Alvin, 25
Jacobs, Henry E., 202n
Jason, Heda, 64n
Jeremiah, 187, 194, 197-99
Johnson, Charles S., 2n, 3n, 209n, 210
Johnson, Clifton, 209
Johnson, Suzan, 35, 64
Johnson, William, 30n, 34
Jones, Henry, 35
Jones, Odell, 27

Jones, William A., 25n, 59, 152n
Jules-Rosette, Bennetta, 207n, 209
Jungkuntz, Richard, 202n

Kellogg, Robert, 93n
Kelly, Otha M., 3n
Kemp, Arthur, 21n, 44, 58, 77, 79-85, 86, 87, 88, 90-92, 95-105, 111, 114
Kermode, Frank, 93n
Kimbrough, Walter, 34, 43, 63
King, Martin Luther, Sr., 3n
Klein, William W., 196n
Knox, John, 196n
Knutsson, Karl Eric, 208n

Labov, William, 65n, 70n, 76
Lakin, Benjamin, 203n
Lavin, Thomas Patrick, 119n
Leonard, Bill J., 203n
Levine, Lawrence W., 210n
Lightner, Ann, 20n, 33, 50, 61, 127, 130
Lincoln, C. Eric, 206n
Little, Meredith, 119n
Lomax, Alan, 3n
Luther, Martin, 202

Mahdi, Louise, 119n
Massey, James Earl, 30, 49
Mays, Benjamin E., 3n, 206n
Mbiti, John S., 207n
McCreary, Carey, 22, 30n, 31, 33-34, 45, 50, 55n, 123-24, 127, 135-47, 152, 154, 158-65, 168, 170, 172-75, 187, 189
McCreary, Leroy, 33, 48, 51, 55, 129
McKenzie, Vashti, 20n, 63, 178-85, 187, 189
McKibens, Thomas R., Jr., 203n
McKinney, Samuel, 63
McMickle, Marvin, 34, 57, 220n
Mead, Sidney E., 203n, 204n
Metz, Christian, 81n
Milligan, Thomas B., 4n
Mitchell, Ella, 35, 49n, 226n
Mitchell, Henry H., 20n, 62, 207n, 208n, 211n
Moody, Dwight Lyman, 59n, 204n
Morgan, Eugene, 35

Moss, Otis, Jr., 25n
Munck, Johannes, 196n

Newberry, Andrew, 21n, 26n, 27n
Newman, Ernest, 35, 36n, 77-81, 87-
    89, 91-92, 95, 111-14, 125, 155-58,
    185-86, 188-89
Nicholson, Joseph W., 206n
Niebuhr, H. Richard, 203n

Ong, Walter, 5n, 69n
O'Rourke, John J., 76n

Paul the Apostle, 7, 53n, 72, 101, 121-
    23, 127, 139, 173, 181, 196-99, 217-
    18, 227, 229-30
Payden, Henry, 34, 59n
Pike, Kenneth, 5
Pitts, Walter, 207n
Pounds, Roderick, 20n, 26n
Powell, Adam Clayton, Jr., 3n
Powell, W. H. R., 3n
Proctor, Sam, 35

Raboteau, Albert J., 207n, 209, 210n,
    211
Ransom, Reverdy C., 3n
Rawick, George P., 3n
Reed, Granville W., 3n
Richardson, Harry V., 206n
Richardson, William, 34
Ricoeur, Paul, 81n
Rivers, Clarence Jos., 208n
Roberts, Joseph L., 21n, 39, 77-81, 85-
    87, 88, 90, 91, 92, 95, 105-11, 147-55,
    156, 159, 174-76, 188-89
Rogers, John, 204n

Sanders, E. P., 196n
Schmidt, K. L., 196n, 198n
Scholes, Robert, 93n
Schweizer, Eduard, 199n
Scott, Manuel, Sr., 25n, 26n, 125,
    185-87, 189
Searle, Mark, 119n, 120
Segal, Dimitri, 64n
Shurden, Walter B., 203n

Smith, Elwyn Allen, 203n
Sobel, Mechal, 3n, 28n, 33n, 210, 211n
Southard, Samuel, Jr., 4n
Spener, Philip Jacob, 202n
Spradley, James, 5, 6
Stagg, Frank, 199-200
Steiner, Roland, 2n, 3n
Stendahl, Krister, 196n, 197
Stepto, Robert B., 3n, 207n
Stone, Burton Warren, 204n
Stuckey, Sterling, 207n
Sweet, William W., 203n

Talley, Thomas W., 207n
Taylor, Gardner, 35, 38n, 49, 124-25,
    127-28
Thurman, Howard, 3n
Todorov, Tzvetan, 69
Tunstall, Charles, 34
Turner, Victor, 119-20

Uspensky, Boris, 74, 75, 76, 78, 79n, 92

Van Gennep, Arnold, 10, 11, 55n, 119,
    120, 131, 232
Van Seters, John, 65n

Waletzky, Joshua, 65n, 76
Walker, Williston, 202n
Waller, Alfred, 27n, 187n
Warren, Robert Penn, 75n, 93, 94, 95n
Washington, Booker T., 2n, 205-6, 216
Watson, Maria-Barbara, 5n, 6n
Watson, Lawrence, 5n, 6n
Weems, Renita, 20n, 25, 109, 216, 219,
    220-24
Wehmeier, Waldemar W., 202n
Wheeler, Ed, 33, 40
Wiggins, Alfreda, 20n, 25, 39n
Williams, Ronald, 29n, 30n, 48, 130
Wright, Jeremiah, 33
Wynn, Prathia Hall, 225n, 226

Young, James, 27, 31n
Young, McKinley, 64
Youngblood, Johnny, 31n, 43
Youngs, William T., Jr., 204n

Index of Subjects

African religion: and black church, 207-10; shaman as callee in, 208-9; spirit possession in, 208-9; traditions of, 205, 207, 212

African-American church: *See* Black church

"Betwixt and between": *See* liminality

Bible: in black church, 195, 206; call narratives in, 121, 194-95, 198; in callees' stories, 8, 101, 176, 181-82, 187, 189, 227-29; Gospel of John, 70, 76n; perspectives of, on call, 193-200; relevance to call debate, 6, 226-30.

Black church: call as issue in, 216-17, 231, 232, 233-37; and callee, 20-22, 147-48, 150-51, 235; perspectives of, on call, 115, 204-6, 222; preaching in, 1, 222-23; traditions of, 2-3, 144, 169, 177, 179, 189; and white Christianity, 165, 210-11. *See also* African religion; Bible; Call; Ministry; Pastor; Rites of passage; Theology; Women

Call: and black church today, 215-24, 231-37; and conversion, 210; definition of, 17, 194; as divine encounter, 227; in history of Christianity, 200-205; "inner" vs. "outer," 202, 205, 212, 217-19, 227; in New Testament, 195, 196; in Old Testament, 194-95, 197, 198, 199; of Paul the Apostle, 196, 197-99; perspectives on, 193-212, 232; to preach vs. to ministry, 3, 179, 186, 190-91, 215, 216-33; as process, 126, 174, 228; and rites of passage, 119-31; as "story" vs. "narrative," 17, 69, 70, 177. *See also* Black church; Callee; Hermeneutics; Holy Spirit; Liminality; Pastor; Signs of call; Stages of call; Types of call; Validation of call; Urge; Women

Callee: and ambiguity, 45, 50, 128; and certainty, 143; in conflict with church, 169; doubting call, 45, 174, 182-83; loneliness of, 45, 168, 177; and predictions of future, 21, 40, 58, 60, 96; resisting call, 37-46, 71, 144, 163, 184; self-understanding of, 154, 164, 177; typical experiences of, 24-36; women's experience as, 158-85; youth of, 17-23, 40, 43, 178, 179, 186, 188. *See also* Call; Education; Family; Liminality; Narrative; "Preacher's Kid"; Women

Demographics: *See* Appendix A

Education: in black church, 206; of callees, 146, 151, 154; as issue today, 219, 220, 223, 235-36; as training, 204n

Family: parents' influence in, 18-19,

263

101-2; of preachers, 88, 147, 155-57; role of, in call, 18, 41, 48, 55-56, 59, 96. *See also* "Preacher's Kid"

Gender issues: *See* women

Hermeneutics, 5-6, 7, 12; in callees' stories, 51-52, 135-91; and implications of call, 187-91, 227, 232-33; and ministry, 215-37; and women's call, 191, 216, 222, 223, 225-30. *See also* Narrative
Holy Spirit: and call, 141, 142-43, 146, 165, 202, 227. *See also* Signs of call
Home: *See* family

Interpretation: *See* Hermeneutics
The Irresistible Urge to Preach: A Collection of African American "Call" Stories (Myers), 2; noted as documentation, 18-22, 24-31, 33-36, 38-59, 61-64, 73, 77-79, 109, 124, 136, 152, 170, 187, 215, 216, 220

Liminality: definition of, 55, 119-20; examples of, 108, 119-31, 136, 139, 141-42, 147, 149, 160-63, 174, 180-85, 190; and narrative, 172, 176; phases of, 11

Ministry: forms of, 220-25, 233-35; as issue today, 215-24, 234-36; and ordination, 236-37. *See also* Black church; Call; Education; Pastor

Narrative: causality in, 104; definitions of, 17, 93-94, 232; as distinct from "story," 7, 108-9, 153, 160, 177, 189-90; elements of, 69-70, 74-77, 81, 89; and narrator, 78, 102, 114; plot in, 10, 93-95, 119-31; point of view in, 74-81; as reconstruction of "story," 17, 81-82, 190; retrospection in, 69-92, 162, 172; spatiotemporal markers in, 106, 112-13; techniques in, 115, 146; theme in, 104-7, 110, 112-13, 115; theories of, 7, 17, 64, 69-70, 74-77, 93-94; time in, 10, 81-92, 178; and truth, 153-54. *See also*

Bible; Hermeneutics; Liminality; Appendix C

Pastor: and callee, 144, 145, 161, 162, 179, 181, 184; examples of, 102-3, 139-40; role of, in call, 47-48, 50, 52-54, 59, 129-31, 189; as teacher, 215, 219, 222-23, 234. *See also* Ministry
Plot: *See* Narrative
"Preacher's Kid": as callee, 21, 26n, 43, 49, 58, 59, 62, 78, 188; examples of, 86, 88, 105-6, 125, 130, 147-49, 155-57

Rites of passage, 7, 119-31; and call, 120-21; and pastor, 48, 64; pattern of, 126

Scripture: *See* Bible
Signs of call, 24, 28-35, 57, 60; in biblical call narratives, 195; terminology of, 32; types of, 28; vision (dream, trance), 28, 33, 61, 140, 157; voice, 28-32, 98, 122, 158-60, 167, 184, 185
Stages of call: early, 17-23; experience, 24-36; sanction, 54-60; search, 47-53; struggle, 37-46, 128, 163, 188; surrender, 61-66. *See also* Appendix B
Story, 7, 131. *See also* Liminality; Narrative

Theology of call, 200-212; in black church, 204-12; in church history, 200-204.
Types of call, 9-10; cataclysmic/reluctant, 71-72, 135-47, 158-77; noncataclysmic/nonreluctant, 73, 155-58, 185-87; noncataclysmic/reluctant, 72-73, 147-55, 178-85

Urge, internal: as element of call, 24-28, 36, 234. *See also* Call

Validation of call, 47-53, 54-60, 151, 164; by God, 165-77, 188-89; by humans, 173, 182, 189, 218; in narrative, 168, 172; role of church in, 145. *See also* Call; Pastor; Stages of call

Women: as callees, 6, 28-32, 33, 34,

35, 38, 226-30; black church's
rejection of, 164-69, 171-72, 188,
229; examples of, 158-77, 178-85;
as influence on male callees, 228;
as role models, 165, 184, 188; and
struggle with call, 42, 43, 45, 228.
See also Black church; Call; Callees;
Hermeneutics; Liminality